2

THE SUPREME COURT AND THE NCAA

THE SUPREME COURT AND THE NCAA

The Case for Less Commercialism and
More Due Process in College Sports

Brian L. Porto

THE UNIVERSITY OF MICHIGAN PRESS
ANN ARBOR

Copyright © by the University of Michigan 2012

Published in the United States of America by
The University of Michigan Press
Manufactured in the United States of America
⊗ Printed on acid-free paper

2015   2014   2013   2012   4   3   2   1

A CIP catalog record for this book is available from the British Library.

Library of Congress Cataloging-in-Publication Data

Porto, Brian L.
    The Supreme Court and the NCAA : the case for less commercialism
and more due process in college sports / Brian L. Porto.
        p.   cm.
    Includes bibliographical references and index.
    ISBN 978-0-472-11804-5 (cloth : alk. paper) — ISBN 978-0-472- 02809-2 (e-book)
    1. College sports—Law and legislation—United States.   2. Antitrust
law—United States.   3. College sports—Economic aspects—United States.
4. United States. Supreme Court.   5. National Collegiate Athletic
Association.   I. Title.
    KF3989.P67   2012
    344.73'099—dc23
                                                            2011028326

To two able lawyers and dedicated sportsmen, Judges William R. Johnson, late of the New Hampshire Supreme Court, and William I. Garrard, formerly of the Indiana Court of Appeals, with fond memories of our wonderful conversations about law and sports.

ACKNOWLEDGMENTS

Although only one name appears on the cover of this book, numerous people helped to make its publication possible. When this project was in its infancy, academic lawyers Peter Goplerud, Raymond Yasser, and David Schultz read the prospectus and offered thoughtful suggestions for improving the manuscript.

At Vermont Law School, my research assistants, Conor Brockett and Brian Jones, mastered the intricacies of microfiche technology on my behalf, dutifully checked the accuracy of my case citations, and made sure those cases were still good law. Lawyer librarian Cynthia Lewis patiently answered my endless questions about how and where to locate a diverse array of research materials. My colleague Philip Meyer offered encouragement on numerous occasions, along with insights into academic publishing. When the manuscript was complete, my colleagues Gilbert Kujovich and Marc Mihaly provided helpful critiques during a presentation I gave to members of the law school faculty. My assistant, Tammie Johnson, put her formidable computer skills to work for me as I revised the manuscript for publication.

At the University of Michigan Press, acquisitions editor Melody Herr believed in the book and shepherded it from proposal to published work expertly and expeditiously. I could not have asked for any more prompt or thoughtful consideration of my proposal than she and the respective reviewers provided.

Finally, as always, my wife, Sherrie Greeley, supported this project wholeheartedly yet knew when I needed to put it aside to hike, ski, or paddle instead. I am deeply indebted to her for her wisdom and sense of perspective.

CONTENTS

The marriage of athletic commerce to higher education in the late nineteenth and early twentieth centuries has had mixed results for American colleges and universities. On the one hand, both individuals and institutions have achieved fame and fortune from big-time college sports. On the other hand, financial excess, academic fraud, and unsportsmanlike conduct by coaches and athletes, on and off the field, plagued college sports a century ago and continue to do so. During the past generation, critics of the college sports industry have assigned most of the blame for such behavior to college presidents and to the National Collegiate Athletic Association (NCAA), the principal governing body for college sports. Both entities deserve criticism for subordinating the educational missions of academic institutions to the twin goals of publicity and profit. But this book does not revisit the history of college sports or that industry's contemporary problems, because other books have addressed those topics thoroughly. Instead, this book explains how, in the 1980s, the United States Supreme Court made the marriage between athletic commerce and higher education even rockier than before.

Two Supreme Court decisions, namely, *NCAA v. Board of Regents of the University of Oklahoma*, 468 U.S. 85 (1984), and *NCAA v. Tarkanian*, 488 U.S. 179 (1988), are the subject of this book. In both cases, the Court struggled to understand the legal implications of the incongruous union between big-time sports and postsecondary education, then reached a decision that favored sports over education. In *NCAA v. Regents*, the Court held that the NCAA's regulation of live telecasts of college football games was an unreasonable restraint of trade in violation of the Sherman Antitrust Act. The justices reasoned that college football should enjoy a free market in which colleges could negotiate directly with television networks to determine if, when, and how often their teams would appear on television and how much they would earn per appearance. In *NCAA v. Tarkanian*, the Court held that the NCAA was a private association, not a "state actor"; therefore, it was not obliged to provide "due process" (principally, notice of charges and a hearing in which to rebut them) to persons whom it accused of rules violations. This arrangement contrasts with government's obligation to provide due process in court and in administrative proceedings such as those determining eligibility for workers' compensation and social security disability benefits.

Taken together, *Regents* and *Tarkanian* have been toxic to the cause of amateur sports played by full-time students in an academic setting. *Regents* raised the financial stakes in college sports considerably, thereby increasing the incentives to subordinate academics to athletics and to cheat in pursuit of a competitive advantage. *Tarkanian* failed to increase the procedural protections available to persons accused of rules violations proportionally to the elevated financial stakes, even though the accused may lose a livelihood, a college education, an opportunity to play professionally, or a good reputation as a result of NCAA-imposed penalties.

Justice Byron White, the only member of the Court who had played big-time college sports, dissented in both cases. In *Regents,* he reasoned that his colleagues had disregarded the fundamental educational purpose of college sports, while in *Tarkanian,* he argued that they failed to recognize the NCAA's quasi-governmental power. Justice White's dissents are the foundation of this book. It argues that *Regents* denied the NCAA power to limit the commercialization of college football, while *Tarkanian* permitted the NCAA to wield great power over the lives of coaches and athletes without protecting them against the arbitrary and capricious exercise of that power.

The NCAA cannot rectify the adverse consequences of *Regents* alone, and it is unwilling to rectify the adverse consequences of *Tarkanian* by affording due process commensurate with the high stakes involved in its enforcement process. Only the United States Congress can soften the impact of both decisions by granting the NCAA an antitrust exemption for rules having a demonstrably educational purpose, while requiring it to enhance procedural guarantees in enforcement cases. To achieve these ends, this book presents a legislative proposal that, if adopted, would make the governance of college sports fairer and more educationally sound.

A clear understanding of the problem must precede the proposed solution, though. With that in mind, chapter 1 discusses current legal arrangements in college sports. Chapter 2 recounts the history of *Board of Regents v. NCAA,* and chapter 3 explains how the Supreme Court resolved that case. Chapter 4 assesses the economic, academic, and social implications for colleges of the high court's decision in *Regents.* Chapter 5 recalls the history of

Tarkanian v. NCAA, chapter 6 discusses the Supreme Court's decision in that case, and chapter 7 examines *Tarkanian*'s implications for college sports. Chapter 8 proposes legislation creating a new legal structure for college sports, featuring an educationally based antitrust exemption for the NCAA and enhanced due process for persons accused of violating NCAA rules.

Thus, *The Supreme Court and the NCAA* is both realistic and hopeful. It is realistic enough to assume the continued viability of big-time college sports, notwithstanding the many problems that beleaguer the college sports industry. But it is hopeful that, even without a major cultural shift by the American public against athletic commerce, the commercial excesses and the legal deficiencies of the existing system can be ameliorated in favor of education and fairness. The Supreme Court abandoned both education and fairness in deciding *NCAA v. Board of Regents* and *NCAA v. Tarkanian.* This book offers Congress a plan for restoring those values to their proper place in college sports. May the Supreme Court's fumble become Congress's slam dunk.

Chapter 1

ANTITRUST AND DISTRUST OF THE NCAA
The Current Legal Structure in College Sports

Punting Amateurism

The commercial boom that has occurred in college sports during the past generation is no secret, even to the casual fan. A vivid illustration of this phenomenon is the increase in the number of college football games available to television viewers on autumn Saturdays. For example, during the 1970s and the early 1980s, the maximum number of games televised in the Minneapolis–St. Paul metropolitan area was two, one on ABC and one on CBS. In 1983 that number rose to three, as cable station WTBS (now TBS) signed a contract with the NCAA to broadcast college games on Saturday evenings.[1] By 2004 viewers in the Twin Cities area could watch up to 13 college football games on one "Saturation Saturday" if they wished. The offerings included up to four Big 10 games on ABC or ESPN, a game featuring the University of Notre Dame on NBC, perhaps a Southeastern Conference (SEC) game on CBS and a Big 12 game on Fox Sports Net, a game from the Mountain West Conference on ESPN 2, and even an Ivy League game on the CSTV (College Sports Television) channel or a game between two historically black colleges on Black Entertainment Television (BET).[2]

Not only rabid college football fans have gorged themselves on this sumptuous smorgasbord of televised games. Coaches have feasted on it, too, but for them, unlike for the fans, the feast has been primarily financial. In 2003 college football coaches in Division I-A, which includes the NCAA's most athletically prestigious colleges, earned an average annual base salary of more than $388,000, an increase of more than 80 percent in real terms over the 1998 average.[3] The most successful coaches enjoy compensation packages that include not only a princely base salary but also fees for television and radio shows and for personal appearances, raising their value to several million dollars. For example, after Nick Saban led Louisiana State University to the national championship in 2003, he signed a contract for 2004 worth at least $2.3 million.[4] By 2009, at least 25 college head football coaches earned $2 million or more annually, more than double the number who had earned that much in 2007. The average salary for a head football coach in the NCAA's 120-member Football Bowl Subdivision (FBS, formerly Division I-A) in 2009 was $1.36 million, a 46 percent increase since 2006.[5]

If these developments are no surprise, their origins are nonetheless likely to surprise most Americans, even those who follow college sports closely. The prime mover behind college football's commercial growth during the past two decades has been the United States Supreme Court's decision in *NCAA v. Board of Regents of the University of Oklahoma* in 1984.[6] In that case the Court invalidated the NCAA's long-standing Football Television Plan, concluding that it violated the Sherman Antitrust Act.[7] The Court's ruling came just as cable television was experiencing explosive growth in the United States. Together, the two events unleashed an "arms race" among colleges in athletic recruiting, facilities construction, coaches' compensation, and conference realignments aimed at increased television exposure for members' football teams.[8] Sports economist Andrew Zimbalist has observed that *NCAA v. Regents* "opened the floodgates of commercialism [in college sports] much wider than before."[9]

At issue in the case was whether the NCAA's Football Television Plan violated the Sherman Act by restraining economic competition among colleges that sponsored big-time football teams. The plan limited the total number of televised college football games and the number of times per season that any particular team could play on television. It also prohibited Association members from selling the rights to televise their games independently of the NCAA.[10] The stated aims of the plan were to (1) reduce the adverse effects of televised college football on live attendance at games not televised, (2) give as many NCAA members as possible a chance to play on television, and (3) provide televised college football to the public in a way that was compatible with the other two aims.[11]

Justice John Paul Stevens, writing for the majority, observed that Congress had intended the Sherman Act to be a device for protecting consumer welfare. Therefore, he reasoned that any restraint on economic competition "that has the effect of reducing the importance of consumer preference in setting price and output is not consistent with this fundamental goal of antitrust law."[12] The NCAA Football Television Plan had precisely that effect, according to Justice Stevens and the Court's majority, because it restricted the number of televised games that fans could enjoy and prevented colleges whose football teams were popular with the fans from responding to public demand for more televised games. Thus, the Court invalidated the NCAA Football Television Plan.

Justice Byron White dissented from the majority's conclusion. He would have upheld the NCAA plan because it prevented the professionalization of college sports, which would allow profits to drive win-at-any-cost practices. White wrote, "The Court errs in treating intercollegiate athletics under the NCAA's control as a purely commercial venture in which colleges and universities participate solely, or even primarily, in the pursuit of profits."[13] In his view, the plan's price and output restrictions were acceptable restraints on competition because they served "the NCAA's fundamental policy of preserving amateurism and integrating athletics and education."[14] Thus, according to Justice White, ending the plan and thereby allowing a few colleges to enjoy unlimited television appearances "would inevitably give them an insuperable advantage over all others and in the end defeat any efforts to maintain a system of athletic competition among amateurs who measure up to college scholastic requirements."[15]

Byron White spoke with authority about professionalism in college sports, because he had been both a college athlete and a professional athlete. In January 1961, shortly after President John F. Kennedy was inaugurated, Deputy Attorney General White went to lunch at a restaurant located near his office at the Department of Justice. A waitress looked carefully at him and asked, "Say, aren't you Whizzer White?" White, who disliked his unshakeable nickname, replied softly, "I was."[16] A consensus all-American as a senior at the University of Colorado, "Whizzer" White was the most publicized football player in the United States in 1937–38. Newsreels then played the role that television plays now, and in White's senior year at Colorado, three newsreel companies provided motion-picture coverage of one of his football games, and *Life* magazine sent a team of photographers to capture his daily routine in pictures.[17] The attention was understandable, because White finished the 1937 season as the leading scorer in the nation, set a record for all-purpose yards per game that would stand for 51 years, and finished second in the balloting for the Heisman Trophy.[18]

White's senior year also presented him with a delicious but difficult choice that few persons will ever have to make. Throughout the spring and summer of 1938, the media and the American public waited anxiously for him to decide whether he would accept a Rhodes Scholarship to study at Oxford University or a lucrative offer to play professional football for the

Pittsburgh franchise in the National Football League (NFL).[19] The then Pittsburgh Pirates, who later became the Steelers, had made White their first draft choice in December 1937 and had offered him a salary of $15,000 plus an $800 bonus to play in exhibition games. That figure was twice the amount earned by any other player in the NFL at that time.[20]

Byron White's football prowess made his academic success much more interesting to the media than it would otherwise have been. He was the first American Rhodes scholar whose selection was published in newspapers from coast to coast, including the *New York Times,* the *Washington Post,* the *San Francisco Chronicle,* and the *Los Angeles Times.*[21] When he chose the Rhodes Scholarship, both Denver newspapers devoted front-page headlines to his announcement, which he made at a news conference.[22] Later, the Rhodes trustees granted White's request to enroll at Oxford in January 1939, which enabled him to play for Pittsburgh during the 1938 season, earning Rookie of the Year honors along with his handsome salary.[23]

England's entry into World War II in 1939 forced Byron White to leave Oxford prematurely, along with many other Americans.[24] He enrolled at Yale Law School in the fall of 1939 but did not graduate until 1946, after taking the fall semesters of 1940 and 1941 off to play pro football and serving in the United States Navy for several years during World War II.[25] His football career ended with his induction into the navy. By then, White had played three seasons of pro football. His most memorable play of those three seasons occurred during the final game of his career, in November 1941. Playing for the Detroit Lions, to whom Pittsburgh had sold his contract in 1938, White intercepted a pass in the first quarter, seemingly swiping it right out of the opposing receiver's hands, and ran 81 yards for a touchdown. The *New York Times* reported that he broke free from the last defender "with a mighty twist" when it appeared that he was about to be tackled.[26]

White's biographer, Dennis Hutchinson, has noted that this play cemented White's celebrity in the minds of members of his generation. Hutchinson has written, "Captured on newsreels, the play would stay with White for years and provide a vivid image to sailors who met him in the South Pacific, to law students when he returned to Yale after the war, and to law clerks at the Supreme Court when he began his first professional job."[27] Francis Allen, who, like White, was a law clerk to chief justice Fred Vinson at the Supreme Court in 1946–47, recalled White's celebrity among his fellow clerks. He said, "Everyone had heard of Whizzer White. The newsreels and the headlines about his last game, especially the long touchdown run with the intercepted pass, made him a permanent celebrity at the time with his contemporaries."[28]

White's experiences as an athlete may have been a source of enjoyment for his friends, but they left him distrustful of the press, averse to publicity, unsentimental about his athletic past, and convinced that college sports should be distinct from professional sports in aim and emphasis. His statements and behavior in the years following his athletic career reflect these views. In an interview with an Associated Press reporter during his navy service, he said, "Football was just a means to an end—education—so far as I was concerned. I went from college to pro football to make money to pay for schooling."[29] In 1947, when he returned to Colorado to practice law after completing his clerkship at the Supreme Court, White told a college friend that his goals were "to establish my practice, contribute to the community, and keep my name out of the goddamn newspapers."[30] For the next 14 years, he succeeded so well at the first two aims that President Kennedy tapped him to be deputy attorney general in 1961 and appointed him to the Supreme Court in 1962.

Years later, White's daughter, Nancy, a member of the 1980 U.S. Olympic Field Hockey Team, which was sidelined by an American boycott of the Moscow games, spoke about her father. "I don't think he ever put a whole lot of emphasis on athletics [with his children]," she remarked. "His main concern was developing strength in whatever I did. The first thing he always asks about is school."[31] This view is consistent with the sentiments about sports that Justice White expressed in an interview with a reporter for *Sports Illustrated* soon after he joined the Supreme Court. After discussing the benefits of playing sports, Justice White observed,

> But there are many ways to get the same kind of [confidence-building] experience. Dramatics, for instance, or music; or working on the school paper, which is certainly competitive and has that aspect of performing before the public.[32]

Byron White's athletic experiences not only made him dubious about celebrity and partial toward amateurism; they also made him a good prognosticator regarding the likely consequences that the Supreme Court's decision in *NCAA v. Regents* would have on college sports. His first prediction— namely, that allowing a few college football teams to appear on television an unlimited number of times would give them an enormous advantage over their peers—has surely come true. Six so-called equity conferences (Atlantic

Coast, Southeastern, Big East, Big 10, Big 12, and Pacific-10), which domi-nate regular-season telecasts and the postseason bowl games, include by far the wealthiest and most visible teams.[33] Beginning in the summer of 1990, conference memberships changed dramatically and often, as institutions plotted and schemed with and against each other to leave conferences that had limited television exposure in favor of conferences promising greater television exposure.[34]

The competition for teams reached its peak in the summer and fall of 2003, when the Atlantic Coast Conference (ACC) lured the University of Miami in Florida, Virginia Tech, and Boston College away from the Big East Conference. Adding three new members gave the ACC a total of 12, which allowed it to create two divisions and to hold a lucrative playoff game be-tween the divisional champions for the first time in 2005.[35] It also enabled the league to sign a seven-year contract with ESPN and ABC, doubling the number of ACC football games that ESPN telecasts each season. The con-tract figure, $258 million, is almost twice the amount that the ACC earned under its previous television contract.[36] But the ACC was not alone among conferences in altering its membership roster. In the fall of 2005, 18 of the 119 members (15 percent) of what was then Division I-A (now the FBS) be-longed to a different conference than they had belonged to a year earlier.[37] Unlike the ACC, though, some of those conferences, notably the Big East, became weaker as a result of the membership changes. The conferences that benefited from the shifts are likely to command a larger share of the profits from bowl games and to attract a higher percentage of the best players, while the remaining FBS conferences weaken and lose money.[38] With these aims in mind, several FBS member institutions participated in a second round of conference "musical chairs" in the spring and fall of 2010. The University of Colorado joined the PAC-10, the University of Nebraska joined the Big 10, Boise State University became the tenth member of the Mountain West Conference, and Texas Christian University (TCU) accepted an invitation to join the Big East Conference.[39]

The equity conferences plus the University of Notre Dame comprise the Bowl Championship Series (BCS), a creation not of the NCAA but of television and the marketplace,[40] which is designed to produce a credible "national champion" each year without resorting to a playoff system that would replace the long-standing bowl games, thereby destroying their eco-nomic viability.[41] The BCS guarantees the equity conferences that their top teams will appear in the most prestigious and financially rewarding bowl games, sometimes even in favor of a more powerful team that does not belong to one of the equity conferences. The BCS also guarantees the equity conferences that their teams will appear in more bowl games than will teams belonging to the other FBS conferences (Mountain West, Western Athletic, Big West, Sun Belt, Mid-American, and Conference USA).[42]

The Supreme Court's bow to the marketplace in *NCAA v. Regents* caused institutions to increase their spending on sports, especially football, to pay their coaches exorbitant salaries, and to assume large amounts of capital debt in order to remain athletically competitive with their peers. College athletic expenses rose approximately 8 percent per year between 2002–3 and 2004–5, according to an analysis by *USA Today* of reports that colleges filed with the federal Department of Education in October 2005.[43] According to the NCAA, expenses rose by a similar percentage between 2000–2001 and 2002–3.[44] The annual rate of increase in athletic spending is twice the annual rate of increase in overall spending by colleges, which, according to the NCAA, was between 3 percent and 4 percent from 2000–2001 through 2004–5.[45]

Commenting on these figures, the then NCAA president, Myles Brand, said, "We have a system under stress. Revenue streams have been increasing as well. But it's unrealistic to believe they will increase at double the rate of the general university [revenue increase] for the foreseeable future."[46] If the existing trend continued, he added, "Funding from the academic budget of the institution will have to be redirected to athletics. Or students will be charged directly with [higher] athletic fees. That is problematic."[47] It is also endemic. Data published by *USA Today* early in 2010 showed that institutional subsidies for athletics at 99 public universities belonging to the FBS grew approximately 20 percent, from $685 million to $826 million, between 2005 and 2008, after adjusting for inflation. At more than one-third of those institutions, the percentage of athletic department revenue that was represented by subsidies grew during that period.[48]

Similarly, a draft report by the NCAA's Fiscal Responsibility Subcommittee calls the recent spending increases "a looming crisis" and argues that if college presidents do not rein in athletic spending soon, "it will be too late to avoid problems that will seriously threaten the survival of intercollegiate athletics."[49] An October 2009 consultant's report to the Knight Commission on Intercollegiate Athletics, a private watchdog group, observed, "It is clear that the question for a majority of presidents of equity and non-equity institutions alike is not whether . . . the current model is sustainable, but, given the forces at work, how long it can be sustained."[50] That commission's own report, released in June 2010, noted that median athletic spending per athlete in the major athletic conferences ranged from 4 to nearly 11 times more than those institutions' median spending per student on education-related activities.[51]

Justice White's second prediction in *NCAA v. Regents*—namely, that allowing some college football teams to make unlimited television appearances would hinder efforts to ensure that college athletes are bona fide college students—has also come true. To be sure, *NCAA v. Regents* is not solely responsible for academic fraud or low graduation rates among college athletes; those problems long preceded the Supreme Court's decision. But that decision has enhanced the financial rewards associated with athletic success, making it difficult for the NCAA to eliminate academic fraud or to improve athletes' graduation rates significantly.

Recent data reflect the continuing problem of low graduation rates among college athletes, the overwhelming majority of whom will not become professional athletes.[52] In December 2005 the Institute for Diversity and Ethics in Sport, located at the University of Central Florida, issued a report titled *APR Rates and Graduation Rates for 2005–06 Bowl-Bound Teams*. It noted that nearly half of the college football teams that participated in bowl games at the end of the 2005 season had failed to graduate at least 50 percent of their players during the past six years.[53] Similarly, a report published jointly by the Institute for Diversity and Ethics in Sport and the Knight Commission in 2004 showed that 44 of the 65 men's college basketball teams participating in the NCAA Tournament that year had graduated less than 50 percent of their players during the preceding six years.[54]

The report also pointed out that 41 percent of the bowl-bound teams had failed to meet a new academic standard established by the NCAA.[55] Under the new standard, known as the Academic Progress Rate (APR), teams earn points based on their athletes' classroom performances and on whether the players are making progress toward obtaining degrees.[56] A score of 925 equates to an expected graduation rate of 50 percent, a standard that 23 of the 56 bowl-bound teams examined in the study failed to meet, meaning that they were not likely to graduate at least 50 percent of their athletes. In March 2006 the NCAA announced that 99 teams from 65 colleges would lose scholarships in the coming year for failure to satisfy the requirements of the APR. Sixty-one of those 99 teams compete in baseball, football, or men's basketball.[57]

Adoption of the APR follows on the heels of another academic rules change by the NCAA, which went into effect in 2003. It increased the academic rigor of the course requirements that incoming freshman must complete during high school, and it required athletes enrolled in college to complete 40 percent of their degree requirements by the end of their second year of college, 60 percent by the end of their third year, and 80 percent by the end of their fourth year.[58] In the fall of 2006, the NCAA began to penalize institutions whose teams failed to meet the new standards, by reducing the number of athletic scholarships that those colleges can offer.[59] According to Dr. Richard Lapchick, who wrote the report on academic progress among the 2005 bowl teams, the APR and the sanctions associated with it are cause for optimism because "[f]or the first time the NCAA can sanction schools for not doing what they are supposed to be doing: educating the people who come to [their] campuses."[60] He added, "My hope is that because there are consequences, institutions will pay more attention to what their athletes are doing."[61]

Perhaps they will; indeed, perhaps they already are. In its March 2006 report, the Institute for Diversity and Ethics in Sport found that of the 65 Division I men's basketball teams selected for the NCAA Tournament that year, 35, or 54 percent (Penn and the Air Force Academy do not report graduation rates), did not graduate at least 50 percent of their athletes within six years of enrollment, an improvement from 42 teams in 2005.[62] Moreover, that 54 percent figure resulted from using the Federal Graduation Rate, a measure devised by the United States Department of Education that understates graduation rates by counting as nongraduates (1) students who transfer out of Division I colleges, (2) transfers from junior colleges who graduate from the four-year colleges to which they transfer, and (3) former athletes who return to school and graduate more than six years after their initial enrollment. When the same 65 teams were studied using the Graduation Success Rate, a measure devised by the NCAA, which counts as graduates athletes who transfer from a college in good academic standing, transfers from junior colleges who graduate from their four-year institutions, and former athletes who earn degrees more than six years after first enrolling, the result was that 41 teams, or 64 percent of the total, graduated at least 50 percent of their basketball players within six years.[63]

But any optimism about the impact of the new standards must be guarded. One reason for caution is what Dr. Lapchick has called "the persistent gap [in graduation rates] between African-American and white basketball student-athletes."[64] Among the 2006 NCAA Tournament teams, 88 percent (51 colleges) graduated 50 percent or more of their white athletes, but only 57 percent (36 colleges) graduated 50 percent or more of their African American athletes.[65] Twenty-five of the teams that participated in the 2006 tournament had at least a 30 percent gap between the graduation rates of their white and African American male basketball players.[66]

This racial disparity remained evident for both men's and women's basketball teams that participated in the 2010 NCAA Tournament. Dr. Lapchick's study of these teams found that white male basketball players graduated at an 84 percent rate, compared to 56 percent for their African American counterparts. This study also found that white female basketball players on the tournament teams graduated at a rate of 90 percent, compared to 78 percent for their African American counterparts.[67] A racial disparity also existed among the college football teams that participated in bowl games at the end of the 2009 season. Dr. Lapchick reported that 22 teams, or 32 percent of those participating in a bowl game after the 2009 season, graduated less than half of their black players, whereas only two teams graduated less than half of their white players. He also reported graduation rates among these teams of 77 percent for their white football players and 58 percent for their black players.[68]

Another reason for caution is that no decrease in the financial incentives for athletic success has accompanied the increased penalties for academic failure in college sports. Absent an abatement of the financial incentives, incentives that increased after *NCAA v. Regents,* sanctions for academic failure are unlikely to succeed as much as Dr. Lapchick and other advocates of college sports reform would like. After all, notwithstanding the APR and its associated sanctions, the expansion of televised college football now includes midweek games, thanks to growing competition for a share of the college sports market, fueled in part by the emergence of three new cable television networks—CSTV, ESPNU, and Fox College Sports—since 2003.[69] These games have academic consequences, as when the University of Louisville, in order to play a Thursday night game against the University of Miami, caught a Wednesday afternoon flight, spent Thursday in Florida, and then returned to Louisville after the 7:45 p.m. game, arriving home at 3:00 a.m. Under these circumstances, said then coach Bobby Petrino, "[i]t's really hard to get [the players up to] go to class [the next day]."[70]

Former TCU quarterback Tye Gunn echoed Coach Petrino's sentiments when he testified before the Knight Commission on Intercollegiate

Athletics in January 2006. Noting that a weeknight football game "is a huge stress on you as far as academics go," he explained that a weeknight game out of state could cause him to return to his campus at 4:00 a.m. on a day when he had a class—and a test—at 8:00 a.m. He added that "[w]hen you go on a football trip there isn't much time for studying."[71]

The time commitment associated with playing big-time college sports continues today, especially in football and basketball, notwithstanding improved graduation rates. Happily, 79 percent of athletes in all sports at NCAA Division I institutions who enrolled between 1999 and 2002 graduated within six years, an increase of 8 percent since 2001. Still, 3 of the top 25 football teams during the 2009 season and 23 of the 65 teams that played in the 2009 NCAA Men's Basketball Tournament graduated fewer than half their players during that six-year period.[72] Under these circumstances, the results of a 2007 NCAA survey of 21,000 college athletes, indicating that most of them viewed themselves more as athletes than as students, are not surprising. Football players at FBS institutions reported spending 44.8 hours a week practicing, playing, or training for their sport. One in five survey subjects reported that playing a sport prevented them from choosing the major they preferred.[73]

The financial incentives for athletic success can also cause coaches and athletes to commit academic fraud in order to keep athletes academically eligible to compete. A prime example of academic fraud for this purpose occurred at the University of Georgia in the fall of 2001. Assistant men's basketball coach Jim Harrick, Jr., whose father, Jim Harrick, Sr., was the head coach, taught a basketball-coaching course that term in which three varsity basketball players were enrolled. Several years later, the university fired the younger Mr. Harrick for awarding As to the three players even though they had not done any work in the course and for encouraging two of them to mislead university and NCAA investigators about his grading policy.[74]

Academic fraud continues in college sports. In 2009 the NCAA ordered Florida State University to forfeit wins and scholarships in 10 sports because of an academic cheating scandal involving 61 athletes in 2006–7. Three staffers in the University's Athletic Academic Support Services Office "gave improper assistance" to the athletes, according to an NCAA report. The report noted that many of the violations occurred in an online music course and that one Academic Support staffer had typed portions of term papers for at least three athletes.[75]

When the Supreme Court decided *NCAA v. Regents,* it made Coach

Petrino's task of ensuring that his players get to class more difficult, and it increased the incentive for unscrupulous coaches, like Jim Harrick, Jr., to cut academic corners in pursuit of athletic, hence financial, success. In the name of markets and consumer welfare, the Court disregarded the academic setting in which college sports operate, thereby rendering the already troubled marriage between athletic commerce and higher education even rockier than it was before. *Regents* did not introduce commercialism to college sports, but it surely intensified that commercialism. Absent *Regents,* for example, Penn State would have lacked a financial incentive to join the Big 10, Notre Dame could not have made its own arrangement (with NBC, beginning in 1991) for the televising of its football games, and the average salary for a head football coach at an FBS institution in 2009 would not have been $1.36 million.[76]

Fumbling Fairness

Ironically, at about the same time that the Supreme Court raised the financial stakes in college football, it also denied to coaches and athletes legal protections that match those high financial stakes. If found guilty of violating NCAA rules, coaches stand to lose their livelihoods, while athletes stand to lose a subsidized college education and the chance to catch the eye of a professional team. The legal protections afforded to coaches, athletes, and other college employees whom the NCAA accuses of rules violations ought to be commensurate with the gravity of the losses that accused persons will sustain if found guilty.

The protections do not match the penalties primarily because of the Supreme Court's decision in *NCAA v. Tarkanian.*[77] That decision held that the suspension by the University of Nevada, Las Vegas (UNLV), a public institution, of head men's basketball coach Jerry Tarkanian, in response to NCAA findings that he had violated its rules and that UNLV should sever its ties with him for two years, did not make the NCAA a "state actor" that must accord Tarkanian due process of law. Writing for the majority, Justice John Paul Stevens noted that the issue to be decided in *Tarkanian* was "whether UNLV's actions in compliance with the NCAA rules and recommendations turned the NCAA's conduct into state action."[78] He concluded that the Court could not fairly attribute the NCAA's conduct to the State of Nevada; although UNLV had followed the NCAA's rules and adopted its recommendations, only UNLV was authorized to suspend Tarkanian and did so.[79] Justice Stevens wrote, "It would be more appropriate to conclude that UNLV has conducted its athletic program under color of the policies adopted by the NCAA, rather than that those policies were developed and enforced under color of Nevada law."[80]

Justice White dissented, noting that private organizations, such as the NCAA, can be held to be state actors if they engaged jointly with state officials in the challenged action.[81] In this instance, he observed, the NCAA acted jointly with UNLV to suspend Tarkanian for violating NCAA rules that UNLV had adopted when it joined the Association.[82] Indeed, he elaborated, "It was the NCAA's finding that Tarkanian had violated NCAA rules, made at NCAA-conducted hearings, all of which were agreed to by UNLV in its membership agreement with the NCAA, that resulted in Tarkanian's suspension by UNLV." "Thus," White concluded, "the NCAA was jointly engaged with [UNLV] officials in the challenged action and therefore was a state actor."[83]

But White's view could not command a majority of the Court. As a result, the NCAA need not (and does not) guarantee due process to persons whom it accuses of violating its rules. Although the *Tarkanian* decision did not reduce the due process protections available in NCAA proceedings, it eliminated any incentive the NCAA might otherwise have had to increase those protections. The lack of independent judges in NCAA enforcement proceedings is especially troublesome because both the Committee on Infractions and the investigative staff that assists the committee owe their allegiance to the NCAA. Under these circumstances, accused persons and institutions often complain that "prosecutor" (investigative staff), "judge" (Committee on Infractions), and "jury" (Committee on Infractions) are all the same in those proceedings.[84] The Infractions Appeals Committee is also comprised of employees of NCAA member institutions, which reinforces the widespread view that the Association has a "home-field advantage" in enforcement cases. This deficiency prompted Gary Roberts (then Tulane University law professor, now dean of the Indiana University School of Law–Indianapolis), an authority on sports law who generally supports the NCAA's enforcement process, to recommend, in testimony to a congressional subcommittee, that the NCAA "establish a 'judiciary' of paid and properly trained 'judges.'"[85] Dean Roberts has written that "in the long run, the image, integrity and mission of the NCAA might well be better served" if the Association used "neutral outside dispute resolution mechanisms" in its enforcement program.[86]

The lack of independent judges is the major flaw in NCAA enforcement proceedings, but those proceedings fall short in other ways, too. No witnesses are permitted to appear at the hearings conducted by the Committee on Infractions, except NCAA staff, individuals representing accused institutions, and coaches and athletes accused of wrongdoing. The committee lacks subpoena power, which means that it cannot compel witnesses to attend hearings and that an accused individual or institution cannot challenge incriminating testimony through cross-examination.[87] This also means that third parties whose allegations precipitated the investigation and the hearing or whom the accused parties claim could exonerate them cannot appear or testify. Neither can third parties who are implicated in the allegations.

The prohibition that prevents third parties implicated in allegations from participating in hearings is especially troubling. Despite having done nothing wrong, athletic department personnel may become scapegoats for institutions under investigation that wish to accommodate the NCAA in order to minimize their anticipated punishment.[88] Nowadays, when the NCAA alleges that an institution has committed major rules violations, the institution typically hires a law firm to investigate the allegations. This investigation is conducted simultaneously with but independently of an investigation by the NCAA's enforcement staff. When the institutional investigation is complete, the institution's leaders and lawyers draft a report and impose their own set of penalties on the athletic department, such as reducing scholarships for the offending team(s) for a defined period of time.[89] The institution also punishes employees whom the investigation has deemed responsible for the wrongdoing, by firing, reassigning, or reprimanding them.[90] But that does not mean that the targeted employees necessarily did anything wrong.

Consider, for example, the case of Dr. B. David Ridpath, formerly the assistant athletic director for compliance and student services at Marshall University in West Virginia. Marshall hired him in 1997, in his words, "to clean up a rules compliance program in disarray."[91] While trying to do so, he discovered several minor violations and two major violations of NCAA rules, which he reported to the Mid-American Conference, of which Marshall was a member, and to the NCAA. One major violation, which became the subject of an NCAA investigation, was "an illegal employment scheme for football and men's basketball athletes."[92] It enabled athletes whose high school grades and standardized test scores made them ineligible for athletic scholarships to earn above-market wages at a machine shop where Marshall coaches had arranged for them to be employed.[93]

The employment scheme predated Dr. Ridpath's arrival at Marshall by seven years, during which time both coaches and administrators kept its existence a secret.[94] They did not inform Dr. Ridpath about it when he began working at Marshall.[95] Moreover, Ridpath alleged, in a lawsuit he filed against Marshall and that the parties settled in 2009, that during Marshall's internal investigation of the employment scheme, the head football coach, the university's general counsel, and the special counsel whom the university had hired to lead the internal investigation prohibited him from interviewing the owner of the machine shop who had employed the athletes.[96] He also alleged that when the NCAA's Committee on Infractions conducted a hearing on Marshall's case, both the general counsel and the special counsel encouraged him to defend the university, its compliance program, and its football coach vigorously.[97]

Ridpath's vigorous defense of persons whom he mistakenly believed to be honest and forthcoming served him to no good end. His lawsuit stated that on or about October 1, 2001, "for numerous reasons both personal and professional, Ridpath agreed to be re-assigned to the position of Director of Judicial Programs at [Marshall]."[98] According to Ridpath, although Marshall's president, Dan Angel, assured him that his removal as compliance director was not the consequence of any wrongdoing by him, university authorities, acting through counsel, "informed the NCAA that [his] re-assignment was a 'corrective action' taken by MU as the result of NCAA rule violations at the University."[99] Thus, Ridpath's lawsuit alleged, despite his lack of involvement in NCAA violations, "he became a convenient scapegoat for MU when his vigorous defense of the University . . . [angered] the NCAA Committee on Infractions."[100]

Commenting on this outcome, Ridpath told a subcommittee of the House Judiciary Committee in 2004, "Although I did everything required by NCAA rules and told the truth throughout the investigation, my career and reputation were in tatters, while those who actually started the [illegal employment] program, maintained the program, and covered up the program are still working in college athletics today."[101] To prevent what happened to him from happening to others, Dr. Ridpath recommended to the lawmakers that when a college's corrective action in response to an investigation by the NCAA is to fire or discipline one or more employees, the employee(s) should have "appeal rights IF the NCAA accepts the sanction as its own."[102] Similarly, chapter 7 of this book recommends a model of due process at NCAA hearings that includes an opportunity for a booster or a college employee whom a college sought to sacrifice in return for leniency to present oral or written testimony during those hearings.

An Act of Congress

Taken together, *NCAA v. Board of Regents* and *NCAA v. Tarkanian* have aided and abetted an expensive entertainment enterprise that is prone to scandal and fails to protect the rights of its workers (coaches and athletes) adequately. The two decisions' joint responsibility for the excessive demands placed on coaches and athletes and for the inadequate protections afforded them accounts for their joint emphasis in this book. To be sure, the cases presented markedly different legal issues (a claimed restraint of trade in *Regents* and an alleged denial of due process in *Tarkanian*), and no evidence indicates that their outcomes reflect a desire by the Supreme Court to structure or restructure college sports in any particular way. On the contrary, the Court seems to have decided each case on its own merits, as evidenced by the closer vote in *Tarkanian* (5–4) than in *Regents* (7–2). Moreover, neither decision created the problem of excessive commercialism or insufficient due process in college sports; the NCAA and its members bear that responsibility, with an assist from media companies regarding commercialism. Still, *Regents* and *Tarkanian* are problematic because they have made college sports more commercialized and less protective of coaches' and athletes' rights and hence less compatible with higher education today than was true a generation ago. In short, these two decisions have exacerbated preexisting maladies in college sports, making those maladies considerably more difficult to treat and cure than they would otherwise be.

Happily, the solution to the commercial excesses precipitated by *NCAA v. Board of Regents* is also the solution to the inadequate legal protections for coaches and athletes resulting from *NCAA v. Tarkanian*. Congress should enact legislation granting the NCAA a limited antitrust exemption for rules designed to serve educational ends and requiring it to provide legal protections commensurate with the high stakes that its enforcement proceedings have for accused parties. The concept of congressionally driven reform of college sports is not new. Indeed, former congressman and professional basketball player Tom McMillen has long advocated granting the NCAA an antitrust exemption and requiring the Association to strengthen legal protections for persons accused of rules violations. Speaking in 2003 at the National Symposium on Athletic Reform sponsored by Tulane University, McMillen analogized college athletic reform to campaign finance reform in politics. In both contexts, he observed, "it's pretty hard to change the rules when the issues are so difficult, the conflicts are so intractable, or the money is so great."[103] Thus, he concluded, "[my] view is that [such change] will probably have to be done externally."[104]

In 1991, while a member of Congress from Maryland, McMillen tried to promote a fundamental change in the administration of college sports by introducing the Collegiate Athletic Reform Act in the House of Representatives.[105] This proposal derived from McMillen's view that the NCAA needed to be "a benevolent dictator of college sports" and that only Congress could "restore the NCAA to its pre-1984 power over TV contracts."[106] His bill would have given the NCAA an antitrust exemption for five years, enabling it to negotiate and approve all major television and radio contracts for college football and basketball during that time. It would also have empowered the Association to expel any member institution that attempted to make its own broadcasting arrangements.[107]

In return for receiving the antitrust exemption, the NCAA would have been required to adopt various reform measures, including establishing (1) a more powerful Board of Presidents to oversee the Association; (2) a more equitable plan for revenue distribution among colleges, namely, one that was less tied to a college's athletic success; and (3) enhanced due process protections for persons accused of violating Association rules.[108] If the NCAA failed to adopt the reform measures within one year after the new law's enactment, the Collegiate Athletics Reform Act would have authorized the Internal Revenue Service (IRS) to begin taxing the revenues that the NCAA and its member institutions earn from sports, under the Unrelated Business Income Tax (UBIT).[109] The UBIT subjects to taxation the revenues that nonprofit entities earn from operating for-profit businesses unrelated to their nonprofit work.[110] McMillen's bill would also have authorized colleges to pay their athletes a stipend of up to $300 a month and to make their athletic scholarships effective for five years as long as the recipient remained in good academic standing during that time.[111]

Implicit in Tom McMillen's proposal, which did not become law, was a recognition that college sports, at least as they operate in the NCAA's Division I, have as much, if not more, to do with commerce as they do with higher education. Economists Arthur Fleischer, Brian Goff, and Robert Tollison captured the hybrid nature of big-time college sports when they wrote in their 1992 book on the NCAA that "[t]he non-profit, educational setting of college sports helps to mask much of its underlying profit-motivated behavior."[112] The NCAA's profit-motivated behavior was evident in its posture toward a lawsuit brought against it several years ago by promoters of early-season college basketball tournaments, *Worldwide Basketball and Sport Tours, Inc. et al. v. NCAA.*[113] The origins of the lawsuit lay in a scheduling rule that the NCAA had adopted for basketball. NCAA rules permit colleges to play a maximum of 28 regular-season games but grant an "exemption" to "certified" multigame, early-season tournaments. These tournaments began as a way to encourage colleges located on the American mainland to schedule games against colleges located in Alaska and Hawaii, which had long had difficulty in scheduling games because of their distance from the mainland.[114]

Over time, the NCAA became concerned that the more successful and visible college basketball teams were appearing in these tournaments with disproportionate frequency. It therefore adopted Proposition 98-92, which increased the maximum number of regular-season games to 28 and counted as just one regular-season game all of the contests played in an "exempt" tournament, even if a team actually played three or four games in that tournament.[115] But this rule limits a team to participating in "not more than one certified basketball event in one academic year, and not more than two certified basketball events every four years."[116]

One would be naive to think that the aim of this "two-in-four rule" was to limit the class time and studying time that college basketball players missed because of travel. Instead, the text of the rule specifies that its purpose is to "address competitive equity concerns . . . so that the inherent recruiting and competitive advantages [of participating in these tournaments] are distributed equally among Division I institutions."[117] Similarly, after a federal appellate court held that the two-in-four rule does not violate the Sherman Antitrust Act, thereby upholding the NCAA's position, NCAA spokesman Erik Cristianson praised the court's ruling by saying,

> It's important for intercollegiate athletics because the two-in-four rule was designed to provide more opportunity for student-athletes and give a broader range of institutions the opportunity to compete in these events.

Thus, despite the NCAA's insistence on calling college basketball players "student-athletes," it showed during the lawsuit over the two-in-four rule, as it had shown in limiting televised college football 50 years earlier, that its rules are often driven more by athletic and commercial motivations than by a healthy desire to integrate athletics into an educational context. Therefore, one can agree with the position argued by the NCAA in both *Worldwide Basketball* and *NCAA v. Regents* but still not celebrate its victory in the former or mourn its defeat in the latter, because even when the NCAA argues for the correct result in court, it seems to do so for the wrong reasons. The NCAA's commercial focus also argues against Tom McMillen's suggestion that Congress should make it a "benevolent dictator" over college sports. The NCAA's capacity to be a dictator is evident, but its inclination toward benevolence is questionable. Under these circumstances, the antitrust exemption that this book recommends for the NCAA is limited and designed to spur the Association to act in the best educational interests of college athletes.

Ironically, the NCAA passed up a chance to obtain an antitrust exemption in 1961, when Congress bestowed one on the NFL so that it could negotiate a collective television contract for its teams.[118] The NCAA chose not to apply for an exemption of its own, believing that was unnecessary because its ties to higher education would shield its rules from antitrust scrutiny.[119] But the NCAA may have outsmarted itself, because in the years since 1961 and especially in the years since *NCAA v. Regents,* big-time college sports have become so commercialized that antitrust scrutiny of NCAA rules has become a reality, as *Regents* and *Worldwide Basketball* demonstrate. In this environment, the need for the NCAA to have some sort of an antitrust exemption so that it can enact rules designed to curb commercial excess has become apparent.[120]

Any such exemption, though, must recognize that big-time college sports, as Gary Roberts has pointed out, are an awkward hybrid of commerce and education.[121] Roberts has written,

> While the NCAA's Division I members are running operations that are primarily driven by commercial motives, they are still strongly influenced by educational values that are often at odds with the Sherman Act's value of promoting competition in the marketplace. Preserving some modicum of educational integrity in the academy is simply not reconcilable with maximizing consumer welfare in the sports entertainment marketplace.[122]

Dean Roberts contends that evaluating college sports according to the requirements of the Sherman Act "will do great violence to" academic values[123] but that creating an antitrust exemption or favoring the NCAA in antitrust cases will "allow athletic programs to profit by the uncontrolled exploitation of student-athletes and consumers."[124]

His points are well taken. Institutions that profit from ostensibly amateur sports played by nominally full-time students probably cannot avoid the charge that they are exploiting athletes by not paying them for their athletic labor. But much of the sting would go out of that charge if the NCAA were to (1) enact rules designed to reduce the commercial pressures that rob college athletes of educational opportunities and (2) adopt procedures designed to ensure that athletes who are accused of violating Association rules receive the same measure of due process as someone who seeks workers' compensation or social security disability benefits. Athletes would still not be paid wages for their athletic labor, but the NCAA could require colleges to increase the value of their athletic scholarships to cover the full cost of attendance if it wished.

An educationally based antitrust exemption would enable the NCAA to prohibit midweek football games and to shorten competitive seasons, thereby enhancing the chances that athletes will earn degrees in a timely way. For most college athletes, who will not play professionally, a degree is the best "wage" that they can possibly earn. This limited antitrust exemption would also enable the NCAA to rein in coaches' salaries, thereby reducing athletic department spending and bringing athletic departments closer to the mainstream of campus life.[125] If robust legal protections accompanied enhanced educational opportunities for athletes, one would be hard-pressed to argue that college athletes were victims of "uncontrolled exploitation," whether or not their respective institutions profited from sports.

This vision is consistent with that articulated by President Scott Cowan of Tulane University, who advocates "continu[ing] to enhance student-athlete welfare, not by paying [athletes] more money, but by reducing time requirements, pressure, and expectations."[126] "[R]educe the length of the schedule," President Cowan urges, "reduce the requirements we have for practice time on athletes, allow them to have some of the free time that they so richly deserve to truly be part of a university community."[127] These changes would be possible if the NCAA had the educationally based limited antitrust exemption that this book advocates.

The limited antitrust exemption would not depart radically from present law, because the courts already treat NCAA rules fostering amateurism more favorably than rules serving purely commercial ends.[128] For example, in *Law v. NCAA,*[129] a federal appellate court affirmed the decision of a federal trial court holding that an NCAA rule limiting certain college basketball coaches to "restricted earnings" of no more than $16,000 a year violated the Sherman Act.[130] The "restricted earnings rule" limited basketball coaching staffs at Division I colleges to four members, including the head coach, two assistant coaches, and one restricted-earnings coach (REC), who could earn no more than $12,000 from coaching during the academic year and $4,000 during the summer.[131] Its purpose was to reduce escalating personnel costs in college basketball.

Both the trial court and the appellate court concluded that the restricted-earnings rule would not contain costs, because it did not prevent colleges from using the money they saved on the salary of the REC to increase the salaries of the head coach and the assistant coaches.[132] Moreover, both courts concluded that the rule was "anticompetitive" under the Sherman Act because it interfered with and reduced economic competition among basketball coaches seeking work and among colleges seeking coaches, by shrinking the price of an assistant coach artificially.[133] Viewing the restricted-earnings rule as strictly commercial, both courts emphasized its interference with economic competition in striking it down.

But courts generally treat NCAA rules designed to preserve the amateur status of college athletes with considerable deference. For example, in *Banks v. NCAA,* the court upheld NCAA rules prohibiting college athletes from entering a professional sports league's draft and from hiring a professional sports agent before completing their college athletic eligibility, under penalty of losing that eligibility.[134] The *Banks* court wrote,

> We consider college football players as student-athletes simultaneously pursuing academic degrees that will prepare them to enter the employment market in non-athletic occupations, and hold that the regulations of the NCAA are designed to preserve the honesty and integrity of intercollegiate athletics and foster fair competition among the participating amateur college students.[135]

Therefore, an antitrust exemption for educationally based rules would preserve the dichotomy between the way in which courts treat predominately commercial NCAA rules and the way in which they treat rules regulating the eligibility of athletes. One might reasonably wonder why the proposed exemption is necessary if courts already defer to NCAA rules relating to amateurism. The answer is that the exemption would ensure that rules enacted for legitimate educational purposes, such as to reduce the number of regular-season games and to restrict them to weekends, would survive judicial scrutiny even if they limited athletic commerce. The burden of proof would be on the party challenging a particular rule on antitrust grounds to show that the rule did not serve a legitimate educational purpose and that it was anticompetitive. The rule's anticompetitive effect would be insufficient to invalidate it if it served a legitimate educational goal.

Moreover, the antitrust exemption proposed here would send a strong signal to the college athletics community that the federal government was genuinely interested in making higher education the managing partner in the long-standing relationship between American colleges and athletic commerce. This signal is crucial in the present environment, where commercial pressures on college sports are increasing and where legal challenges to the NCAA's efforts to preserve amateurism are likely to increase, too. The growing commercialism of college sports and the growing profitability of the NCAA increase the likelihood of antitrust challenges to the NCAA. For the past several years, commentators on sports law have predicted that if present patterns continued, the NCAA would face challenges to its rules limiting (1) the number of athletic scholarships that institutions can award, (2) the amount of income that athletes can earn from jobs during the competitive season, (3) the size of coaching staffs, and (4) the dollar amounts of athletic scholarships.[136]

These predictions proved prescient in February 2006, when two former football players and one former men's basketball player at NCAA Division I colleges filed an antitrust lawsuit against the NCAA in a federal district court in Los Angeles.[137] The suit, *White et al. v. NCAA,* alleged that athletes at Division I institutions often must pay $2,500 or more each year to meet basic expenses that their athletic scholarships do not cover.[138] The plaintiffs asked the court to certify a class of 98 present and former athletes at each of 116 institutions (or a total of 11,638 class members) who are eligible to receive damages from the NCAA of $10,000 each, or $2,500 per year for four years.[139] The plaintiffs also asked the court to allow colleges to pay their athletic scholarship recipients in revenue-producing sports additional funds above the limit of the scholarship if they wished.[140] The plaintiffs contended that "[w]hile big-time college sports have become a huge commercial enterprise generating billions in annual revenues, the NCAA and its member institutions do not allow student athletes the share of the revenues that they would obtain in a more competitive market."[141] Accordingly, besides asking the court for damages, the plaintiffs sought an injunction restraining the NCAA from enforcing the cap that it imposes on athletic financial aid by limiting the reach of athletic scholarships to "tuition and fees, room and board, and required course-related books."[142]

The plaintiffs' argument raised more questions than it answered. For example, if, as the plaintiffs wished, the NCAA permitted institutions to pay stipends of $2,500 per year or more to athletic scholarship recipients, would the athletes receiving these stipends become employees who would be eligible to receive workers' compensation for injuries sustained in practice or competition?[143] Would colleges then be required to pay social security taxes for these athletes, and could the athletes unionize and demand the right to bargain collectively?[144] Would colleges be held legally responsible for injuries resulting from negligent or reckless behavior by athletes that occurred within the scope of their athletic employment (e.g., a locker-room fight or a "late hit" during a football game)?[145] Employment issues aside, would colleges engage in illegal sex discrimination if they awarded the $2,500 stipends only to male athletes because only men's teams were profitable,[146] and would male athletes in revenue sports be entitled to the stipends even in years when their teams were not profitable?[147]

In light of the serious implications of these questions and the federal courts' historic deference to the NCAA in "personnel" matters, the plaintiffs' prospects for success were questionable. But if the plaintiffs succeeded, the costs of maintaining big-time college sports programs would increase, and the institutions that could afford to pay the stipends would gain a significant recruiting advantage over those that could not, thereby exacerbating the gap between the BCS colleges and their less affluent rivals. Alternatively, the less-affluent rivals would sink deeper into debt to pay the stipends and stay competitive.

No such consequences occurred, though, because the parties settled *White v. NCAA* in 2008. Under the settlement, the NCAA agreed to make available $218 million over five years to help more than 150,000 Division I athletes in all sports meet basic expenses not covered by their scholarships. The NCAA also agreed to create a separate fund of $10 million to provide career-development services for and to reimburse former college athletes who were members of the class of plaintiffs and who qualify under and comply with the requirements associated with the fund. Both pots of money are time-limited, though. If the benefits to current athletes are to continue beyond five years, institutions will have to pay for them, and if former athletes are to obtain reimbursements and career-development services, they must do so within three years.[148]

Although *White v. NCAA* ended in a settlement, another antitrust action, *Agnew v. NCAA,* soon followed. Former Rice University football player Joseph Agnew alleged that the NCAA has violated antitrust law by (1) making athletic scholarships annually renewable one-year grants instead of multiyear grants and (2) placing caps on the number of athletic scholarships that institutions can offer. Filed in March 2011, the *Agnew* case is pending in a federal district court in Indianapolis.[149] Regardless of the outcome in *Agnew,* other antitrust challenges to NCAA rules are likely to follow it if commercial goals continue to drive the governance of college sports in the United States. In light of these conditions, Congress should blunt such challenges by giving the NCAA an antitrust exemption for educationally based rules changes, thereby alerting the college sports community that greater educational integrity, not a "more competitive market," must be the wave of the future in college sports.

Like the limited antitrust exemption, additional due process protections for persons accused of violating NCAA rules would not represent a radical departure from present practices. The NCAA already provides accused persons with some process, including notice of the allegations against them and of the witnesses and evidence on which the Association will rely, the right to counsel, and the right to an appeal.[150] Additional protections, including independent judges who possess subpoena power, prehearing discovery, the right of cross-examination, and an opportunity for hearing testimony by third parties (boosters, college employees, etc.) who are implicated in NCAA investigations, would build on the existing structure to increase the fairness and enhance the legitimacy of NCAA enforcement proceedings. Increased fairness and enhanced legitimacy would make the additional expenses associated with paid judges and longer hearings (necessitated by cross-examination and third-party participation) a relatively small price to pay for good public relations, especially for a wealthy organization like the NCAA.

This book urges Congress to enact legislation giving the NCAA a limited antitrust exemption and requiring it to adopt the due process protections just discussed. Before unveiling this proposed legislation, though, the book examines the circumstances that led to *NCAA v. Board of Regents.* That is the task of chapter 2.

Chapter 2

A REVOLT OF THE "HAVES"
The Road to *NCAA v. Board of Regents*

Football, Television, and the NCAA

The NCAA was founded in 1906 in response to the violence that plagued college football during the 1905 season, after which the *Chicago Tribune* reported that 18 college and high school students had died and 159 had been injured while playing football that season.[1] The cause of many injuries was the "mass play," which saw offensive players link arms to protect the ball carrier while they alternately pushed and pulled him toward the opponent's goal line. Late in the season, on November 25, Union College end Harold Moore died after receiving a blow to the head from another player's knee while making a tackle during a game with New York University (NYU).[2]

Moore's death spurred Henry B. MacCracken, the chancellor of NYU, to organize a meeting of college officials in New York City to discuss ways to end the brutality in college football. On December 5, 1905, the presidents of 13 colleges attended this meeting, during which they voted against abolishing football on their respective campuses but in favor of reform and of holding a general meeting of all football-playing colleges.[3] The second, larger meeting, which convened in New York City on December 28, 1905, attracted representatives from 68 colleges and resulted in the creation of the Intercollegiate Athletic Association, which was formalized the following year and ultimately became the NCAA.[4]

At its founding, the NCAA was firmly committed to amateurism. It believed that coaches should pick their athletes from among members of the student body instead of recruiting them by offering financial assistance. It opposed the notion of member colleges providing athletes with financial inducements from any source, including the faculty and financial aid committees. The NCAA's commitment to amateurism was reflected in the statement issued during its annual convention in 1922, which said, "An amateur sportsman is one who engages in sport solely for the physical, mental, or social benefits he derives therefrom, and to whom the sport is nothing more than an avocation."[5] But the NCAA could not enforce amateurism among its members, because it lacked enforcement power until 1948; therefore, it relied on colleges and conferences to police themselves, with predictably uneven results.[6]

The era of self-policing coincided with the rise of radio in the United States. The National Broadcasting Company (NBC) began network radio coverage of college football in 1926, and on November 1, 1927, it broadcast the first Rose Bowl game. In 1935 the University of Michigan signed a $20,000-per-year radio contract to broadcast its football games, and Yale signed a contract for the same amount the following year.[7] The NCAA's fear that radio broadcasts of college football games would hurt live attendance at games prompted the Association to establish a three-member committee in 1935 to study the likely impact of radio on attendance at college games.[8] But in 1936, after conducting a yearlong study, the committee announced that it could not determine whether radio broadcasts of college football games reduced live attendance.[9] Therefore, the NCAA opted not to set a national policy on radio broadcasting but, instead, to allow each college to decide for itself whether or not to broadcast its football games.[10] That turned out to be a wise strategy, because by 1940 live-attendance figures at college football games had showed that the NCAA's fear that radio broadcasts might hurt ticket sales was unfounded. On the contrary, the broadcasts increased the popularity of college football by expanding the audience for the games, thereby proving to be an unexpected source of income and publicity for the participating colleges.[11]

Based on its experience with radio, the NCAA initially treated television similarly, allowing individual colleges to negotiate their own contracts with individual stations or with networks as they saw fit. In 1949, for example, the University of California, Los Angeles (UCLA), and the University of Southern California (USC) signed television contracts worth $34,500 apiece, and in 1950 the University of Pennsylvania (Penn) signed a $75,000 contract for telecasts of its home football games.[12] But, unlike radio, television seemed to reduce game attendance, as 1,403,000 fewer fans attended college football games in 1950 than had done so in 1948, when no telecasts occurred.[13] Consequently, the NCAA banned live telecasts of college football games in the hope of boosting attendance and gate receipts.[14]

Still, the NCAA did not reject television entirely. Instead, at its 1951 convention in Dallas, the membership approved a plan to test the impact of televised college football on live attendance. This plan was a compromise, because the ban on televised college football that the membership favored threatened to trigger an antitrust investigation by the United States Department of Justice.[15] NCAA members were aware that attendance at college games had increased between the coasts, where few households could enjoy televised football in the early 1950s, while it had declined in areas of the United States where television sets were becoming commonplace. Accordingly, the Association feared that televising games would reduce live attendance and gate receipts. But it also wished to avoid an antitrust inquiry, so it agreed to a limited package of televised games to test the effects of televised football on live attendance.[16]

Under this arrangement, the Westinghouse Corporation paid the NCAA $679,800 in rights fees to televise a limited schedule of games on the 52-station Westinghouse network, which served about 58 percent of the American public.[17] The schedule called for three nationally televised games during the 1951 season and up to four regional games on most Saturdays.[18] No games would be telecast on two Saturdays in the fall, and the regions would be blacked out on a rotating basis during the season, to assess the impact, if any, of televised games on live attendance.[19] Moreover, colleges who had negotiated their own television contracts in 1950 (Penn, Notre Dame, Georgia Tech, and others) were prohibited from doing so in 1951.[20] The 1951 experiment also included a detailed attendance survey, the results of which convinced the NCAA membership that the best way to preserve live attendance at college football games was to control telecasts of the games. Accordingly, the membership voted 163–8 to authorize the Television Committee to create a package of televised games for the 1952 season.[21] The NCAA then signed a television contract with NBC for the 1952 season, worth $1.14 million.[22]

The NCAA's control over televised college football transformed what had been a relatively weak advisory body into a regulatory body wielding tremendous economic power, and with economic power came rule-making power. That was evident when Penn attempted to defy the NCAA by signing its own television contract for the 1951 college football season, despite the ban on such arrangements. The NCAA declared Penn a member not in good standing and pressured several of the Quakers' 1951 opponents, including Cornell, Columbia, Dartmouth, and Princeton, to announce that they would cancel their games with Penn unless it joined the NCAA's Football Television Plan. Fearing the demise of its football program, Penn capitulated by canceling its contract with ABC on July 19, 1951.[23] In 1952 the NCAA created an enforcement division and asserted its new power by suspending the University of Kentucky's basketball team from NCAA play for participating in a point-shaving scandal.[24] Kentucky did not contest the punishment, and the NCAA emerged from this episode more powerful than ever before.[25]

For three decades, the NCAA controlled televised college football. The Football Television Plan called for one game to be telecast nationally and for several games to be telecast regionally every Saturday during the fall. No institution could appear on television more than twice during the regular season, but only those institutions whose teams played on television received television revenue directly from the NCAA.[26] The NCAA received 12 percent of the proceeds of the 1952 television contract but usually 4 or 5 percent in succeeding years.[27] It distributed the rest among the colleges whose teams had appeared on television; teams that had participated in games telecast nationally earned about 30 percent more than teams whose games had been telecast regionally.[28]

The Football Television Plan increased the NCAA's wealth along with its power, which is ironic because the NCAA had long feared the impact of televised games on live attendance. But the plan also made college football more expensive for the television networks to provide and for the fans to consume than it would have been if the colleges were free to negotiate their own television deals. The plan restricted fans' access to televised games, thereby raising the prices of the rights fees the networks paid to the NCAA and increasing both the Association's revenues from college football and the colleges' revenues from television appearances by their respective teams.[29] It also turned the NCAA into a "cartel," which is a combination of producers that exists to control the production, sale, and price of its members' product.[30] A cartel seeks to maximize the price of its product by limiting the product's availability to consumers, which is achieved by the producers' agreement to restrict competition.[31] Whether or not price maximization was the NCAA's aim when it created the Football Television Plan, price maximization was certainly a major result of the plan for 30 years.

The NCAA's increased wealth resulted from a phenomenon that its members could not foresee in 1951, namely, television's enormous capacity to increase the nationwide audience for college football, including both live attendees and armchair fans. The greatest growth occurred among people who were neither alumni nor students, which was a double-edged sword for the institutions and the NCAA. The increased fan base enriched the NCAA and the most athletically successful institutions, but, as journalist Keith Dunnavant has written, it also made the institutions and the NCAA "more beholden to a group who saw college football as separate and distinct from the academic mission" of the colleges that sponsored the teams.[32] In this environment, the athletically preeminent colleges sought to maintain their status by hiring talented coaches, recruiting gifted players, and upgrading their football facilities regularly. By the late 1970s and early 1980s, they viewed the NCAA's control of televised college football, which limited their opportunities to play on television, as a barrier to earning the revenues necessary to "stay on top." A "clash of titans" was imminent.

Dissension in the Ranks

To the college football powerhouses, the NCAA's Football Television Plan increasingly felt like a yoke around their necks. Under the plan, no team could appear on television more than twice per season, regardless of its popularity with the fans, and the NCAA guaranteed a small number of television appearances each season to teams from less athletically prestigious conferences, such as the Ivy League, the Southern Conference, and the Mid-American Conference.[33] A team could earn no more than $267,000 per television appearance.[34] The 1978–81 NCAA-ABC contract required the network to televise the championship games in Divisions I-AA, II, and III; four regular-season games in Division II; three regular-season games in Division III; and the national championships of wrestling, swimming, gymnastics, volleyball, and indoor track.[35] A game featuring two popular teams could generate the same payment for the participating colleges as a game featuring two lackluster teams. On one weekend in 1981, for example, a "super regional" game between Oklahoma and USC aired on nearly 200 stations reaching 98 percent of the country. The NCAA added the concept of the super regional to its Football Television Plan in the late 1970s.[36] On the same weekend, a contest between the Citadel and Appalachian State was televised in just a few media markets in the Carolinas. All four institutions received the same fee for their respective appearances, because under the rules of the Football Television Plan, both games were "regional" telecasts.[37] To add insult to injury, the NCAA's democratic voting structure, which permitted members of Divisions II and III, including non-football-playing members of those divisions, to vote on the football television contract, prevented the football powerhouses from claiming a larger share of the burgeoning broadcast revenues for college football.[38]

The restiveness of the football powerhouses was somewhat ironic because, despite the NCAA's efforts to spread television appearances out among as many colleges as possible, an elite group—including Notre Dame, Alabama, Texas, Ohio State, Michigan, USC, Oklahoma, and Nebraska—always made the maximum number of television appearances allowed per season. Lesser teams from the same conferences to which the elite group belonged and teams from less prestigious conferences rarely, if ever, appeared on television.[39] Still, if the football powerhouses could be criticized during the 1970s for emphasizing commerce over education, they were surely not alone. As the decade progressed and fees for television rights skyrocketed, the NCAA's annual football contract generated enough revenue that the Association increasingly appeared to be a for-profit cartel rather than the nonprofit educational organization it claimed to be.[40] The NCAA's financial success caused the football powerhouses to chafe under the yoke that the Association imposed on them, as they became increasingly aware of the revenues they could earn absent NCAA restrictions.

As the 1980s dawned, cable television began to challenge the long-standing preeminence of ABC, CBS, and NBC. The football powerhouses, most of which belonged to the College Football Association (CFA), founded in 1976, believed that the new competition for sports programming would reward them handsomely if they could shed the restrictions imposed by the NCAA.[41] This environment spurred the CFA's executive director at the time, Chuck Neinas, a former NCAA employee, to negotiate a contract with NBC in the summer of 1981. NBC agreed to pay the CFA $180 million for the telecasts during a three-year period beginning in the fall of 1982.[42] Under the contract, each CFA member's football team would appear on television at least once and not more than seven times in a two-year period. The colleges would not have to pay an "assessment" to the NCAA, as they were required to do under the NCAA's Football Television Plan, and "independents," like Notre Dame, which did not belong to a conference, could keep virtually the entire proceeds of their TV appearances.[43]

The NCAA responded to this challenge from the CFA on two fronts. One front, which was reminiscent of the Association's reaction to Penn's apostasy in 1951, featured a threat by the NCAA to expel any member that honored the contract with NBC. Specifically, NCAA president James Frank of Lincoln University in Missouri announced that any member seeking to televise a football game under rules other than the NCAA Football Television Plan would become ineligible to participate in any NCAA-sponsored championship.[44] The second front featured a measure of conciliation, although the conciliation aimed to sabotage the NBC-CFA contract by making the NCAA's contract more appealing to CFA members than it had been to date. Two months before the deadline of September 10, 1981, set by the NCAA for CFA members to abandon the deal with NBC, NCAA executive director Walter Byers signed a contract with ABC, CBS, and TBS (cable pioneer Turner Broadcast Sports) that sought to meet the needs of CFA members without abandoning the long-standing Football Television Plan.[45]

Under this contract, the three networks would pay a total fee of $285 million over four years to televise college football games.[46] This represented a dramatic increase over the 1978–81 contract with ABC, which paid the NCAA $30 million during the period of the agreement.[47] The new contract would pay teams $500,000 for appearing in a nationally telecast game.[48] Moreover, the new contract deflated the CFA's argument that the NCAA refused to negotiate with more than one network, while seeking to meet the CFA's needs by steering more money to a smaller number of athletic powerhouses, which would no longer have to tolerate regular television appearances by low-profile teams.[49]

The NCAA's carrot-and-stick response to the CFA-NBC contract succeeded. For CFA members in 1981, as for Penn in 1951, the prospect of expulsion from the NCAA, followed by athletic isolation, forced grudging compliance with the Association's wishes. Expulsion would have ended participation by CFA members in the NCAA's lucrative men's basketball tournament, and the CFA did not include enough highly visible college basketball teams to enable it to run a successful tournament independently of the NCAA.[50] Few CFA member institutions were willing to honor the NBC contract and call the NCAA's bluff, especially after the University of Georgia and the University of Oklahoma filed one lawsuit and the University of Texas filed another, challenging the NCAA's authority to negotiate a football television contract for its members.[51] Even after a federal district court in Texas dismissed the University of Texas's suit, the Georgia-Oklahoma suit moved forward, and most CFA members assumed that it would either resolve this issue or give them leverage to make a more advantageous deal with the NCAA in the future.[52] Thus, the CFA abandoned its contract with NBC and awaited the outcome of *Board of Regents v. NCAA,* which a federal district court in Oklahoma City would hear soon. All CFA members had an enormous stake in the outcome of this lawsuit, not only because their freedom to negotiate television contracts for themselves was at issue, but also because the group had agreed to share in the expenses incurred by Georgia and Oklahoma in connection with the suit.[53]

College Football on Trial

Regents v. NCAA went to trial in the United States District Court for the Western District of Oklahoma in June 1982.[54] In a testament to the powerful hold that college football has on American hearts and minds, Judge Luther Eubanks, who was originally assigned to hear the case, recused (i.e., disqualified) himself because he was a graduate of the University of Oklahoma and a well-known fan of its football team.[55] None of the other judges in the Western District of Oklahoma wanted to hear the case either, so the chief judge of the United States Court of Appeals for the Tenth Circuit, which includes Oklahoma, assigned district judge Juan Burciaga of New Mexico to hear it.[56]

As these events suggest, *Regents v. NCAA* involved high stakes for the parties to the case, and it attracted keen interest from the television industry, sports journalists, and college football fans nationwide. But it was not unprecedented; that is, it was not the first case in which a plaintiff challenged an NCAA rule as violating one or more antitrust laws. Indeed, by the time that *Regents v. NCAA* went to trial, the NCAA had compiled an impressive winning streak in antitrust challenges to its rules and regulations.

In *Jones v. NCAA,*[57] plaintiff Stephen Jones sought an injunction that would have prevented the NCAA from declaring him ineligible to play ice hockey at Northeastern University and from penalizing Northeastern for letting him play or for awarding him an athletic scholarship.[58] Jones ran afoul of NCAA rules that made a college student ineligible to compete in a sport if the student had previously received pay of any kind for participating in that sport, had entered into a contract to compete in the sport, or had played the sport outside the United States on a team including other athletes who had received compensation in excess of NCAA limits. These rules made ineligible for college competition any athlete who was given financial aid to play a sport while not attending school. Jones had played on various Canadian and American hockey teams during his last three years of high school and for two years after high school, and he had received compensation from the teams during this five-year period, which preceded his enrollment at Northeastern. The NCAA denied Jones's request for a waiver that would have permitted him to play for Northeastern despite the earlier compensation, so he sued the NCAA in federal district court in Massachusetts.

In Jones's view, the NCAA's declaration that he was ineligible to play college hockey was an unreasonable restraint of trade in violation of Section 1 of the Sherman Antitrust Act.[59] The court disagreed, observing that the Sherman Act did not govern efforts by the NCAA to set eligibility standards for athletes at its member institutions. The Sherman Act, the court noted, was enacted at a time (1890) when large commercial enterprises joined together to control the market for, hence the price of, their products by "suppress[ing] competition in the marketing of goods and services."[60] Therefore, the court continued, antitrust regulation "[wa]s aimed primarily at combinations with commercial objectives and is applied only to a very limited degree to other types of organizations."[61] Quoting a decision of the United States Supreme Court, the *Jones* court added that the Sherman Act was "tailored for the business world" and that it was not designed to resolve controversies in the arts, academe, or the "learned professions" (law, medicine, etc.).[62]

Besides, Jones's principal argument was that the NCAA's refusal to let him play college hockey amounted to a "group boycott," which violated Section 1 of the Sherman Act. The court rejected this argument, pointing out that a plaintiff claiming to be the victim of a group boycott had to show that the defendant sought to exclude the plaintiff from competing in the marketplace or to accomplish another anticompetitive aim. The court then reasoned that unlike group boycotts, NCAA rules were designed not to limit economic competition but, rather, "to implement the NCAA['s] basic principles of amateurism, principles which have been at the heart of the Association since its founding."[63] The court added that "[a]ny limitation on access to intercollegiate sports" that flowed from those rules "[wa]s merely the incidental result of the organization's pursuit of its legitimate goals."[64] Consequently, the court concluded that the NCAA's denial of athletic eligibility to Jones did not "rise to the level of a violation" of the Sherman Act.[65] Thus, Stephen Jones failed to demonstrate a substantial likelihood of success on the merits of his lawsuit, as would be necessary to obtain a preliminary injunction against the NCAA. The court therefore denied Jones's request for a preliminary injunction.

Two years after *Jones*, the NCAA won another lawsuit, *Hennessey v. NCAA*,[66] in which an Association rule was the subject of an antitrust challenge. The plaintiff, Lawrence (Dude) Hennessey, was an assistant football coach at the University of Alabama whose full-time position was reduced to part-time on August 1, 1976, when the NCAA adopted Bylaw 12-1, which imposed limits on the number of assistant coaches Division I colleges could employ in football (eight) and in basketball (two). Hennessey argued that Bylaw 12-1 unreasonably restrained trade, in violation of Section 1 of the Sherman Act, by inhibiting colleges' economic freedom to hire coaches as they wished. The NCAA countered that it was a nonprofit, voluntary association whose activities and objectives were educational, thereby exempting it from regulation under Section 1 of the Sherman Act.

The United States Court of Appeals for the Fifth Circuit adopted a middle ground between these two positions, observing that despite the amateurism of college sports, "there is a business aspect in the providing of coaching for the athletes or in the providing of athletic events to an interested public."[67] Under these circumstances, the court reasoned, "the NCAA [wa]s not entitled to a total exclusion from anti-trust regulations" based on its claimed educational mission.[68] Moreover, the court noted that the Association's adoption of Bylaw 12-1 would "curtail the extent of coaching services which previously flowed from one state to another" and would "reduc[e] the movement of coaches between institutions located in different states."[69] Therefore, the court concluded, Bylaw 12-1 would affect interstate commerce sufficiently to bring it within the reach of Section 1 of the Sherman Act.

The court's refusal to grant the NCAA an exemption from the antitrust laws did not signal an intention to treat the NCAA like IBM or General Motors. Indeed, the court observed that "given the nature and purposes of the NCAA and its member institutions, this particular restraint, limiting the number of assistant coaches who may be employed at any one time by the institutions, is not a per se [i.e., on its face or automatic] violation of the antitrust laws."[70] The test of the new bylaw's legality, then, would be the "rule of reason," that is, whether it merely regulated economic competition between the colleges for coaches, thereby perhaps even promoting competition by allocating talented coaches among many colleges, or whether it suppressed or even destroyed this competition. In applying this test to Bylaw 12-1, the court, which acknowledged that Bylaw 12-1 would have commercial consequences in the college coaching market, nevertheless concluded that "the fundamental objective in mind was to preserve and foster competition in intercollegiate athletics."[71] In the court's view, the new bylaw would achieve that goal by preventing the most athletically prominent institutions from hiring the best and the most coaches, thereby putting their less prominent and less wealthy rivals at a competitive disadvantage. Thus, Bylaw 12-1 would promote competition in college sports, not stifle it.

The court, conceding that Bylaw 12-1 would cause some coaches to lose their jobs, added that it might benefit coaches in the long run by enabling less wealthy institutions to continue competing in Division I, which they might not be able to do otherwise, thereby "preserving the number of institutions which remain as potential employers of such coaches."[72] The court agreed with the NCAA that no less restrictive measure was available to the Association to accomplish the aim of Bylaw 12-1, namely, to cut the costs of operating football and basketball programs at Division I institutions. Thus, the court in *Hennessey* concluded that the NCAA's Bylaw 12-1 was not an unreasonable restraint of trade in violation of Section 1 of the Sherman Act, because, when examined under the rule-of-reason standard, it showed itself to have procompetitive, rather than anticompetitive, consequences for college sports.

The NCAA also prevailed in *Justice v. NCAA,*[73] in which football players at the University of Arizona sought a preliminary injunction to prevent the NCAA from enforcing penalties that made their team ineligible for postseason bowl games in 1983 and 1984 and for television appearances in 1984 and 1985. The NCAA had imposed these penalties on Arizona after discovering that the football coaches had given their players benefits prohibited by NCAA rules, including "free airline transportation between school and their homes, free lodging, and cash and bank loans for the athletes' car payments, rental payments, and personal use."[74] The plaintiffs in *Justice* argued that the penalties the NCAA imposed on Arizona violated Section 1 of the Sherman Act because both the vote by the NCAA's Committee on Infractions to penalize the Wildcats and the rule that prompted the vote were agreements among Association members who competed against Arizona to exclude it from the market for televised and postseason college football. According to this view, the NCAA's actions against Arizona constituted a "group boycott," which was a per se violation of Section 1 of the Sherman Act.

The court rejected the plaintiffs' argument for several reasons. First, to obtain a preliminary injunction against the NCAA, they had to show that the sanctions had caused them to suffer a demonstrable injury, which the court concluded they could not do. The plaintiffs contended that the sanctions would bar Arizona from appearing on television and in bowl games, which would injure them by reducing their chances of being seen in action by scouts for professional football teams and of eventually signing a contract to play for one of those teams. The court regarded this claimed injury as being too speculative to qualify as an actual injury; in order for it to become an actual injury, the court reasoned, the plaintiffs would have to continue playing football, their team would have to have a successful regular season and be invited to participate in a bowl game, they would have to perform well in the game, and professional scouts would have to conclude that they were talented enough to play professional football. Based on the evidence presented, the court determined that "there [wa]s little more than a remote possibility that the plaintiffs' 'value' in the professional football trade would be substantially different but for the [NCAA] sanctions, or would improve were [the court] to grant the injunctive relief."[75]

Second, the NCAA's actions against the University of Arizona did not amount to a group boycott in violation of the Sherman Act. The court noted that actual cases of group boycott "have typically involved a concerted attempt by a group of competitors at one level to protect itself from competition from nongroup members who [we]re attempting to compete at the same level."[76] In other words, a group boycott exists only "when the exclusionary or coercive conduct is a direct affront to competition, or 'naked restraint,' rather than action that merely has an incidental effect on competition."[77] No group boycott existed in this case, the court reasoned, because the plaintiffs could not show that the NCAA, its members, or its Committee on Infractions intended to insulate itself from competition by imposing sanctions on the University of Arizona or any other institution "on probation" for violating Association rules. Indeed, the court continued, the purpose of NCAA sanctions was not to quash competition but, rather, to promote fair competition among member institutions in an amateur setting. Moreover, the imposition of these sanctions did not result from an agreement among traditional business rivals, nor did the sanctions lack redeeming virtue. Thus, according to the court, the NCAA's punishment of Arizona was neither a group boycott nor a per se violation of Section 1 of the Sherman Act.

Third, the NCAA's actions satisfied the rule-of-reason test, too. Citing the *Jones* and *Hennessey* decisions favorably, the court noted that "NCAA regulations designed to preserve amateurism and fair competition have previously been upheld as reasonable restraints under the rule of reason."[78] The court added that the sanctions levied against the University of Arizona lacked an anticompetitive intent and flowed directly from the NCAA's aims to preserve amateurism and promote fair competition, respectively. Any anticompetitive effect they had on coaches and athletes who were connected to penalized teams was "incidental."[79] Thus, the court concluded, "Because the sanctions evince no anti-competitive purpose, are reasonably related to the association's central objectives, and are not overbroad, the NCAA's action does not constitute an unreasonable restraint under the Sherman Act."[80]

For all three reasons, the court rejected the plaintiffs' antitrust claim against the NCAA and denied their request for a preliminary injunction. The court was satisfied that the NCAA actions challenged in *Justice,* like those challenged in *Jones* and *Hennessey,* respectively, were compatible with the Sherman Act because (1) they aimed to preserve amateurism in college sports, not to stifle economic competition, and (2) any anticompetitive result they produced was incidental to and offset by the laudable goal of enhancing amateur athletic competition among colleges and universities. But the court in *Justice* recognized that the NCAA's goal of preserving amateur athletics did not make the Association immune from antitrust claims. "It is clear," the court wrote, "that the NCAA is now engaged in two distinct kinds of rulemaking activity."[81] "One type," the court noted, "exemplified by the rules [challenged] in *Hennessey* and *Jones,* is rooted in the NCAA's concern for the protection of amateurism; the other type is increasingly accompanied by a discernible economic purpose."[82] This distinction was important because the first type of rule was compatible with the antitrust laws, but the second type of rule might not be. In *Regents v. NCAA,* Judge Burciaga would conclude that the NCAA's Football Television Plan possessed a discernible economic purpose, namely, to limit the supply of televised college football in order to maximize its price, which violated antitrust law.

Judge Burciaga's decision was dramatically different from the conclusion that a federal district court in Ohio had reached in an earlier antitrust challenge to the NCAA's Football Television Plan. In *Warner Amex Cable Communications, Inc. v. American Broadcasting Companies, Inc. et al.,* the plaintiff claimed that the defendants, who included the NCAA, had violated the Sherman Act by preventing it from airing Ohio State University's football games on cable television in the Columbus, Ohio, area during the 1980 season.[83] The plaintiff, Warner Amex, sought a preliminary injunction to restrain the defendants from barring the cable telecasts. This lawsuit challenged the Football Television Plan because a part of the plan was a clause whereby the NCAA and ABC agreed that cable telecasts of college football games would be permitted only if they did not occur at the same time as ABC telecasts.

This lawsuit was Warner Amex's second challenge to the restriction on cable telecasts in the NCAA plan. In both 1977 and 1978, Warner Amex had sought to televise Ohio State football games not aired by ABC, but ABC and the NCAA insisted that the Football Television Plan and the ABC-NCAA contract prohibited any other network from showing live college football games. Warner Amex challenged that prohibition in a lawsuit filed in 1978. But shortly before a court hearing on Warner Amex's request for a preliminary injunction in the earlier suit, the parties settled, enabling the cable company to air five Ohio State games not aired by ABC in 1978 and five more in 1979 in return for agreeing to drop the lawsuit and to refrain from further litigation until after the 1979 season. But Warner Amex filed a new lawsuit in 1980, after ABC and the NCAA once again prohibited it from airing any Ohio State football games.

Early on, the court in *Warner Amex* signaled that it would not view the NCAA plan as a purely commercial or even a predominately commercial venture. The court conceded that if the plan were "viewed as an agreement among horizontal competitors to limit output, [it] would be a per se violation of the Sherman Act by virtue of its restrictions upon the amount of college football that can be televised."[84] But, the court added, "a practice that would be declared invalid per se if it occurred in a purely commercial context should not be subject to a per se rule in the context of singularly integrated commercial and educational activities with which no court has had considerable experience."[85] Therefore, the court opted to analyze the Football Television Plan and its prohibition on cable telecasts of college games under the rule of reason, noting that the challenged practices were not "unequivocally pernicious in their effect upon competition, or totally lacking any redeeming virtue."[86]

Applying the rule of reason, the court concluded that Warner Amex was unlikely to prevail in its antitrust challenge to the NCAA. This conclusion was fatal to the cable company's request for a preliminary injunction, because courts are loath to grant a preliminary injunction to a plaintiff who cannot show a substantial likelihood of winning its lawsuit on the merits. To win on the merits, Warner Amex had to show that the NCAA possessed monopoly power in a particular market and acquired or maintained that power willfully. But the court pointed out that the identity of the relevant market was unclear, hence Warner Amex was unlikely to win on the merits because it would presumably be unable to establish that the NCAA monopolized any particular market.

Besides, the court added, the potential injury to Warner Amex from being unable to televise Ohio State's football games was theoretical, not actual, because the evidence contradicted the cable company's contention that televising the games enabled it to acquire and retain subscribers. The court noted that the Ohio State telecasts had not earned a profit for Warner Amex in 1978 or 1979. ABC, however, would suffer a real injury if Warner Amex's request for a preliminary injunction were granted, namely, a loss of its exclusive right to televise Ohio State football games in the Columbus area. Additionally, small colleges located in that area would likely suffer a reduction in live attendance at their games if Warner Amex were permitted to televise Ohio State games live. Taken together, the public interest in honoring contract rights and in maintaining the viability of college football as an amateur activity favored ABC and the NCAA. Thus, based on Warner Amex's inability to show that the NCAA was a monopoly, the theoretical nature of the cable company's claimed injury, and the public interest in preserving contract rights and amateurism, the court rejected Warner Amex's request for a preliminary injunction against ABC and the NCAA.

The NCAA Football Television Plan survived *Warner Amex* unscathed, but it would not be so lucky in Judge Juan Burciaga's courtroom in *Regents v. NCAA*. Instead of seeking to preserve contract rights and amateurism, Judge Burciaga sought to bring the benefits of free-market economics, especially consumer choice, to televised college football. He issued his decision in *Regents v. NCAA* on September 15, 1982, in a long, detailed opinion reflecting the complexity of the case and the length of the trial, which had lasted nine days. The opinion began by chronicling the history of the NCAA's Football Television Plan and of the resulting dispute between the NCAA and the CFA. Then it focused on the contract that ABC and the NCAA had agreed to for the 1978–81 college football seasons. That contract commanded the court's attention because it was similar to the 1982–85 deal the CFA was challenging in *Regents*.

Under the earlier contract, ABC paid the NCAA a "minimum aggregate fee" of $29 million to televise regular-season college football games during the 1978 season. The total was allocated as follows, at the NCAA's direction:

$730,000 as the rights fee for the Division I-AA playoffs;

$670,000 as the rights fee for the Division II and III playoffs, respectively;

$165,000 as the rights fee for regular-season telecasts of Division II and Division III games; and

$250,000 as the rights fee for televising five NCAA championship events in sports other than football and basketball.

The remainder, after these distributions, was $27,165,000, of which the NCAA's share was 8 percent, or $2,173,000. Deducting the NCAA's share left $24,991,800 to be divided among the Division I teams that appeared on ABC in 1978. ABC televised 13 games between these teams nationally and 45 games between them regionally and paid the participants a total of $533,600 (or $266,800 each) for a nationally televised game and $401,222 (or $200,611 each) for a regionally televised game. No team could appear on television more than five times in two seasons.

Turning his attention to the 1982–85 contract, Judge Burciaga noted that the basic features of the previous agreement would remain in force in the new contract. Although the new contract appeared to provide for competition between ABC and CBS for the right to televise any particular game, the "ground rules" developed by the NCAA for administering the contract eliminated any possibility of competitive bidding between the networks.[87] The best evidence of this was that one network would have exclusive rights to televise any particular game. Beyond that, each network was required to televise a game on at least 14 different dates and to show at least 35 games per season. Each network also had to televise at least seven games nationally and six games regionally per season, and at least one network was required to televise a game on each Saturday during the season. No team could appear on television more than six times in two years or more than four times nationally in two years, and at least 82 teams had to appear on each network during that time period. Furthermore, a team's television appearances during those two years had to be divided equally between ABC and CBS.

After identifying the ground rules of the 1982–85 contract, Judge Burciaga took pains to explain their practical effects. Before the college football season began, the networks would submit to the NCAA Television Committee their preferences for at least three "special dates" per network.[88] If both networks chose the same date, a coin flip would determine which network got its first choice of special dates. The winner would choose a special date, then the other network would choose one, and they would alternate choosing dates until each network had all the "special dates" it wanted. These dates included (1) the first Saturday of the college football season, (2) the Friday and the Saturday after Thanksgiving, (3) Labor Day, (4) Veterans Day, (5) the first Saturday in December, (6) Monday through Thursday nights, and (7) any Saturday night approved by the Television Committee. After choosing their special dates, the networks would select the games they wished to televise on these dates and the time of each telecast. Both networks could show a game on the same special date, but the rules of the contract made it unlikely that more than one game would air simultaneously.

Once the special dates were set, the networks would engage in a so-called equity draft, whereby each network would be permitted to select at least two "equity games" to televise during the season.[89] The purpose of the equity draft was to enable the networks to televise an equal number of comparably popular and lucrative games.[90] The network that had second choice in the earlier selection of special dates chose first in the equity draft. ABC and CBS alternated in choosing equity games until they had chosen the allotted number of games.[91] Just as with the special dates, the rules covering the equity games made it unlikely that both networks would show equity games simultaneously. Following the equity draft, the networks would alternate in picking dates over which they would have a "right of control," that is, the first right to choose any particular game. For example, if CBS chose Saturday, October 30, it would have its pick of all the games to be played that day. Judge Burciaga noted that if a particularly attractive game were scheduled for that date, the contract theoretically allowed the participating institutions to negotiate for more money than CBS offered, thereby spurring competitive bidding between the networks. He added that, according to the NCAA, this potential for competitive bidding made the challenged contract compatible with the antitrust laws.

But the judge quickly concluded that the evidence did not support the NCAA's argument. He reasoned that the networks did not intend to engage in competitive bidding. The best indication of this, he observed, was that once the network holding first choice for any given date had made its choice and agreed to a rights fee for the game, NCAA rules prohibited the participating institutions from selling or threatening to sell the broadcast rights to another network. "The evidence is clear," Judge Burciaga wrote; under the new contract, as under prior football television contracts, "the NCAA controlled the price to be paid to participating teams and made it impossible for the teams to negotiate any higher price by restricting dealings to a single network."[92] "The evidence is also clear," he continued, that under the new contract, as under prior contracts, "some teams would have received [or would receive] larger fees [if] allowed to negotiate with any and all potential broadcasters."[93]

Under these circumstances Judge Burciaga determined that the new contract featured NCAA price-fixing for televised college football, just as the previous contract had done. He wrote,

> After the network having the right of first choice on any given date has made its agreement with the teams playing the most attractive game of the week, the other schools are left in the same position as they were in under previous contracts. They will be selling in a market where there is only one eligible buyer.[94]

In his view, "the setting of a minimum aggregate fee, in combination with the 'ground rules' restricting competition between the networks and the limitations on each team's appearances, only perpetuate[d] the monopsony situation [i.e., price fixing resulting from the existence of just one buyer] which NCAA has created."[95]

These arrangements violated antitrust law, Judge Burciaga continued, because they produced results such as identical rights fees for the two 1981 college football games noted earlier, a highly visible one between Oklahoma and USC and a largely ignored one between the Citadel and Appalachian State. Identical fees for these two games amounted to, in the judge's words, "a gross distortion of free-market forces."[96] Besides fixing prices for college games, the judge reasoned, the NCAA, "by making agreements with the networks for exclusive national television rights and placing severe restrictions on local broadcasts of college football, . . . has agreed to limit production of televised college football."[97] In other words, he added, "Were it not for the NCAA controls, many more college football games would be televised."[98]

As if fixing prices and artificially limiting production were not bad enough, the NCAA Football Television Plan was also a group boycott, in Judge Burciaga's estimation, and group boycotts, like price-fixing and colluding to limit production, are per se violations of the antitrust laws. In the judge's view, NCAA members colluded to produce a group boycott in two different ways. First, they granted exclusive rights to certain networks to televise college football, meaning that they "essentially agree[d] not to bargain or to make [their] product available to other broadcasters."[99] Second, they authorized the Association to punish any member institution that sought to make its football games available to the highest bidder, and the likely punishment—namely, a refusal to compete against the outcast—would itself be a group boycott.

In reaching his conclusions, Judge Burciaga rejected the NCAA's argument that its restraints on televised college football were necessary to protect live attendance at games. He voiced skepticism that televised college football affected live attendance, partly because the NCAA continued to base its conclusion that televised games hurt live attendance on studies conducted by the National Opinion Research Center at the University of Chicago in the 1950s. Moreover, those studies had failed to show that televised games had caused the decline in live attendance during the time period studied. Pointing out that college enrollment had declined during the period of the study, Judge Burciaga hypothesized that declining enrollment, rather than television, could have caused the drop in live attendance at college football games during those years. Even if televised football and reduced live attendance were linked, the judge reasoned, the 1982–85 television contract was obviously not geared toward protecting live attendance, because under it, fans in many regions of the United States would be able to see up to nine hours of televised college football on several Saturdays during the 1982 season. Thus, Judge Burciaga concluded that the challenged contract was incapable of protecting live attendance at college football games. The judge also rejected the NCAA's argument that the need to preserve "competitive balance" among college football teams justified its Football Television Plan. He reasoned that the Football Television Plan was a "much too far-reaching" method of improving competition in college football and that the NCAA's "regulations on recruitment, the limitations on the number of scholarships each team may award, and the other standards for preserving amateurism found in NCAA legislation [we]re sufficient to achieve this goal."[100]

Based on this reasoning, Judge Burciaga concluded that the NCAA's Football Television Plan amounted to price-fixing and a group boycott, both of which were per se violations of the Sherman Act. He could have ended his analysis with that conclusion, because it would have justified invalidating the NCAA plan without further adieu. But, undoubtedly anticipating an appeal by the NCAA and careful examination of his reasoning by the appellate court, Judge Burciaga opted to make his opinion as unassailable as possible by analyzing the NCAA plan according to the rule of reason, too. He maintained that the unique nature of college football, as both a commercial venture and an educational activity, justified the additional analysis. Still, the application of the rule-of-reason test would offer little solace to the NCAA. Judge Burciaga observed that this analysis "does not open the field of antitrust inquiry to any argument in favor of a challenged restraint that may fall within the realm of reason."[101] "Instead," he added, "it focuses directly on the challenged restraint's impact on competitive conditions."[102] Under the rule of reason, then, a restraint is compatible with the antitrust laws if it merely regulates competition and perhaps thereby promotes that competition, but not if it suppresses or destroys competition.

Applying the rule of reason to the NCAA Football Television Plan, the judge concluded that "the controls [imposed by the plan] [we]re unreasonable restraints on competition and therefore illegal."[103] Instead of protecting live attendance, as the NCAA claimed, the plan sought, according to Judge Burciaga, "to enhance the television revenues of less prominent members [of the NCAA] and to provide [the] NCAA with income." Moreover, he noted, if the NCAA were serious about preserving live attendance, it would presumably not have approved a contract under which nine hours of college football would be televised on several Saturdays during the coming season. Under these circumstances, he concluded that "the goal of maximizing revenues is far more important to [the] NCAA than that of protecting gate attendance."[104]

Judge Burciaga was equally dismissive of the NCAA's contention that its Football Television Plan was necessary to preserve "competitive balance" among its football-playing members. "[W]hatever marginal contribution the controls make to preservation of competitive balance," he reasoned, "is overwhelmed by the violence which the controls inflict on the free market economy."[105] In other words, the Football Television Plan was aimed primarily at increasing the price of televised college football, which aim it achieved by restricting the number of games televised and setting the price for the rights to show them. Therefore, in Judge Burciaga's view, the plan did not merely regulate and promote competition, as the controls at issue in *Jones* and *Hennessey* did, but instead "suppress[ed] competition to the point of destruction."[106] The worst implication of the plan, he continued, was that "the market [wa]s not responsive to viewer preference."[107] Many games for which there was a high viewer demand were not televised, and many games for which little viewer interest existed were nonetheless televised. Thus, Judge Burciaga determined that the NCAA Football Television Plan was not only a per se violation of the Sherman Act but also violated the act when examined under the rule of reason.

Accordingly, he held that Georgia, Oklahoma, and their fellow NCAA members were entitled to sell their football games for telecast without interference from the NCAA. He therefore voided the contracts the Association had entered into with ABC, CBS, and TBS and enjoined the NCAA from trying to enforce them and from making similar contracts in the future. Bloodied but still standing, the NCAA quickly appealed to the United States Court of Appeals for the Tenth Circuit, located in Denver, which stayed Judge Burciaga's decision pending the outcome of the appeal. The stay left the NCAA Football Television Plan in place for the 1982 season.

As is customary in federal appellate courts, a three-judge panel of Tenth Circuit judges heard oral arguments in *NCAA v. Board of Regents,* whose name change on appeal reflected the NCAA's status as the appealing party. On May 12, 1983, the panel announced its decision, which affirmed Judge Burciaga's decision by a 2–1 vote. The first question the appellate court addressed was whether the Football Television Plan and the related network contracts amounted to illegal price-fixing and hence were per se violations of the Sherman Act or whether they should be analyzed under the rule of reason. Its answer was that "the plan and contracts constitute per se illegal price fixing."[108] The majority wrote, "The NCAA television arrangement is so fraught with anti-competitive potential that it appears to be one that would always or almost always tend to restrict competition."[109]

The appellate court majority was as dismissive of the NCAA's argument that the plan preserved live attendance as Judge Burciaga had been. If the plan increased live attendance, the majority wrote, it did so "by restricting the availability of other options," most notably, popular games that the fans wanted televised.[110] Like Judge Burciaga, the appellate majority rejected the NCAA's argument that the plan promoted competitive balance in college football. It noted that this argument was a noneconomic justification for an anticompetitive practice and that the United States Supreme Court had held that noneconomic considerations, however worthy they might be, could not be used to justify anticompetitive restraints.[111] Moreover, the appellate court reasoned, the evidence introduced in the trial court had shown that competitive balance could be achieved by other means (e.g., the eligibility restrictions featured in *Jones* and the limits on the number of coaches at issue in *Hennessey*) that were not anticompetitive. However, the NCAA's exclusive contracts with ABC, CBS, and TBS and its establishment of "minimum aggregate compensation," were, in the court's view, decidedly anticompetitive. The former stifled competition, and the latter was price-fixing. Thus, the majority voted to affirm Judge Burciaga's ruling that the NCAA Football Television Plan was a per se violation of the Sherman Act.

The majority opted to consider the plan under the rule of reason, too. Like Judge Burciaga, the Tenth Circuit panel anticipated an appeal by the NCAA, this time to the United States Supreme Court, so it wished to analyze the issues at hand as thoroughly and comprehensively as possible. Also like Judge Burciaga, the appellate majority concluded that the Football Television Plan violated the Sherman Act under the rule of reason. It observed that the NCAA's enormous market power, based on dominance of the airwaves by college football on Saturday afternoons in the fall, resulted in "price enhancement" that was plainly anticompetitive. Furthermore, football fans were restricted to watching NCAA-sanctioned telecasts because no alternative existed, another anticompetitive result. Thus, the appellate court majority affirmed Judge Burciaga's conclusion "that the television plan [wa]s unreasonably restrictive of competitive conditions and therefore unlawful."[112] The court wrote,

> It increases concentration in the marketplace; it prevents producers from exercising independent pricing and output decisions; it precludes broadcasters from purchasing a product for which there are no readily available substitutes; it facilitates cartelization. Against this array of antitrust injuries the NCAA's justifications are insufficient.[113]

Nevertheless, the appellate court agreed with the NCAA that Judge Burciaga had erred in finding the Football Television Plan a group boycott and hence a per se violation of the Sherman Act. The key to a group boycott, the majority reasoned, is an effort by one competitor to cut its rivals off from trade relationships and opportunities. In the majority's view, NCAA members were not trying to shield themselves from competition with broadcasters, because NCAA members were not in competition with broadcasters. Moreover, all broadcasters had a chance to purchase rights to the NCAA television package. Based on this reasoning, the appellate court concluded that "the NCAA's practices do not constitute a boycott of the networks not awarded broadcast rights."[114] This conclusion was cold comfort to the NCAA, of course, because the appellate court had already invalidated the Football Television Plan, determining that it was per se illegal price-fixing and anticompetitive, therefore illegal, under rule-of-reason analysis.

The majority's conclusion sparked a dissenting opinion from Judge James Barrett, who rejected his colleagues' view that the purpose of the Football Television Plan was to limit the availability of televised college football in order to raise the price of the telecasts. Instead, he wrote, the plan was designed to maintain college football "as an amateur sport and an adjunct of the academic endeavors of the institutions."[115] These purposes were "so compelling," he continued, that "under the rule of reason analysis the public interest and that of the parties is served by sustaining the restraint as reasonable." Judge Barrett's reasoning reflected two conclusions the majority had rejected: that the NCAA Football Television Plan should not be judged by the same standards as a conventional commercial enterprise and that its restraints, however anticompetitive they might be, "[we]re fully justified under the rule of reason in that they [we]re necessary to maintain intercollegiate football as amateur competition."[116] He observed that "all of the reported cases wherein the *per se* rule has been applied have involved true competitive *business enterprises* operating in the interstate market where the goal is exclusively that of seeking a profit from the product or service offered to the public."[117] In contrast, he noted, the NCAA's television contracts were not business enterprises, because "they [we]re not designed to render the greatest profit for a *business purpose*."[118]

Judge Barrett conceded that the college football powerhouses would earn a much higher price for their televised games "in the so-called 'open market.'"[119] Still, he argued that the NCAA restraints were permissible under the rule of reason because "they insure[d] that [the powerhouses] confine[d] [their football] programs within the principles of amateurism so that intercollegiate athletics supplement[ed], rather than inhibit[ed], academic achievement."[120] Viewed from this perspective, the restraints were more procompetitive than anticompetitive, because they insured fair competition among colleges bound by identical strictures born of a desire to preserve amateurism in college sports. He added that the restraints also increased television viewership for college football by enabling fans of teams in Divisions I-AA, II, and III to see their favorite teams play on television occasionally, which presumably would not occur absent those restraints. In the context of the NCAA's educational goals, he continued, setting nearly equal payments per game to member institutions, regardless of the popularity of their football teams, "[wa]s no more 'price-fixing' than . . . a law partnerships's division of profits."[121]

For Judge Barrett, the statement in the NCAA Constitution indicating that the "fundamental policy" of the Association is to "maintain intercollegiate athletics as an integral part of the educational program" of its members dictated that college football and the NCAA's regulation of it should be viewed as educational activity beyond the reach of the antitrust laws. He concluded that "the district court [and, by implication, his colleagues on the Tenth Circuit] erred by subjugating the NCAA's educational goals . . . to the purely competitive commercialism of [an] 'every school for itself' approach to television contract bargaining."[122] Thus, Judge Barrett's view of the Football Television Plan flowed from the NCAA's stated educational mission for college football, whereas his colleagues' view flowed from the Association's tendency to use the plan to enrich itself and control its members. The conflict between the two conclusions reflected the troublesome hybrid status of big-time college sports.

Had Judge Barrett's view commanded a majority, he would have reversed Judge Burciaga's decision, thereby preserving the NCAA Football Television Plan. But Judge Barrett's view did not prevail, and the NCAA plan clung to the ropes after sustaining severe body blows from both the trial court and the appellate court. Still game for a fight, though, the NCAA petitioned for a stay of the Tenth Circuit's decision pending a planned appeal to the United States Supreme Court. The Tenth Circuit denied the stay, but Justice Byron White of the Supreme Court granted it, keeping the NCAA plan in place through the 1983 college football season and giving the Association time to file an appeal in the high court. The Supreme Court agreed to hear the NCAA's appeal, which meant that the CFA members who had abandoned their contract with NBC in 1981, hoping the courts would resolve this issue, had played their cards right, at least in the short run. The Supreme Court would indeed resolve the conflict between the NCAA and the CFA once and for all. The high court's decision is the focus of chapter 3.

Chapter 3

FREE-MARKET FOOTBALL
The Supreme Court Decides *NCAA v. Board of Regents*

Competitive Balance versus Consumer Welfare

The United States Supreme Court heard oral arguments in *NCAA v. Board of Regents* on March 20, 1984, and announced its decision in the case on June 27, 1984. Justice John Paul Stevens, whom President Gerald Ford appointed to the Court in 1975, wrote the majority opinion for himself and six colleagues. The opinion began by describing the basic features of the 1981 NCAA Football Television Plan, noting that "it retained the essential features" of its predecessors, "limit[ing] the total amount of televised intercollegiate football and the number of games that any one team may televise," and that "[n]o member [could] make any sale of television rights except in accordance with the basic plan."[1] Under the plan, Justice Stevens explained, ABC and CBS each had the right to televise "14 live exposures" and, in return, agreed to pay a specified "minimum aggregate compensation" of $131,750,000 to the institutions whose teams appeared on television during the four-year period of the networks' contract with the NCAA.[2] The 14 live exposures referred to the Saturday time slots in which each network was entitled to broadcast college football, which amounted to approximately one time slot per network per Saturday.[3]

Justice Stevens emphasized that except for higher payments to institutions participating in national, as opposed to regional, telecasts, the compensation that a team received under the NCAA plan would not change to reflect the size of the viewing audience, the number of media markets in which a game were telecast, or the particular characteristics of the game or the participating teams.[4] He also stressed that the appearance limitations in the plan prohibited the football teams from NCAA-member institutions from appearing on television more than six times in toto (and more than four times nationally) during a two-year period and required the networks to show games involving at least 82 different colleges during that time.[5] The contract between the networks and the NCAA also capped the total number of games that could be telecast during the regular season.[6]

These practices, Justice Stevens observed, "share characteristics of restraints we have previously held unreasonable."[7] More precisely, he continued, the practices featured in the NCAA plan, namely, "prevent[ing] member institutions from competing against each other on the basis of price or kind of television rights that can be offered to broadcasters," created a "horizontal restraint" on economic competition, which is usually a per se violation of the Sherman Antitrust Act.[8] A horizontal restraint is an agreement among economic competitors about the way in which they will compete with one another.[9] In this case, Stevens explained, the horizontal restraint limited the number of college football games to be televised, thereby "plac[ing] an artificial limit on the quantity of televised football that is available to broadcasters and consumers."[10] In other words, the NCAA Football Television Plan limited the "output" of televised college football, which was problematic because, in Justice Stevens's words, "our cases have held that such limitations are unreasonable restraints of trade."[11] To make matters worse, the minimum aggregate price that the networks paid to televise college football prevented any price negotiation between the institutions and the networks. In Justice Stevens's view, this amounted to "horizontal price-fixing, perhaps the paradigm of an unreasonable restraint of trade."[12]

Justice Stevens pointed out that horizontal price-fixing and limitations on output are ordinarily per se violations of the Sherman Act because "the probability that these practices are anti-competitive is so high."[13] He reminded his readers that the per se rule applies when "the practice [at issue] facially appears to be one that would always or almost always tend to restrict competition and decrease output."[14] In those circumstances, he added, a restraint on competition is presumed to violate the Sherman Act, and courts typically do not bother examining the particular industry involved to see if the restraint is somehow justified.[15]

Despite this grim assessment of the NCAA plan's anticompetitive features, Justice Stevens and the Supreme Court majority opted not to apply the per se rule and stop the plan dead in its tracks. Instead, they used the rule of reason, because, in Stevens's words, "this case involves an industry in which horizontal restraints on competition are essential if the product is to be available at all."[16] Justice Stevens and his colleagues in the majority recognized that in order to market athletic contests between competing institutions, the NCAA had to impose "rules on which the competitors agreed to create and define the competition to be marketed" or the games would not occur.[17] To ensure the availability of college football, the NCAA established rules concerning, for example, "the size of the field, the number of players on a team, and the extent to which physical violence is to be encouraged or proscribed."[18] These rules, and others like them, Justice Stevens acknowledged, were necessary "to preserve the unique product known as 'college football,' the popularity of which derives from its distinctiveness from professional sports."[19] In other words, the players' amateur and student status were essential to the uniqueness and the continued popularity (and profitability) of college football, and only rules imposed by mutual agreement among the competitors would ensure that the players remained amateurs and students.[20]

Therefore, Justice Stevens observed, NCAA rules enabled college football "to preserve its character" and to thrive as a commercial product because of its unique blend of high-quality athleticism, amateurism, and academic tradition.[21] "In performing this role," he continued, the NCAA "widen[ed] consumer choice—not only the choices available to sports fans but also those available to athletes—and hence can be viewed as procompetitive."[22] Indeed, he noted, the University of Georgia and the University of Oklahoma conceded that most of the NCAA's rules promoted competition between member institutions rather than stifling it.[23] Under these circumstances, Justice Stevens determined, "despite the fact that this case involves restraints on the ability of member institutions to compete in terms of price and output, a fair evaluation of their competitive character requires consideration of the NCAA's justifications for the restraints."[24] That consideration would proceed under the rule of reason; the "essential inquiry," Justice Stevens wrote, would be "whether or not the challenged restraint enhances competition."[25] That was because "[u]nder the Sherman Act the criterion to be used in judging the validity of a restraint on trade is its impact on competition."[26]

Keeping the competitiveness criterion firmly in mind, Justice Stevens proceeded to describe the "anticompetitive consequences" of the Football Television Plan, namely, its price-fixing and limitations on output. He observed that under the plan, "individual competitors (i.e. colleges) lose their freedom to compete. Price (i.e. the cost to televise games) is higher and output (number of games televised) lower than they would otherwise be, and both are unresponsive to consumer preference."[27] Unresponsiveness to consumer preference was a serious problem because, Stevens noted, "Congress designed the Sherman Act as a 'consumer welfare prescription.'"[28] "A restraint that has the effect of reducing the importance of consumer preference in setting price and output," he explained, "is not consistent with this fundamental goal of antitrust law."[29] He called restraints on price and output "the paradigmatic examples of restraints of trade that the Sherman Act was intended to prohibit."[30] Regarding the output restrictions, he observed that only the largest broadcasters, such as ABC and CBS, which could afford to bid on an entire season's package of NCAA games, could compete for the football television contract, hence "many telecasts that would occur in a competitive market are foreclosed by the NCAA's plan."[31]

Justice Stevens rejected the NCAA's argument that the Football Television Plan was compatible with the Sherman Act, because, despite the plan's arguably anticompetitive features, its effects were minimal as a result of the NCAA's lack of "market power," that is, the ability to affect supply and demand in the television marketplace.[32] Specifically, the NCAA argued in its brief that even if it wished to artificially raise the price of televising college football games by restricting the number of games to be telecast, it could not achieve that goal, because "advertisers would switch to other shows or other media."[33] The NCAA added that its football programming was "a trivial fraction of all T.V. programming" and hence that the Association had no power (over advertisers) to set prices by restricting output.[34]

In response, Justice Stevens observed, first, that even if the NCAA were correct about its claimed lack of market power, it would still not be entitled to place "a naked restriction on price or output."[35] Market power aside, he explained, the NCAA plan was contrary to the Sherman Act's requirement that price and output (i.e., supply) respond to consumer preference.[36] But then he wrote that the NCAA "does possess market power."[37] He based that conclusion on the trial court's finding that "intercollegiate football telecasts generate an audience uniquely attractive to advertisers (i.e., young adult and middle-aged males with college degrees and relatively high incomes) and that competitors are unable to offer programming that can attract a similar audience."[38] Perhaps the best evidence for that finding was the lack of competitive programming offered by networks not showing college football games on Saturday afternoons in the autumn; their standard fare during that time slot was cartoons and old movies.[39] Indeed, during several recent seasons, when ABC was the only network showing college football games, CBS actually "went dark" on half of the Saturday afternoons in the autumn rather than try to compete with college football on ABC.[40] In Justice Stevens's view, these factual findings by the trial court compelled the conclusion that the NCAA possessed market power sufficient to make its price and output restrictions problematic.

According to Justice Stevens, those restrictions were "hallmarks of anticompetitive behavior" that, when examined under the rule of reason, required the NCAA to bear "a heavy burden of establishing an affirmative defense which competitively justifies this apparent deviation from the operations of a free market."[41] In his view, the NCAA failed to show any "procompetitive" justification for the restraints imposed by the Football Television Plan. That was not for lack of trying by the NCAA to show that the plan provided what Justice Stevens called "procompetitive efficiencies."[42] One of the documents the NCAA submitted to the Court in connection with this case was its Television Committee's 1981 briefing book, which listed the following "primary objectives and purposes" for the Football Television Plan: "1. To reduce, insofar as possible, the adverse effects of live television upon football game attendance and, in turn, upon the athletic and education programs dependent upon that football attendance; 2. To spread television among as many NCAA member colleges as possible; and 3. To provide football television to the public to the extent compatible with the other two objectives."[43] These objectives, the NCAA argued in its brief, were sufficiently procompetitive to justify the restrictions on price and output imposed by the Football Television Plan.

In the NCAA's view, the plan increased competition in the college football market by spreading national and regional television appearances among more teams than would appear on television without the plan. Specifically, the plan's limitation on the number of television appearances a college football team could make (six during a two-year period, including four national appearances) allowed access to television for teams that would not otherwise enjoy it.[44] According to the NCAA, access to television enabled lesser-known teams to recruit athletes whom they would not otherwise have been able to recruit and to enjoy financial support from donors that would not have been forthcoming had the teams not played on television.[45] As a result, college teams were more evenly matched on the field than they would have been without the plan, and more games were competitive and exciting than would otherwise have been true, thereby expanding the audience for college football on television, where it competed with other forms of entertainment.[46]

Thus, argued the NCAA, the plan was procompetitive (and hence compatible with the Sherman Act) because it promoted competitive balance between teams and increased both the television audience and live attendance at college stadiums across America.[47] The NCAA's brief maintained that college football teams, like professional teams, "are rivals on the field and have separate 'owners'"[48] (either colleges or entrepreneurs); therefore, in college football, as in the National Football League, "[j]oint action produces balance; teams and colleges cannot do this alone. Cooperation thus increases competition."[49] Accordingly, the NCAA concluded, even if it enjoyed market power, its Football Television Plan and associated network contracts "[we]re not unreasonable restraints of trade [because] they expand[ed] rather than reduc[ed] output."[50] In effect, then, *NCAA v. Regents* pitted competitive balance and consumer welfare squarely against each other, and the Supreme Court's job was to pick the winner once and for all.

The Case for Consumer Welfare

Justice Stevens disagreed with the NCAA's view that its Football Television Plan was "procompetitive." He reasoned that if the plan were indeed procompetitive, it would increase the number of games televised and reduce the price of televising them.[51] On the contrary, he noted, the trial court found that the plan had precisely the opposite effects: the networks televised fewer games than they would televise absent the plan, and the price of each telecast was higher than it would be absent the plan.[52] Therefore, Justice Stevens reasoned, the plan stifled economic competition in the college sports industry instead of promoting it.

Economic competition is dear to the heart of Justice Stevens, who retired from the Supreme Court in 2010. In antitrust cases, one commentator has written, Justice Stevens "repeatedly identifies the goal of the antitrust laws as the preservation of competition in the ultimate service of enhancing consumer welfare."[53] In this respect, Justice Stevens's view reflects the modern interpretation of antitrust law, namely, that its aim is not just to ensure price competition but, rather, to foster market conditions that make a wide array of goods and services available to consumers. In other words, the antitrust laws should ensure that the economy responds to consumer demand instead of to governmental directives or the preferences of individual businesses.[54] According to this view, if those laws are working properly, they will promote both consumer choice and product innovation.[55] An antitrust violation, then, is an activity that unreasonably distorts or restricts the options that would otherwise be available to consumers.[56]

During his 35 years on the Supreme Court, Justice Stevens sought to promote competition by using the antitrust laws to quash "the broadest range of activity that is harmful to competition, whether it be undertaken by private individuals or firms or by entities supervised by federal or state governments."[57] He criticized Supreme Court decisions limiting the reach of the antitrust laws and tended to interpret antitrust exemptions narrowly.[58] Another key feature of Justice Stevens's antitrust opinions was deference to the findings of the "trier of fact" in the trial court, regardless of whether a judge (i.e., in a bench trial) or a jury performed that function.[59] He relied heavily on the facts found in the trial court and expressed his displeasure when, according to him, his Supreme Court colleagues substituted their own judgments about the facts of a case for those of the trier of fact.[60]

Each of these components of Justice Stevens's antitrust philosophy was evident in his majority opinion in *NCAA v. Regents*. In rejecting the NCAA's overall claim that the plan enhanced competition, Justice Stevens also rejected the Association's more narrowly tailored argument that the plan protected live attendance at college football games, thereby promoting competition by ensuring audiences for teams whose games were not televised. This argument failed in part because the NCAA did not appear to be sincere about achieving the stated goal. "Under the current plan," Justice Stevens wrote, "games are shown on television all hours that college football games are played."[61] Therefore, he concluded, "[t]he plan simply does not protect live attendance by ensuring that games will not be shown on television at the same time as live events."[62]

But the NCAA's halfhearted effort to protect live attendance was not the only reason or even the principal reason why Justice Stevens rejected its argument that the Football Television Plan was necessary to fill stadiums. "[A] more fundamental reason for rejecting this defense," Stevens wrote, was that "it [wa]s not based on a desire to maintain the integrity of college football as a distinct and attractive product, but rather on a fear that the product will not prove sufficiently attractive to draw live attendance when faced with competition from televised games."[63] In Stevens's view, this amounted to an admission by the NCAA that "ticket sales for most college games are unable to compete in a free market."[64] That admission and the restriction on televised games flowing from it were, according to Justice Stevens, "inconsistent with the basic policy of the Sherman Act," which is to promote, not to restrict, economic competition.[65]

Justice Stevens was equally dismissive of the NCAA's argument that the Football Television Plan was procompetitive because it produced a competitive balance among rival college football teams, thereby ensuring exciting contests on the field and large, enthusiastic audiences, both at the stadium and in front of the TV set. He acknowledged that "most of the regulatory controls of the NCAA are justifiable means of fostering competition among amateur athletic teams and [are] therefore procompetitive because they enhance public interest in intercollegiate athletics."[66] Then he drew a sharp distinction between rules that preserved amateurism or fostered competitive equity, on the one hand, and the Football Television Plan, on the other. "The specific restraints on football telecasts that are challenged in this case," he wrote, "do not . . . fit into the same mold as do rules defining the conditions of the contest, the eligibility of participants, or the manner in which members of a joint enterprise shall share the responsibilities and the benefits of the total venture."[67]

Echoing the opinion of the trial court, he added that "the NCAA imposes a variety of other restrictions designed to preserve amateurism which are much better tailored to the goal of competitive balance than is the television plan, and which are 'clearly sufficient' to preserve competitive balance to the extent it is within the NCAA's power to do so."[68] Among these were rules that (1) limited the number of games each team could play in a season, (2) capped the number of coaches and players a team could have, (3) regulated the recruitment of high school athletes, (4) established academic standards for initial and continued athletic eligibility, and (5) set the maximum number of athletic scholarships a college could award in any particular sport, including football.[69] Moreover, Justice Stevens observed, the trial court had found that "many more games would be televised in a free market than under the NCAA plan," so the NCAA's restrictions on televised football prevented, rather than promoted, competitive balance among college football teams.[70] In Stevens's view, the best means of promoting competitive balance was to abandon the Football Television Plan, thereby increasing the number of televised games and the number of college teams that would appear on television and reap the associated financial and recruiting benefits.

Thus, Justice Stevens concluded that "by curtailing output and blunting the ability of member institutions to respond to consumer preference, the NCAA has restricted rather than enhanced the place of intercollegiate athletics in the Nation's life."[71] Accordingly, the Court majority affirmed the decision of the court of appeals. The Court thereby invalidated the NCAA Football Television Plan as a violation of the Sherman Antitrust Act and ended more than three decades of NCAA control of televised college football.

A Plea for Amateurism

Not every member of the Supreme Court shared Justice Stevens's emphasis on consumer welfare in antitrust law. Justice White, joined by then justice William Rehnquist, who would become chief justice in 1986,[72] penned a vigorous dissent in which he charged that the majority had erred by treating college sports "as a purely commercial venture in which colleges and universities participate solely, or even primarily, in the pursuit of profits."[73] This charge reflected White's view that the NCAA performed a unique function, namely, "to enhance the contribution made by amateur athletic competition to the process of higher education as distinguished from realizing maximum return on it as an entertainment commodity."[74] That function was necessary, in White's estimation, because the marketplace, if left to its own devices, would rob college sports of their amateurism, which was the source of their unique appeal to fans. "The NCAA ensures," Justice White wrote, "the continued availability of a unique and valuable product, the very existence of which might well be threatened by unbridled competition in the economic sphere."[75]

Toward that end, White noted, the NCAA had long limited the compensation of college athletes and the number of coaches an institution could hire.[76] It barred from intercollegiate competition athletes who had played professionally in their respective sports, restricted the number of athletic scholarships its members could award, and established minimum academic standards for recipients of athletic scholarships.[77] In Justice White's words, it also "pervasively regulated the recruitment process, student eligibility, practice schedules, squad size, the number of games played, and many other aspects of intercollegiate athletics."[78] Those regulations, White observed, prevented the most athletically successful institutions from using their success to build athletic programs with which their rivals could not compete.[79] In other words, he continued, the NCAA's regulations were designed "to keep university athletics from becoming professionalized to the extent that profit making objectives would overshadow educational objectives."[80] The Football Television Plan shared this aim and, in Justice White's view, did not differ "fundamentally" from NCAA rules limiting squad sizes and regulating athletic eligibility.[81]

White reasoned that the plan "reflect[ed] the NCAA's fundamental policy of preserving amateurism and integrating athletics and education";[82] therefore, the trial court's finding that the plan also aimed to "maximize television revenues" did not mean that the NCAA ignored its stated educational objectives in the pursuit of those revenues.[83] In his view, the Court majority disregarded the NCAA's educational objectives, "trap[ping] itself in commercial antitrust rhetoric and ideology and ignor[ing] the context in which the [NCAA's] restraints [on economic competition] have been imposed."[84] Absent the Football Television Plan, he wrote, "unlimited appearances by a few schools would inevitably give them an insuperable advantage over all others and in the end defeat any efforts to maintain a system of athletic competition among amateurs who measure up to college scholastic requirements."[85]

But Justice White was not afraid to confront the majority on its own turf, namely, economics. He reasoned that his colleagues had erred in concluding that the appropriate measure of "output" in this case was the number of games televised; in his view, the proper measure was the total number of persons who watched college football games on television.[86] The NCAA plan increased the latter number by selling the rights to televise its games only to the established networks, resulting in national and regional (instead of local) broadcasts, thereby expanding the total television audience for college football games.[87] Accordingly, White wrote, the University of Oklahoma and the University of Georgia had not "carried their burden of showing that the television plan has an adverse effect on output and is therefore anticompetitive."[88]

Neither, in his estimation, had they proved that the plan produced an anticompetitive increase in the price of television rights for college football games. On the contrary, he pointed out, because of the limited number of games televised under the plan, "the purchasing network can count on a larger share of the audience, which translates into greater advertising revenues and, accordingly, into larger payments per game to the televised teams."[89] "In short," he continued, "by focusing only on the price paid by the networks for television rights rather than on the nature and quality of the product delivered by the NCAA and its member institutions, the District Court, and this Court as well, may well have deemed anticompetitive a rise in price that more properly should be attributed to an increase in output, measured in terms of viewership."[90]

Staying with economics, Justice White added that under the NCAA plan, the "minimum aggregate compensation" the networks paid to televise college football promoted competition rather than stifling it, by redistributing total television revenues for college football among less competitive teams. In his view, this revenue redistribution was "a wholly justifiable, even necessary, aspect of maintaining truly competitive college teams."[91] It reflected the reality that the games of some college football teams that were especially popular with fans "contribute[d] disproportionately to the total value of the package" of televised college football games during the regular season.[92] Under these circumstances, the NCAA sought to foster competitive balance among its football-playing members by distributing the "minimum aggregate compensation" paid by the networks in such a way that, in Justice White's words, "less prominent schools receive more in rights fees than they would receive in a competitive market and football powers like [Oklahoma and Georgia] receive less."[93] In other words, according to Justice White, the minimum aggregate compensation the networks paid to the institutions "reflected the average value to the networks of the games they anticipated televising," some of which would feature marquee teams, while others would not.[94] In his view, this arrangement was compatible with the Sherman Act. He wrote,

> As long as the NCAA cannot artificially fix the price of the entire package and demand supercompetitive prices, [the redistribution aspect] of the plan should be of little concern. And I find little, if anything, in the record to support the notion that the NCAA has power to extract from the television networks more than the broadcasting rights are worth in the marketplace.[95]

Then Justice White shifted his attention away from economics and back to education. "Like Judge Barrett, who dissented in the Court of Appeals," he wrote, "I believe that the lower courts erred by subjugating the NCAA's educational goals ... to the purely competitive commercialism of [an] 'every school for itself' approach to television contract bargaining."[96] Justice White reminded his colleagues in the majority that Congress had aimed the Sherman Act at entities having commercial objectives, intending it to apply only to a limited extent to organizations, like the NCAA, whose principal objectives are noncommercial.[97] "The legitimate noneconomic goals of colleges and universities," he reasoned, "should not be ignored in analyzing restraints imposed by associations of such institutions on their members, and these noneconomic goals 'may require that a particular practice, which could properly be viewed as a violation of the Sherman Act in another context, be treated differently.'"[98]

In making this point, Justice White cited a decision that the Court had handed down almost a decade earlier, *Goldfarb v. Virginia State Bar,* in which the Court considered whether a minimum fee schedule set by a state bar association for certain legal services violated the Sherman Act.[99] Like *NCAA v. Regents, Goldfarb* required the justices to decide whether price restraints imposed by an organization whose aims were predominately noncommercial violated antitrust law. The plaintiffs, a husband and wife, had contracted to buy a house in Fairfax County, Virginia. The lender from whom they obtained financing required them to obtain title insurance, necessitating a title search, which only a licensed Virginia lawyer could perform. The plaintiffs contacted 37 lawyers, none of whom would charge them less than the minimum fee schedule published by the Fairfax County Bar Association, namely, 1 percent of the value of the property purchased.[100] The fee schedule was a list of recommended minimum prices for common legal services, and the Virginia State Bar Association enforced it.[101] The plaintiffs, who sued both the Virginia State and Fairfax County bar associations, charged that "the operation of the minimum fee schedule, as applied to fees for legal services relating to residential real estate transactions, constitute[d] price fixing in violation of [Section 1] of the Sherman Act."[102]

The Supreme Court agreed with the plaintiffs, rejecting the two bar associations' arguments (1) that Congress had not intended to include the "learned professions," such as law, under the category "trade or commerce" in Section 1 of the Sherman Act and hence that "the sale of professional services [wa]s exempt from the Act" and (2) that competition was contrary to the practice of a profession, the purpose of which was to provide services necessary to the community, not to earn profits.[103] Writing for the majority, Chief Justice Warren Burger observed that previous Supreme Court decisions had included sales of services within the reach of Section 1. "Whatever else it may be," he wrote, "the examination of a land title is a service; the exchange of such a service for money is 'commerce' in the most common usage of that word."[104] Moreover, he noted, "it cannot be denied that the activities of lawyers play an important part in commercial intercourse, and that anticompetitive activities by lawyers may exert a restraint on commerce."[105] Thus, the *Goldfarb* Court invalidated the Virginia State Bar's recommended minimum fee schedule.

Nevertheless, Chief Justice Burger's majority opinion in *Goldfarb* put up a hook that Justice White would hang his hat on almost a decade later in *NCAA v. Regents.* That hook was the following language, which appeared in a footnote in *Goldfarb* and which indicated that some activities ordinarily regarded as anticompetitive under the Sherman Act might be exempt from antitrust regulation because of the professional or organizational context in which they occurred. Burger wrote,

> The fact that a restraint operates upon a profession as distinguished from a business is, of course, relevant in determining whether that particular restraint violates the Sherman Act. It would be unrealistic to view the practice of professions as interchangeable with other business activities, and automatically to apply to the professions antitrust concepts which originated in the other areas. The public service aspect, and other features of the professions, may require that a particular practice, which could properly be viewed as a violation of the Sherman Act in another context, be treated differently. We intimate no view on any other situation than the one with which we are confronted today.[106]

In *NCAA v. Regents,* Justice White used the language of the *Goldfarb* footnote to support his view that intercollegiate athletics was a context in which activities like the NCAA Football Television Plan, which would surely constitute illegal price-fixing in a purely commercial setting, should be permissible because of the predominately noncommercial (i.e., educational) setting in which they occurred. Quoting the footnote in part, he wrote,

> The legitimate noneconomic goals of colleges and universities should not be ignored in analyzing restraints imposed by associations of such institutions on their members, and these noneconomic goals 'may require that a particular practice, which could properly be viewed as a violation of the Sherman Act in another context, be treated differently.[107]

Justice White also used another Supreme Court precedent, *National Society of Professional Engineers v. United States,*[108] to support his argument that the majority was "mistaken" in refusing to consider noneconomic justifications for the Football Television Plan.[109] This portion of White's dissent harkened back to a question he had posed during the oral argument to NCAA counsel Frank Easterbrook, who had pressed the point that the NCAA lacked sufficient market power to limit output and drive up the price of televised college football. Frustrated by Easterbrook's emphasis on economics, White interrupted him, asking,

> But your suggestion, Mr. Easterbrook, suggests that the NCAA is in the business of manufacturing widgets and that its only motive is to maximize profits. But if it's a nonprofit association, might it not have other, noneconomic goals?[110]

That question produced a brief colloquy, which went as follows:

EASTERBROOK: It might well, Your Honor. As you know, we have not argued that any educational or amateurism goals of the NCAA are a good reason for the NCAA to engage in monopolistic practices, practices that increase the price paid by viewers.[111]

WHITE: Why haven't you argued that?[112]

EASTERBROOK: We haven't argued that because as we read this Court's cases, including *Engineers* and others, the goals other than economic are not reasons for monopolistic practices.[113]

Justice White rejected the view reflected in the majority opinion in *NCAA v. Regents*, namely, that *National Society of Professional Engineers v. United States* had held that noneconomic goals could not justify anticompetitive activities that violated antitrust law. His emphasis on *Professional Engineers* warrants a short detour to examine that case. At issue there was an ethical canon by which the engineering society prohibited competitive bidding on engineering projects by its members, which the Justice Department believed violated the Sherman Act. Under the society's Code of Ethics, specifically Section 11(c), an engineer agreed to refuse to negotiate or even to discuss fees with a potential client until the client had selected that engineer to do the work.[114] This prohibition reflected the society's desire to preserve the traditional method of selecting professional engineers, namely, on the basis of background and reputation, not price.[115]

Responding to the federal government's lawsuit, the society defended its ethical canon by arguing that competitive pressure to offer engineering services at the lowest possible price would reduce the quality of those services and, therefore, that awarding engineering contracts to the lowest bidder would endanger the public health, safety, and welfare.[116] Accordingly, the society maintained that Section 11(c) of its Code of Ethics was not an unreasonable restraint of trade.[117] Both the district court and the court of appeals disagreed, concluding that Section 11(c) was a per se violation of the Sherman Act, hence "illegal without regard to claimed or possible benefits."[118] But the Supreme Court, considering the society's noneconomic defense of Section 11(c), examined the ethical canon according to the rule of reason, just as it would later do for the NCAA Football Television Plan.[119]

Writing for the Court in *Professional Engineers*, Justice Stevens remarked, concerning the rule of reason,

> Contrary to its name, the Rule does not open the field of antitrust inquiry to any argument in favor of a challenged restraint that may fall within the realm of reason. Instead, it focuses directly on the challenged restraint's impact on competitive conditions.[120]

He observed that the rule of reason rejects "the argument that because of the special characteristics of a particular industry, monopolistic arrangements will better promote trade and commerce than competition."[121] "That kind of argument," he continued, "is properly addressed to Congress and may justify an exemption from the statute for specific industries, but it is not permitted by the Rule of Reason."[122] In other words, the supposed benefits of the society's restraint on price competition—enhanced public safety and improved product quality—were not the kinds of benefits that courts should consider when conducting a rule-of-reason analysis.[123] Instead, Justice Stevens pointed out, in language similar to that which he would later use in *NCAA v. Regents*, "the inquiry mandated by the Rule of Reason is whether the challenged agreement is one that promotes competition or one that suppresses competition."[124] Therefore, the Sherman Act prohibited reducing competition in order to produce results different from those that would occur in a competitive market.[125]

Justice Stevens then determined that the ban on competitive bidding failed the rule-of-reason test. The society could not properly invoke the rule of reason, he wrote, while arguing that "its restraint on price competition ultimately inures to the public benefit by preventing the production of inferior work and by insuring ethical behavior."[126] He noted that the Court had never accepted such an argument under the rule of reason, which insists on procompetitive outcomes and does not tolerate noneconomic justifications for anticompetitive outcomes.[127] Then he observed that "the cautionary footnote in *Goldfarb* [stating that otherwise anticompetitive practices by professions could possibly survive antitrust scrutiny for noneconomic reasons] cannot be read as fashioning a broad exemption under the Rule of Reason for learned professions."[128] Thus, Justice Stevens concluded in *Professional Engineers,* in language reflecting his deep philosophical attachment to economic competition, "The Rule of Reason does not support a defense based on the assumption that competition itself is unreasonable."[129] Based on Stevens's reasoning, the Supreme Court affirmed the district court's order prohibiting the Society of Professional Engineers from adopting any official opinion, policy statement, or guideline stating or implying that competitive bidding is unethical.[130]

Justice White joined Justice Stevens's majority opinion in *Professional Engineers,* but he rejected Stevens's extension of the reasoning in that case to the world of college sports. "The primarily noneconomic values pursued by educational institutions," Justice White wrote, "differ fundamentally from the 'overriding commercial purpose of [the] day-to-day activities' of engineers, lawyers, doctors and businessmen, and neither *Professional Engineers* nor any other decision of this Court suggests that associations of nonprofit educational institutions must defend their self-regulatory restraints solely in terms of their competitive impact, without regard for the legitimate noneconomic values they promote."[131] "When these values are factored into the balance," he continued, "the NCAA's television plan seems eminently reasonable."[132] He explained, "Most fundamentally, the plan fosters the goal of amateurism by spreading revenues among various schools and reducing the financial incentives toward professionalism."[133]

Quoting Judge Barrett's dissent in the court of appeals, Justice White added that "[t]he restraints upon Oklahoma and Georgia and other colleges and universities with excellent football programs insure that they confine those programs within the principles of amateurism so that intercollegiate athletics supplement, rather than inhibit, educational achievement."[134] In White's view, the Football Television Plan, like the NCAA rule that prohibited paying college athletes, could encourage high school seniors to choose their colleges partly on the basis of "educational quality," by de-emphasizing the economic implications of that choice.[135] The Football Television Plan also helped to preserve the "economic viability" of athletic programs at colleges with weaker football teams and "promoted competitive football among many and varied amateur teams nationwide," by giving a wide array of colleges a chance to play on television.[136] "These important contributions," Justice White concluded, "[we]re sufficient to offset any minimal anticompetitive effects of the television plan."[137]

That conclusion reflected Justice White's philosophy of antitrust law. For White, one commentator has written, "the touchstone of antitrust law [wa]s not solely consumer welfare," and "deciding antitrust cases require[d] more than economic theory."[138] In *NCAA v. Regents,* according to this commentator, "[t]he educational purpose of nonprofit institutions such as the NCAA member universities outweighed all other factors" for White; therefore, to him, "analysis of the NCAA policies under antitrust and economic terms was inappropriate."[139] In other words, "[t]he member schools were not individual businesses trying to compete, as the Court majority presupposed, but rather educational institutions with largely noneconomic goals."[140]

Another force may also have helped to drive Justice White's dissent in *NCAA v. Regents.* When antitrust cases arose in purely economic contexts, a commentator has written, White "str[ove] to protect small businessmen from restrictions imposed by others who would unfairly exploit their own market power."[141] The same commentator has speculated that Justice White may have "based his view of [*NCAA v. Regents*] on his own experience with professional sports."[142] Taken together, these comments call to mind the circumstances under which Byron White played college and professional football, which may well have influenced his emphasis on the NCAA's educational mission in *NCAA v. Regents.*

College athletics were less commercialized when White played than they were in 1984, when the Court decided *NCAA v. Regents.* Moreover, in White's day, the University of Colorado football team was analogous to the small businessperson struggling to compete, as the eastern colleges that had invented football dominated the national rankings. Nobody knew that better than Byron White, who finished second to Yale's Clint Frank in the Heisman Trophy balloting in 1937.[143] Perhaps these factors, along with the clearer distinction that existed during White's undergraduate years between college and professional football, helped to inform his dissent in *NCAA v. Regents.* Journalist Keith Dunnavant has written that in his dissent, "White clearly pined for a simpler era, before commercialism became such an undeniable fact of life in college athletics."[144] Maybe so, but if those feelings spawned the dissent, they did not diminish its cogency. After all, if Justice White's dissent resulted from an antiquated view of college sports, Justice

Stevens's majority opinion arguably resulted from an antitrust ideology that ignored the values of higher education, where college sports reside.

Whatever forces drove Justice White's dissent, though, his largely noneconomic defense of the NCAA Football Television Plan garnered only two votes, and the Court invalidated the plan. Both inside and outside the Supreme Court, economic arguments about efficiency and consumer welfare carried the day regarding the NCAA Football Television Plan, as is reflected in reactions to the decision by two judges who are also scholars of antitrust law. Richard Posner observed that the NCAA had failed to bear its burden of showing that the plan primarily enhanced, rather than stifled, economic competition. "The rule against price-fixing would quickly erode," he wrote, "if the existence of a *plausible* justification [e.g., enhancing overall competition by giving less visible teams a chance to play on television] were a complete defense and the defendant did not have to prove that the restriction had brought about a *net* improvement in efficiency."[145] This conclusion reflects Posner's philosophy of antitrust law, which maintains that no justification exists for "using the antitrust laws to attain goals unrelated or antithetical to efficiency, such as promoting a society of small tradespeople."[146] His view is consistent with that of the Supreme Court majority in *NCAA v. Regents,* which refused to allow the NCAA's goal of ensuring access to television for less visible teams to trump traditional antitrust aims, notably economic efficiency and consumer welfare.

Robert Bork also supported the Supreme Court's decision, but for a different reason than Judge Posner cited. To Bork, the Football Television Plan might have been worth preserving had it been truly procompetitive by protecting competitive balance "across all of college football" instead of moving timidly in that direction by giving a few less prestigious teams a chance to play on television occasionally.[147] The NCAA plan, Bork noted, "did nothing to bring Yale and Notre Dame to a condition of competitive equality,"[148] nor did it "enhance[] economic efficiency in any other way."[149] Interestingly, though, he added that had a particular athletic conference, such as the Big 10, imposed a similar restraint on its members, that restraint might have withstood antitrust scrutiny because it would have had "an obvious relationship to competitive balance" among the league's members and could have enhanced economic efficiency and consumer welfare by producing more competitive, exciting football games between them.[150] Thus, Bork concluded, the Football Television Plan lacked a truly procompetitive purpose, hence the Supreme Court was correct in invalidating it.

Consumer Welfare Prevails

In retrospect, the Supreme Court's emphasis in *NCAA v. Regents* on economic efficiency and consumer welfare was predictable, even defensible, because the NCAA failed to make an educational argument for the Football Television Plan. It relied instead on arguments about preserving gate receipts through encouraging live attendance, ensuring a competitive balance among teams, and its lack of market power to drive up the price of televising college football by limiting the number of games that could be televised. Indeed, Frank Easterbrook, who argued for the NCAA in the Supreme Court, so emphasized the NCAA's claimed lack of market power that Justice White chided him for virtually ignoring what White saw as the procompetitive effects of the Football Television Plan.[151] The criticism from the bench forced Easterbrook to reply, "Justice White, we have not abandoned in any way the first two arguments we made in the brief [about preserving live attendance and ensuring competitive balance]."[152]

Perhaps the NCAA's emphasis on economics over education, though, is best reflected in its failure to respond to a theme introduced by the advocate for the University of Georgia and the University of Oklahoma in the Supreme Court, attorney and Oklahoma City mayor Andy Coats. He told the Court that college basketball was a good model for the way in which college football could operate on television without NCAA regulation. The NCAA did not restrict the televising of college basketball as it restricted the televising of college football. "And the reason basketball has worked so well," Coats argued, "was that lots of teams were on [television]" and "they were on in local and regional areas."[153] Justice White interjected, "Of course, they're on at 12:00 o'clock at night, too, with basketball," to which Coats responded, "Yes, sir, they're on just nearly any time of day."[154]

Coats proceeded to argue that if the Court struck down the NCAA Football Plan, more college football games would be televised, including many on a regional basis, as occurred in college basketball. "The people in the local area," he argued, "will identify with the product, they'll identify with the school, they'll identify with the players."[155] "They will then want to go and see the games in person," he added, thereby enhancing live attendance, contrary to the NCAA's allegations.[156] "And we really believe," he added, "that the decision by this Court affirming the lower courts would be very healthy for football, will indeed cause a lot of teams that are never on [television] these days to be able to be on, to display their wares, their products, and their teams, and indeed return us to the free market, which is where we think this matter should rest."[157] This statement echoed an argument that the University of Georgia and the University of Oklahoma had made in their brief, namely, that the NCAA's claim that the Football Television Plan was necessary to promote competitive balance among teams was incorrect, because dismantling the plan would spread television appearances among more teams, including less visible teams from smaller colleges, resulting in a fair distribution of revenues from televised football.[158] The universities had also argued in their brief that, regardless of the wisdom of trying to protect gate attendance by restricting the number of games televised, the plan had not affected gate attendance whatsoever and should be eliminated for that reason alone.[159]

The NCAA's emphasis on economics may have resulted from overconfidence born of its long record of victories in previous antitrust cases. But those victories occurred when the economic restraints at issue (e.g., barring athletes who had previously played professionally, limiting the number of assistant football or basketball coaches a college could employ, or declaring a team ineligible for postseason competition for violating Association rules) served the NCAA's stated goal of preserving amateur sport in an educational setting. In this connection, one commentary observes,

> The NCAA has power to restrict participants' economic freedom in order to maintain principles of amateurism and education within intercollegiate sports, but when rules fall outside of this grant of authority, an antitrust violation will arise. Thus, in [NCAA v. Regents], the Court found that the NCAA had violated the antitrust laws because reducing the number of college football broadcasts was not related to NCAA efforts to ensure that student-athletes maintain their status as academic-amateurs.[160]

Drawing on NCAA v. Regents, this commentary notes that "the most vulnerable [NCAA] regulations are those which have a direct and immediate economic impact on student-athletes, coaches, or schools, but do not serve any related educational goal."[161]

That commentary postdates NCAA v. Regents, so perhaps the NCAA could not have anticipated that its failure to advance an educational rationale for the Football Television Plan would sound the plan's death knell. But the NCAA should not be let off the hook for that failure so easily, because the brief for the University of Georgia and the University of Oklahoma advanced an argument that was remarkably similar to the argument just quoted. According to the brief,

> The courts below properly recognized that this case has nothing whatever to do with the validity or desirability of NCAA's rules relating to amateurism, rules of play or conditions of competition. [The universities] do not challenge NCAA's rule-making powers in these traditional areas of concern. What respondents do challenge is NCAA's venture away from its heritage and into *economic* regulatory functions—a venture which NCAA has seen fit to undertake in only one of the numerous intercollegiate sports which it regulates.[162]

The NCAA could have responded to this argument in its reply brief, but it did not. Instead, the reply brief concentrated on the NCAA's claimed lack of market power[163] and on the differences between basketball and football that made the former unsuitable for economic restraints comparable to the Football Television Plan.[164]

But the NCAA is responsible for a far greater failure than just neglecting to use its reply brief to cite educational justifications for the Football Television Plan. The greater failure was its refusal to make educational justifications the centerpiece of its defense of the plan in its principal brief and during oral argument. The precedents showed that courts deferred to NCAA rules designed to maintain a system of college sports played by full-time students who are amateurs. Under these circumstances, it is surprising that the veteran lawyers who represented the NCAA in this litigation apparently failed to anticipate that courts would not defer to the NCAA when its arguments neglected to identify a legitimate educational justification for the economic restraints imposed by the Football Television Plan.

The NCAA left the task of articulating an educational justification for the plan to the National Federation of State High School Associations, which filed an amicus curiae (friend of the court) brief on the NCAA's behalf. The National Federation was not a party to *NCAA v. Regents,* but Supreme Court rules permit third parties to file amicus curiae briefs on behalf of one side or the other, so long as the parties to the case agree or the Court itself approves.[165] According to its brief, the National Federation's membership included "the state high school activities associations of the 50 states and the District of Columbia and their counterparts in the 10 Canadian provinces, the Philippines, Guam, Okinawa, and the Virgin Islands."[166] The brief noted that "the National Federation serves as the voice of the athletic interests of the nation's high schools and can be characterized as the 'NCAA' of high school sports."[167]

To be sure, the National Federation's support for the NCAA Football Television Plan turned in part on educational considerations. Its brief argued,

> Uncontrolled competition for revenues distorts the function of athletics in an educational program. Among the successful, such competition threatens to ele vate a portion of the educational program to an unhealthy predominance over all others. Among the unsuccessful, the threat is to their financial ability to continue a broad athletic program for students and to maintain the athletic aspect of the schools' curricula.[168]

"Domination by a few at the expense of all others," the brief continued, "destroys the system within which all operate and upon which all rely."[169] "From both perspectives," it claimed, "the conclusion that the NCAA television plan lacks any redeeming virtue and is plainly anticompetitive is unsupportable."[170]

But even the National Federation had an economic motivation for supporting the NCAA. Early on in its brief, the National Federation explained that the elimination of the Football Television Plan would "expose[] the high schools to the prospect of live intercollegiate [football] telecasts on Friday nights in direct competition with high school stadium attendance."[171] In the National Federation's view, live college football telecasts on Friday nights would amount to "collegiate encroachment upon high school football night."[172] That would cripple high schools' efforts to earn income necessary for funding student extracurricular activities, the National Federation maintained, because high school football, the principal source of this income, lacked a television audience, thereby making it dependent on stadium attendance for its revenue.[173] Under these circumstances, the National Federation wished to preserve the NCAA Football Television Plan, which provided that college football games telecast during the regular season would be played on Saturdays only, except for the Friday following Thanksgiving and at other times when "no appreciable damage [would] be done to a conflicting high school game by the telecast."[174] Thus, unlike the NCAA, the National Federation offered an educational rationale for preserving the Football Television Plan, but like the NCAA, it supported the plan principally for an economic reason. In the National Federation's case, that reason was to preserve the viability of Friday night high school football as a revenue source for high schools across the United States.[175]

Of course, Justice White also identified an educational justification for the plan, noting that absent restrictions on televised college basketball, television stations aired basketball games virtually every day of the week, at all times of the day. The NCAA could have seized on Justice White's comment to argue that the Football Television Plan prevented the proliferation of televised games in football that had occurred in basketball, where players routinely missed classes because of midweek travel, returned to campus in the wee hours of the morning, and struggled to get up a few hours later to attend morning classes. The NCAA could have argued that by precluding such consequences for college football players, the plan fostered the NCAA's stated purpose of ensuring college sports were compatible with higher education. That argument would have linked the Football Television Plan to judicially approved NCAA rules, such as the rule barring players who had previously been paid for playing their sports, on the ground that both rules promoted amateurism and properly subordinated sport to academics in higher education.

Instead, the NCAA cited no educational justifications for restricting telecasts of college football, choosing to concentrate on its claimed lack of market power and its desire to preserve gate receipts through encouraging live attendance and to ensure a competitive balance among teams. Moreover, unlike Justice White, who argued in his dissent that competitive balance assured top high school athletes that their college teams would appear on television, thereby freeing them to choose a college based on educational as well as athletic criteria,[176] the NCAA stressed that competitive balance ensured closer games and greater fan interest.[177] These arguments portrayed the NCAA as just another profit-hungry corporation in the entertainment marketplace, making it easy for the Supreme Court to focus on the anticompetitive aspects of the Football Television Plan, namely, a tendency to produce higher prices and less product availability, thereby restricting consumer preference. Under these circumstances, the Court disposed of the NCAA's arguments rather quickly.

It is impossible to know whether the Football Television Plan would have survived antitrust scrutiny if educational, rather than economic, concerns had been front and center in the NCAA's argument. Perhaps the Supreme Court majority would still have concluded that the plan was anticompetitive and violated the Sherman Act. However, if the NCAA had demonstrated a compelling educational justification for the plan, Justice White may have secured a majority for his view. The hybrid nature of college sports lent credence to both Justice Stevens's view and Justice White's view of the NCAA Football Television Plan. But as decided according to Stevens's view, *NCAA v. Regents* was followed by major negative implications for the welfare of college athletes and their institutions and by adverse economic consequences for less athletically prominent colleges and conferences, which could have been avoided had Justice White's view prevailed. Chapter 4 discusses these outcomes.

Chapter 4

THURSDAY NIGHT GAMES AND
MILLIONAIRE COACHES
The Implications of *NCAA v. Board of Regents*

The End of an Era

Reaction to the Supreme Court's decision was swift and dramatic. The NCAA and its Division I-A members met in Chicago shortly after the decision was announced, and in the words of a contemporary news report, "they frantically sought to avoid chaos and the dread consequences of T.V. over-saturation."[1] According to this report, "There seemed to be strong sentiment for some sort of voluntary T.V. package put together by the NCAA."[2] "In the meantime," this report observed, "pressure for some schools to make private deals [was] already formidable."[3]

The pressure to make private deals proved impossible to resist. The Big 10 and the Pacific-10 conferences recommended a less restrictive version of the old NCAA Football Television Plan, which would have allowed more television appearances by the most popular teams. It featured an "open window" concept that would have given individual conferences the freedom to assemble noncompeting regional television packages.[4] Specifically, this plan featured three "windows," or time periods, during which football games would be telecast. One window would have been set aside for network broadcasts. A second window would have accommodated syndicators, who purchased packages of games the networks chose not to telecast and distributed them to independent television stations. A third window, the Saturday evening time slot, would have belonged to syndicators and to cable television companies.[5] The network window (3:30 on Saturday afternoon) would have featured full competition, with the networks and the CFA or conferences freely negotiating the terms of television contracts, including price.[6] Once a particular network purchased the rights to a game, it would have the exclusive right to air the game; it would still have to compete with the other networks for sponsors and viewers, though.[7] Most colleges thought they could make more profitable arrangements on their own, so the proposal offered by the Big 10 and Pac-10 failed by a vote of 64–44.[8] The vote was significant because it meant that after 32 years the NCAA had lost control of televised college football.[9]

It also meant that individual colleges and conferences had to scramble to arrange for their games to be televised, because the 1984 college football season was scheduled to start in two months. Most colleges opted to have either the CFA or their respective conferences negotiate television deals with the networks. Individual colleges and conferences then negotiated separate contracts with television syndicators and with cable and local broadcasters for the rights to games the networks had not selected; those games could be telecast so long as they did not air at the same time as a game telecast on a network.[10] The new contracts were less lucrative than the Division I-A colleges had anticipated, as the increased supply of potential games for telecast caused the rights fees for telecasting them and hence the colleges' revenue projections to plummet.[11] Thus, the NCAA appeared to have the last laugh. "A lot of people felt that the open market would be a golden market," said John Swofford, who chaired the NCAA's football television committee in 1984. "I don't think that's going to be the case. I see more games being broadcast, but I see those games with fewer dollars."[12] Mr. Swofford's comment was prophetic, at least in the short run.

Short-term Losses, Long-term Gains

Liberation was sweet success for the powerhouses of college football, but it brought unforeseen consequences that soon turned the sweet taste of victory sour. In the first year of deregulation, as the supply of games increased and viewers' demand for them declined, college football's combined revenue from network television dropped by more than 60 percent.[13] The colleges had sought to control their own television destiny in order to put more games on the air and earn more money. Ironically, they succeeded so spectacularly in getting more games on the air that they made it impossible to earn more money.[14] Indeed, despite having three times as many games on television in 1984 as in 1983, colleges earned $25 million less in 1984 than they had earned in 1983.[15] In that same period, football revenue for the Big 8 (now Big 12) Conference fell from $6.1 million to $3.8 million, and football revenue for the Southeastern Conference dropped from $11.2 million to $7.5 million.[16] The University of Alabama's earnings declined from $1.924 million to $764,000, UCLA's take declined from $1.238 million to $735,000, and the revenue of the University of Oklahoma, which had carried the banner of free-market football all the way to the Supreme Court, sank from $1.276 million to $753,208.[17]

No school felt the impact of declining revenues brought on by the Supreme Court decision more than Boston College. In 1983, led by the inspiring play of its creative quarterback Doug Flutie, Boston College made four regular-season television appearances, from which it earned $1,585,000. Only Alabama, Texas, and UCLA earned more television revenue that year.[18] Until the Supreme Court handed down its decision, Boston College, with Flutie returning for his senior season, had every reason to believe that it would do just as well in 1984. But the Court's decision changed all that. An anticipated $800,000 payment from CBS to Boston College for its game on November 23, 1984, against the University of Miami (which Flutie won for the Eagles by throwing a last-second touchdown pass to wide receiver Gerard Phelan) became $400,000, and an expected $700,000 payout from ABC for a game against the University of Alabama became $250,000.[19] Overall, Boston College played on television about 50 percent more often in 1984 than in 1983 and earned about 50 percent less money for its efforts.[20]

The colleges' reduced football revenues in 1984 reflected a decline in the Nielsen ratings for college football, resulting from a glut of televised games that year. As the Nielsen ratings declined, so did advertising rates. In 1983 advertisers had paid the networks $813 million to reach more than 100 million viewers, and a 30-second advertisement during a CFA game on ABC cost $60,000.[21] A year later, the same ad on ABC cost only $27,500, and ads during games telecast by syndicators on independent stations cost even less.[22] Recalling these conditions sometime later, former NCAA executive director Dick Schultz remarked, "The drop in T.V. revenues had a tremendous impact on college sports across the board. It made the financial crisis even worse, and it didn't take long for everybody to wish we could turn the clock back to before 1984."[23]

Still, some teams and conferences that had not fared well under the NCAA Football Television Plan benefited from the tremendous increase in the number of televised college football games after *NCAA v. Board of Regents*. For example, the University of Kentucky's football team appeared on television nine times in the first two years after deregulation, which equaled its total number of appearances under the NCAA plan from 1952 through 1981.[24] Similarly, in the first year after deregulation, Atlantic Coast Conference teams played on television nearly as many times as they had during the entire decade of the 1970s. Gene Corrigan, who became the conference's commissioner in 1988, observed, "For the ACC, the lawsuit was the best thing that ever happened. We were so rarely on the NCAA package. We never would have had our syndication package without the lawsuit, so from that standpoint, it was a good thing."[25]

Exacerbating the financial crisis to which Schultz referred was the growing pressure on colleges to comply with the "equal educational opportunity" mandate of the Education Amendments Act of 1972, more commonly known as Title IX, by upgrading the athletic offerings and facilities for their female students.[26] University of Georgia president Fred Davison saw a direct link between increasing the profitability of college football and improving athletic opportunities for women on campus. He observed, "Title IX was beginning to put a pretty severe financial strain on our program and others like it. Football had to do it all, and football could only do so much unless we exploited it to a greater degree. I saw [free-market television] as a way for us to alleviate some of the financial strain on our programs, especially in regard to the funding of women's sports."[27]

But football could not even support itself, let alone bankroll women's sports, unless colleges found a way to make it more profitable. So the colleges worked hard to devise new ways of earning revenue through football. With entrepreneurial zeal born of financial necessity, they built luxury suites in their stadiums, solicited corporate sponsorships, and pursued more inventive forms of product licensing. Increasingly, athletic directors spoke the language of the corporate boardroom, as they discussed "branding," "corporate synergy," the need to find new "revenue streams," and the need to "reach consumers."[28]

The new entrepreneurial orientation in college football extended to the postseason bowl games, too. The Supreme Court decision had only applied to regular-season games, but beginning in 1984, the bowl games also experienced a decline in television rights fees. The glut of regular-season games gave advertisers many more chances than they had in the past to reach the college football audience, making the advertisers less eager to buy time during bowl games and causing rights fees for bowl games to drop precipitously.[29] The glut of regular-season games also caused the television ratings for bowl games to tumble by more than 20 percent in three years.[30] Bowl promoters responded by pursuing corporate sponsors; as a result, by 1989 more than half of the bowl games had signed up title sponsors, turning the

Sun Bowl into the John Hancock Sun Bowl and the Sugar Bowl into the USF&G Sugar Bowl.[31] The bowl games used their new corporate revenues to keep themselves viable by steadily increasing their "payouts" to participating teams. In 1989, for example, bowl games paid out a total of $56 million, which represented a 30 percent increase in five years.[32]

Gradually, conferences and colleges also began to profit from free-market football. In 1991 members of the CFA earned about $42 million from their contract with ABC, finally exceeding, after eight years, the highest total earned under the NCAA plan.[33] In search of more television sets and hence more profits, conferences began to exploit an NCAA rule allowing conferences with at least 12 football-playing members to hold a championship game between the winners of the two divisions within the conference.[34] Toward the same end, colleges caught what Keith Dunnavant has described as "realignment fever" in the summer and fall of 1990.[35] According to Dunnavant, "Colleges started plotting and scheming with each other and against each other, determined to enhance their strength with regard to television, scheduling, marketing, and competitive balance."[36] "It was like a high-stakes game of musical chairs," he observed, "[a]nd no one wanted to be left without a seat when the music stopped."[37] By the time the music stopped, more than 40 colleges had changed their conference affiliations, in a realignment that was unprecedented in the history of college sports.[38]

Former independents Penn State and the University of Miami joined the Big 10 and the Big East, respectively.[39] Florida State joined the ACC for football in 1990 and for all sports in 1992, instantly turning that basketball-rich conference into a prominent football conference, too.[40] South Carolina joined the Southeastern Conference in 1990, giving the league 12 teams, which enabled it to create two divisions and to hold a championship game at the end of the regular season between the two divisional winners.[41] By the late 1990s, the SEC was earning more money from its championship game alone than it had earned from a season of televised games in the years immediately following the Supreme Court's decision in *NCAA v. Regents.*[42]

In 1994 the Southwest Conference (SWC) disbanded, and four of its members—Texas, Texas A&M, Baylor, and Texas Tech—joined the former members of the Big 8 to form the Big 12 Conference.[43] The Big 12 was arguably the clearest winner among the revamped conferences. As the Big 8, it had lacked for television exposure because its members were located in small media markets between Missouri and Colorado, but when the Texas colleges joined, the Big 12 signed a lucrative contract to televise its football games.[44] Several years later, it joined the other five major football conferences (Big East, ACC, Southeastern, Big 10, and Pac-10) in signing a seven-year contract worth $700 million for ABC to televise the Bowl Championship Series.[45] Meanwhile, the defection of Texas, Texas A&M, Baylor, and Texas Tech from the SWC forced the less prestigious former members of that conference (Texas Christian University, Southern Methodist University, Rice University, and the University of Houston) to join second-tier conferences (the Western Athletic Conference and Conference USA) whose members had limited access to television.[46]

Conference realignments continued in the new millennium. In 2004 the University of Miami and Virginia Tech left the Big East and joined the ACC. Boston College followed in 2005, bringing the ACC's membership to 12 teams, which qualified it to hold a lucrative championship game between its divisional winners.[47] After the ACC expanded, it signed a seven-year contract for $258 million with ESPN and ABC that doubled the number of ACC football games aired each season and nearly doubled the amount the conference had earned from its previous television contract.[48] Not everybody profited from conference realignments, though. For example, Conference USA lost nine teams to other conferences in 2004. Three of those teams, the University of Cincinnati, the University of Louisville, and TCU, had made a total of 13 appearances in postseason bowl games between 1999 and 2004, whereas just one of the six replacement teams Conference USA added in 2005 (Marshall University) had earned bowl bids consistently in recent years.[49] Acknowledging the growing gap between rich teams and poor teams in Division I-A, Conference USA commissioner Britton Banowsky told a reporter before the 2005 college football season, "We are not projecting a lot of postseason football revenues."[50] It was safer to predict a lot of new road trips and rivalries, as 18 of the 119 Division I-A institutions competed in a new conference during the 2005 college football season.[51]

Along with defections from former conferences came defections from the CFA and from its television contract, too. The first defector from the CFA contract was Notre Dame, the only institution whose football team consistently enjoys a nationwide television audience. In 1991 the CFA signed contracts with ABC and ESPN to televise college football.[52] ABC also won a separate contract to televise Big 10 and Pac-10 games, as those two conferences did not belong to the CFA. The dual contracts created a delicious dilemma for ABC, namely, how to broadcast all the games it had agreed to air. The solution was to air mostly regional games, which angered Notre

Dame, whose national following caused it to favor national telecasts of its games.[53] Consequently, Notre Dame left the CFA in 1991 and signed its own four-year contract for $38 million with NBC, thereby more than doubling its annual revenue from football telecasts.[54]

In 1995 the SEC followed suit, striking out on its own and signing a five-year contract for $85 million with CBS, which was desperate for football because, earlier that year, it had lost to the Fox Network its long-time contract to televise pro football.[55] CBS's eagerness to embrace the SEC was reflected in the generosity of the new contract, which paid more than double the average amount per team that the CFA-ABC contract had paid. The CBS contract also guaranteed the SEC six national telecasts, which thrilled the conference's coaches and athletic directors, who believed that such national exposure would help them to recruit top athletes and to market SEC football.[56]

The SEC's defection from the CFA resulted from Penn State's departure in 1990 to join the Big 10 Conference, which did not belong to the CFA, and from Notre Dame's departure a year later. After Penn State and Notre Dame left and after the SEC added the University of Arkansas and the University of South Carolina to its membership in 1991, thereby expanding its annual inventory of televised games from 35 to 48, the SEC concluded that it was the "cash cow" for the CFA and soon opted to graze in the greener pastures offered by CBS.[57] The SEC's departure proved fatal to the CFA; without Notre Dame and the SEC, the CFA lacked sufficient appeal to attract another network television contract. The CFA disbanded in 1996, a casualty of its own success, as its members with the greatest television appeal jumped ship in search of an even larger bounty than the CFA could provide.[58] After returning temporarily to its role as an advocacy group within the NCAA, the CFA closed its books permanently on June 30, 1997, and distributed its net worth to its member institutions.[59]

As the demise of the CFA suggests, the free-market football that followed the Supreme Court's decision in *NCAA v. Regents* did not benefit everybody; like any free-market economy, the free-market college football economy produced rather pronounced winners and losers. The greatest beneficiaries, as reflected in the conference realignments after 1990, were the largest, most prominent conferences (ACC, SEC, Big 10, Big 12, and Pac-10) and their coaches, who are likely to reap ever larger shares of the revenue to be earned from college football and basketball and to attract the best players, while the less prominent Division I-A conferences weaken for lack of television exposure.

Coaches of prominent teams have profited handsomely from free-market football. For example, after he led Louisiana State University (LSU) to the national championship of college football in 2003, Nick Saban signed a contract guaranteeing him a record $2.3 million annually.[60] Late in 2006, Saban, who had moved from LSU to the NFL's Miami Dolphins soon after winning the NCAA championship, returned to the college ranks, signing an eight-year contract for $32 million to coach the University of Alabama's football team.[61] During the 2003–4 season, Bob Stoops, the University of Oklahoma's head football coach, earned more than $2.2 million dollars to lead the Sooners.[62] On average, head football coaches at Division I-A colleges earned an annual base salary of $388,000 in 2003, an increase of more than 50 percent in real terms over the comparable figure in 1998.[63] Reaching for this pot of gold, coaches and teams from less prestigious conferences travel far and wide, often missing two days of classes and being overmatched on the field against a powerful opponent, just to play a weeknight game on ESPN.

The windfall that some coaches, colleges, and conferences have enjoyed from free-market football is a result of the almost simultaneous occurrence of the Supreme Court's decision in *NCAA v. Regents* and the explosive growth of cable television in the United States. Together, the Court decision and cable television triggered an "arms race" among colleges in recruiting, facilities construction, and coaching salaries, in addition to spawning the conference realignments noted earlier.[64] These events prompted sports economist Andrew Zimbalist to observe that *NCAA v. Regents* "opened the floodgates of commercialism much wider than before."[65] Most of the flood flows into coaches' salaries and athletic facilities, because the colleges do not have to pay—indeed, are prohibited from paying—their athletes.[66]

When the gates opened, cable television was ready to take advantage of the economic opportunity their opening represented, because the number of cable subscribers was rising rapidly when the Court announced its decision. In 1980 the United States had 15.5 million cable subscribers, who represented 19.9 percent of households with television sets; by 1983, those numbers had risen to 25 million and 34 percent, respectively.[67] By 1990 there were 52 million cable subscribers in the United States, representing 56.4 percent of homes with a television set.[68] The increase in homes equipped with cable television brought a commensurate increase in televised sports generally and in televised college football particularly.[69] With the latter increase came windfall profits for some coaches, institutions, and conferences, a growing disparity between rich and poor members of Division I-A, and an endless quest by both groups to attract more television sets so as to earn a larger share of the bounty from free-market football.

A Prophesy Fulfilled

As the preceding section shows, free-market football after *NCAA v. Regents* did its best to fulfill Justice White's prophesy about the likely consequences of the majority's decision in that case. According to Justice White, "Permitting a small number of colleges, even popular ones, to have unlimited television appearances, would inevitably give them an insuperable advantage over all others and in the end defeat any efforts to maintain a system of athletic competition among amateurs who measure up to college scholastic requirements."[70] Both the inequity and the professionalism Justice White predicted have come to pass. So have the adverse academic consequences he predicted, as evidenced by the NCAA's recent efforts to combat low graduation rates among college athletes, especially football players and men's basketball players.

In the fall of 2003, the NCAA began requiring athletes to complete 40 percent of their coursework toward a degree by the end of their second year of college, 60 percent by the end of their third year, and 80 percent by the end of their fourth year.[71] But even this new standard acknowledged that the time demands of big-time college sports are so great that an athlete is unlikely to complete an undergraduate degree in the customary four-year time period. In 2005 the NCAA instituted the Academic Progress Rate, which, for the first time, authorizes the Association to penalize institutions whose athletes fail to graduate at acceptable rates. The APR is complicated, but the gist of it is that at the conclusion of a particular term, an athlete earns one point by remaining enrolled and a second point by satisfying the NCAA academic standards previously noted. Each team at each NCAA member institution earns an APR that is equal to the number of points earned by its athletes divided by the total number of points they could have earned during an academic year.[72] An APR of 925 means a team's athletes earned 92.5 percent of all possible points, putting the team on a path toward seeing 50 percent of its athletes graduate within six years of their enrollment.[73]

Teams with APRs below 925 risk losing scholarships. Teams lose scholarships by failing to earn the requisite APR 2 years in 4, and they will be banned from postseason play if they fail to do so for 3 years in 10. In other words, after failing to earn an APR of 925 once, a team must earn at least that score for 3 consecutive years to avoid punishment.[74] In 2007 the NCAA penalized 112 teams for failing to satisfy the APR and announced that 81 of them would lose scholarships in 2007–8.[75] Of the 112, 49 (including 18 of those losing scholarships) received warning letters for their repeated failure to earn a satisfactory grade. If athletes on those 49 teams failed to improve their academic records in 2007–8, their teams would face restrictions on postseason play and on the numbers of games and practices they could schedule.[76] Not surprisingly, 75 of the 112 penalized teams were football, baseball, and men's basketball teams; football and men's basketball teams face considerable pressure to win and be profitable, and baseball teams make numerous road trips during a relatively short season.[77]

Unfortunately, the NCAA has increased its academic expectations of college athletes without reducing their coaches' athletic expectations of them or the coaches' demands on their time. Under these circumstances, it is fair to ask whether coaches and athletic directors will subvert the APR by steering athletes into courses and majors that will enable them to earn passing grades and remain eligible for athletic competition but not to obtain a worthwhile degree. Even an insider like veteran Penn State football coach Joe Paterno has doubts about the utility of the APR. In March 2005, he told the *Philadelphia Inquirer,* "I'm not naive. If you tell Whatsammata U they've got to graduate 50 percent of their kids in order to go to a bowl game, then 50 percent of the kids are going to graduate from Whatsammata U."[78]

The jury is still out on whether the APR will trigger more soft majors than hard studying, but some of the evidence makes one suspicious. Even before the APR took effect, athletes tended to cluster in certain majors at many colleges in Division I. For example, in November 2003 the *Chronicle of Higher Education* reported that nearly 25 percent of the football players at Texas A&M were majoring in either agricultural development or agricultural and life sciences, as compared to only 3 percent of the overall student body.[79] At Georgia Tech, 56 percent of football players were majoring in management.[80] While almost one-third of the football players at the University of Southern Mississippi were majoring in coaching and sport administration, 23 percent of their counterparts at the University of Louisville majored in justice administration, and 22 percent of their counterparts at the University of Central Florida majored in liberal studies.[81]

These suspicions grow after considering the survey results the NCAA disclosed at its annual convention in January 2007, which revealed that one in five college athletes claimed that participating in sports has prevented them from choosing the major they preferred. The survey, which involved more than 20,000 athletes at 627 colleges, representing all three NCAA divisions, found that time demands on many athletes have increased in the past 20 years and that athletes often spent as many hours on their sport during the off-season as they spent during the competitive season.[82] Those time demands are imposed not only by coaches but also by the increased role of the mass media in covering and marketing college sports, especially football, in the current, free-market environment. Consider, for example, the comments of Dave Brown, ESPN's director of programming and acquisitions, which reflect no sensitivity whatsoever to the academic implications of Thursday night college football games: "We see the Thursday-night package as a mini Monday Night Football. It's a great showcase that everyone involved with the game is watching, and it's like the unofficial start of the football weekend."[83]

Unfortunately, this "show business" view of college sports has expanded well beyond coverage of the games to a greater focus on off-season events such as National Signing Day, held every February, when top football-playing high school seniors announce their college plans. Media outlets now give this event the same sort of publicity and scrutiny they have long given to the NFL and NBA drafts of college players into the pro ranks.[84] Self-appointed talent scouts have established recruiting Web sites that showcase athletes in their early teens and younger, ranking them based on how much weight they can bench-press and how fast they can run the 40-yard dash. University of Maryland football player Andrew Crummey is painfully familiar with the high-tech talent scouts. "These sites," he told the Knight Commission on Intercollegiate Athletics in February 2007, "they all want the numbers—what's your bench [press], your squat. You end up thinking that those numbers are all that matter."[85]

In this atmosphere, it is not surprising that the NCAA has recently had to investigate and pass legislation to combat bogus "preparatory schools" established to help academically deficient high school athletes obtain the grades necessary to qualify for an athletic scholarship. Since 1986 the NCAA has required college freshmen to achieve a minimum grade point average in high school and a minimum standardized test score to compete in sports. The test score requirement angered officials at historically black colleges because a disproportionately high percentage of the athletes whom it disqualified were African Americans. To quell the controversy, the NCAA adopted a sliding scale of grades and test scores to determine freshman eligibility. A freshman with a GPA of only 2.0 but an SAT score of 1010 could compete, as could a classmate with a GPA of 2.5 or above and only 820 on the SAT. In 2003 the NCAA modified the scale, permitting a freshman with an SAT score of 400 (meaning no correct answers) to compete if he or she had a high school GPA of at least 3.55 in 14 core courses.

This rule change spawned bogus private "high schools," often little more than storefronts, that enabled high school athletes to boost their grades by reading brief passages from a workbook and then taking untimed "tests" based on those passages. Newspaper reports about these "schools" in 2006 prompted the NCAA to investigate, and the investigation revealed that some athletes were dropping out of high school when their sports seasons ended and enrolling in the bogus prep schools instead in order to complete their college course requirements.[86] The NCAA responded by passing a rule in the spring of 2007 allowing incoming freshmen to count only one course taken after graduation from high school toward the academic requirements necessary to play college sports.[87]

But just as there never seems to be enough money in college sports to satisfy the colleges' lust for it, there never seem to be enough or strong enough rules to deter the cheaters, either. This is because the professionalization of college sports, to which *NCAA v. Regents* gave a big assist, has raised the stakes of winning and losing to an all-time high. Charli Turner Thorne, the women's basketball coach at Arizona State University, made this point beautifully when she told the *Chronicle of Higher Education* why big-time college coaching is difficult to balance with a family life. "It's not O.K. not to win," she said. "Too much money is being spent."[88]

No better example exists of the professionalization and of the inequity that Justice White predicted would occur in college sports as a result of *NCAA v. Regents* than the Bowl Championship Series, which controls the postseason in college football. The BCS is a compromise arranged by the television networks and the operators of the traditional bowl games. It "aims to crown a credible 'national champion' without instituting a playoff system that would render the bowl games irrelevant, causing them to fold, and would likely extend the college football season well into January."[89] Thus, both bowl executives and college presidents regard the BCS as "an acceptable, albeit imperfect, alternative to a playoff system."[90] It is surely imperfect; indeed, the BCS is the realization of Justice White's worst fears about free-market football. A creation not of the NCAA but of television and the marketplace, it responds to consumer demand irrespective of concerns about equity or professionalism in college sports.

The greatest imperfection in the BCS is the inequity it produces regarding the opportunities for Division I-A teams to participate in the most prestigious and lucrative bowl games. Formed in 1996 from a predecessor known as the Bowl Alliance, the BCS consists of the six major college sports conferences, including the ACC, Big 10, Big 12, Big East, Pac-10, and SEC, along with the University of Notre Dame, which does not belong to any conference in football.[91] These institutions and conferences command the most fan and media interest in college football, and they use their clout to guarantee BCS members six of the eight spots in the four most lucrative bowl games every year (the Rose Bowl, FedEx Orange Bowl, Nokia Sugar Bowl, and Tostitos Fiesta Bowl).[92] Unlike most bowl games, then, which have agreements with specific conferences and feature the winners of the same conferences every year, the BCS bowls feature the champions of the six major conferences, who are assigned to a particular game based on where they finished in the national rankings at the end of the regular season.[93]

The BCS and the NCAA are legally independent of each other. The NCAA participates in the BCS to the extent of monitoring compliance with NCAA playing rules and certifying the bowl games. The BCS participants are NCAA members, but each bowl game is a private entity independent of the NCAA. The NCAA cooperates with the BCS, but neither one has legal authority over the other.[94] In other words, college football's postseason is an amalgam of teams, bowl games, and the BCS, all of which are legally independent of each other, but which cooperate in temporary relationships under the operating bylaws of the NCAA.[95] The formula by which the participating teams in the BCS bowls are chosen has five major components, namely, polls of the coaches and sportswriters, computer rankings, strength of schedule, win-loss record, and wins against any of the top 10 teams in the BCS standings.[96] Originally, four BCS bowls existed, but after the 2003 college football season, when the NCAA and the BCS crowned co-national champions, the BCS added a fifth bowl game, to appease non-BCS colleges, and modified its selection process to emphasize human polls and de-emphasize the computer rankings of college teams.[97]

Two additional slots in BCS bowl games did not satisfy the critics of the BCS. They argue that non-BCS colleges are unlikely to appear in BCS bowls, because 6 of the now 10 slots in those games are reserved for colleges belonging to one of the six conferences affiliated with the BCS. Notre Dame's entitlement to one of the remaining slots when it finishes the season ranked in the top 10 reduces access even more.[98] Financial data support the critics' argument. Between 1998 and 2003, the 63 BCS colleges shared approximately $500 million in proceeds from bowl games, whereas the non-BCS colleges shared approximately $17 million during the same period.[99]

But proponents of the BCS contend that without it, the best college football teams would revert to playing in the bowls with which they traditionally have had a contractual relationship, which means they would not necessarily compete against each other, thereby denying the fans a national championship game and a true national champion.[100] BCS proponents add that the BCS produces a true national champion while preserving the traditions and the financial viability of the postseason bowl games.[101] Finally, adopting a less diplomatic stance, BCS proponents argue that non-BCS teams are inferior on the field to BCS teams, so their exclusion from the most prestigious bowl games produces better-quality contests that fans are more likely to attend or watch on television.[102]

Even if the latter point is generally true, it is not always true. Indeed, the strongest argument against the BCS flows from its unfortunate history of excluding non-BCS teams from its bowl games even when they have enjoyed highly successful seasons. For example, in 1998 Tulane University won all 12 of its regular-season games, making it just one of two teams in Division I-A that went undefeated. Moreover, the Green Wave scored between 42 and 72 points in 8 games and won 10 games by double-digit margins. Nevertheless, it did not qualify for a BCS bowl and was relegated instead to the non-BCS Liberty Bowl, which it won by a large margin, while eight BCS teams played in the four prestigious BCS bowls.[103] In 1999 Marshall University won all 13 of its games, making it one of two undefeated teams in Division I-A. It even won a road game at Clemson University, a significant accomplishment. Yet it could only qualify for the Motor City Bowl, while eight BCS teams played in the four BCS bowl games.[104]

In 2001 Brigham Young University won its first 12 games, making it one of two undefeated teams in Division I-A as the college football season entered its final week. But several days before BYU's final game, BCS officials informed coach Gary Crowton that they had eliminated the Cougars from consideration for a BCS bowl game. Oddly, the quality of BYU's team had nothing to do with that decision; Paul Holahan, the executive director of the BCS Sugar Bowl acknowledged that "marketing issues" had influenced the choice to exclude BYU.[105] In other words, BYU fans' reputation for not spending money like drunken sailors in bowl game cities contributed to keeping their team out of a BCS bowl. Instead, the Cougars went to the Liberty Bowl, where they shared total proceeds of $1.3 million, having missed a chance to split approximately 10 times that much for playing in a BCS bowl.[106]

The inequities of the BCS have spawned the charge from some of its critics that it violates antitrust law. The gist of this argument is that the BCS "restrains the trade of college football by limiting competition for births in the prestigious and profitable BCS bowl games."[107] According to this view, the BCS agreement gives its members access to its games, while excluding nonmembers. In excluding the nonmembers, this argument goes, the agreement refuses to deal with them and denies them access to the upper echelons of college football, thereby diminishing their stature and reducing their opportunities to compete, succeed, and profit. The inevitable result, say critics of the BCS, is that the gap between the rich and the poor in college football grows steadily larger.[108] In the critics' view, the two-tier system created by the BCS is self-perpetuating because the profits earned from participating in BCS bowls give the top-tier colleges the resources necessary to continually upgrade their facilities and the prestige required to recruit top high school players year after year.[109]

Despite its obvious inequities, the BCS would likely survive antitrust scrutiny, because courts would probably conclude that it enhances, rather than limits, economic competition in college football. For example, unlike the NCAA Football Television Plan, which limited the number of college football games that could be televised, the BCS does not limit the number of bowl games played during the postseason. Indeed, the number of bowl games has increased since the advent of the BCS, hence a court hearing an antitrust challenge to the BCS would likely conclude that it satisfies the antitrust laws by enhancing economic competition.[110]

To be sure, alternatives to the BCS exist. One alternative would be "to place the top two teams, from an agreed-upon formula, in a national championship game."[111] Under this arrangement, "[t]he remaining teams and bowls would exist in a form similar to their existences prior to the . . . BCS, with open-market bargaining among conferences, bowls and television networks."[112] A second alternative would be a playoff system, whereby "each Division I-A team would be equally eligible to qualify for the playoffs by merit."[113] For example, the top eight teams could qualify for the playoffs, with the first round being played in four different bowl games. The first-round winners would meet in two second-round bowl games, and the two semifinal winners would meet in the championship bowl game. The existing bowl games that were not part of the playoff system would remain in place.[114]

Notwithstanding the alternatives, the BCS is likely to remain in effect for the foreseeable future. Its 63 members lack an impetus to change it, because they earn more than 90 percent of the revenue from the BCS bowl games.[115] As noted, a successful antitrust challenge appears unlikely. A court faced with an antitrust challenge to the BCS would presumably evaluate the antitrust implications of the BCS only, instead of comparing it to a hypothetical alternative, such as a playoff. This means that while the court would examine the BCS to make sure its anticompetitive effects did not outweigh its procompetitive effects, the court would not try to determine whether an alternative mechanism would be more procompetitive or less anticompetitive than the BCS. Under these circumstances, because the BCS gives consumers a product not otherwise possible—a true national championship game every year—a court would probably find the BCS to be compatible with the antitrust laws.[116]

But the BCS's presumed compatibility with the antitrust laws merely means that it responds to consumer demands. That responsiveness is why the BCS confirms Justice White's worst fears about free-market football. The BCS responds to consumer demands irrespective of concerns about equity or professionalism in college sports. It symbolizes the triumph of commercialism and professionalism over educational values and amateurism in college sports, a triumph the Supreme Court's decision in *NCAA v. Regents* made possible.

A Schizophrenic Industry

Under these circumstances, it is no wonder that scholar of sports law Gary Roberts has characterized college sports as a "schizophrenic industry driven by inherently conflicting values"[117] and has observed that "[p]reserving some modicum of educational integrity in the academy is simply not reconcilable with maximizing consumer welfare in the sports entertainment marketplace."[118] To be sure, the college sports industry showed signs of schizophrenia long before *NCAA v. Regents*. A study titled *American College Athletics* and published in 1929 by the Carnegie Foundation for the Advancement of Teaching concluded that professionalism was rampant in college football. In the late 1920s, before the advent of athletic scholarships, professionalism typically took the form of "subsidies," which the "Carnegie Report" defined as "any assistance, favor, gift, award, scholarship, or concession, direct or indirect, which advantages an athlete because of his athletic ability or reputation, and which sets him apart from his fellows in the undergraduate [student] body."[119] But *NCAA v. Regents* exacerbated the schizophrenia in college sports considerably.

One symptom of this malady is rampant commercialism. For example, in 1996, Alltel, a technology and telecommunications company, bought the naming rights to a stadium that hosts the annual game between the University of Florida and University of Georgia football teams along with the NFL's Jacksonville Jaguars. Alltel also agreed to sponsor all of the sports teams at the University of Florida and to provide cellular phone service to the university's coaches in order to associate itself with the Gators' highly successful athletic programs. Apparently, this marriage of convenience has been a dream come true for Alltel; a company spokesperson has said, "Nobody knew our name [before the company's involvement in college sports] and now everybody knows the name Alltel."[120] Similarly, Mark Kidd, the former president and CEO of Host Communications, which has long participated in televising college basketball, has said, "The reality is that corporations and athletics are intertwined. The right partners can help you advance your message and what you're trying to accomplish."[121] The link between commerce and college sport became noticeably stronger in the years after *NCAA v. Regents*.

As that link has grown and as the NCAA has become increasingly wealthy, it has argued more frequently and insistently that its product is amateur sport. Insisting that college athletes are amateurs, the NCAA maintains that paying them for their athletic services would destroy the uniqueness of college sports, equating them with less popular athletic ventures, such as minor-league baseball or arena football.[122] In other words, notes Professor Stanton Wheeler, "the only way to make the billions of dollars now generated by varsity athletic programs is to protect the athletes from receiving any of it."[123] He adds,

> By extending normal seasons into preseasons and postseasons, by converting playoffs into media events, by collaborating with the NBA and NFL to feature star athletes as they make their move to the pros while the great bulk of varsity football and basketball players must find their careers elsewhere, the NCAA and its Division I-A presidents put themselves in a difficult moral position from which to trumpet the virtues of amateurism.[124]

But perhaps the clearest evidence of the schizophrenic nature of the college sports industry is the spate of lawsuits since *NCAA v. Regents* that have challenged various NCAA rules on antitrust grounds. These lawsuits reflect the increasingly commercial nature of college sports, and they illustrate the wisdom of Gary Roberts's comment that "[t]he more you commercialize what you do, the more you make judges think that antitrust laws apply to you."[125] Four lawsuits in particular illustrate this phenomenon; they are *Gaines v. NCAA, Banks v. NCAA, Law v. NCAA,* and *Worldwide Basketball and Sport Tours, Inc. et al. v. NCAA.*[126]

In *Gaines* the plaintiff challenged NCAA rules that had rendered him ineligible to play football for Vanderbilt University during the 1990 season and sought a preliminary injunction to bar the NCAA from enforcing the challenged rules against him. Bradford Gaines had played football at Vanderbilt on athletic scholarship from 1986 through 1989. After his junior season (1989), he had declared himself eligible for the NFL draft to be held on April 22 and 23, 1990.[127] If drafted, Gaines planned to forgo his senior football season at Vanderbilt. Unfortunately for him, though, no NFL team drafted him, so he sought to play football at Vanderbilt in the fall of 1990.[128] Therein lay the source of his lawsuit.

By pursuing the NFL draft, Gaines had run afoul of three NCAA rules, thereby losing his eligibility to play college football. Article 12.2.4.2, the NCAA's "no-draft rule," rendered Gaines ineligible to play college football once he placed his name on the list of players seeking to be drafted, even though no team drafted him. Article 12.1.1(f) stripped him of his amateur status for the same reason, and Article 12.3.1 (the "no-agent rule") rendered him ineligible for allowing an agent to contact professional teams on his behalf, though no money had changed hands and though Gaines had not signed a professional sports contract.[129] In Gaines's view, these rules, by preventing a college football player from returning to the college game after an unsuccessful foray into the pro draft, were "an unlawful exercise of monopoly power in violation of [the Sherman Antitrust Act]."[130]

The federal district court in Tennessee hearing Gaines's case observed that because he was requesting "mandatory relief which would change the status quo" (i.e., restore his eligibility and permit him to play in 1990), he had to bear an especially heavy burden in convincing the court that an injunction was appropriate.[131] The court was openly skeptical of Gaines's claim, because, in its view, "[t]he overriding purpose of the eligibility rules, . . . is not to provide the NCAA with commercial advantage, but rather the opposite extreme—to prevent commercializing influences from destroying the unique 'product' of NCAA college football."[132] "Even in the increasingly commercial modern world," it added, "this Court believes there is still validity to the Athenian concept of a complete education derived from fostering full growth of both mind and body."[133] In the court's view, the purpose of the rules Gaines challenged was to "preserve the unique atmosphere of competition between 'student-athletes.' "[134] As a result, the court rejected the notion that those rules violated antitrust law, and it denied Gaines's request for a preliminary injunction, saying that the NCAA's eligibility rules "are not subject to scrutiny under § 2 of the Sherman Act."[135]

But, the court reasoned, even if the antitrust laws applied to NCAA eligibility rules, the Association would still prevail, because "[t]his Court is convinced that the NCAA Rules benefit both players and the public by regulating college football so as to preserve its amateur appeal."[136] "Moreover," the court added, "this regulation by the NCAA in fact makes a better 'product' available by maintaining the educational underpinnings of college football and preserving the stability and integrity of college football programs."[137] In other words, instead of being anticompetitive, the no-draft and no-agent rules, in the court's estimation, "ha[d] primarily procompetitive effects in that they promote[d] the integrity and quality of college football and preserve[d] the distinct 'product' of major college football as an amateur sport."[138]

Thus, the court concluded that even if it granted Gaines a preliminary injunction and his case proceeded to trial, he had failed to show a substantial likelihood of obtaining a permanent injunction that would have enabled him to play for Vanderbilt in 1990.[139] Therefore, the court did not pause long to consider the other three criteria for winning a preliminary injunction (i.e., immediate and irreparable injury to Gaines, hardship to the NCAA and Vanderbilt if the injunction were granted, and the public interest in free and open competition in the marketplace).[140] Noting that the public interest in "preserving amateurism and protecting the educational objectives of intercollegiate athletics" outweighed the public interest in a free and open marketplace, the court denied Gaines's request for a preliminary injunction.[141]

Two years after *Gaines*, *Banks v. NCAA* also featured an antitrust challenge to the NCAA's no-draft and no-agent rules.[142] Braxton Banks had one year of college eligibility remaining at Notre Dame when he entered the NFL draft; like Bradford Gaines before him, Banks was not drafted, and no pro team signed him to a free-agent contract either.[143] He then tried to rejoin the Fighting Irish football team, but the NCAA's no-draft and no-agent rules blocked his path.[144] A federal district court in Indiana dismissed Banks's claim because he had failed to allege that those rules stifled economic competition in any identifiable market.[145] Banks then appealed to the United States Court of Appeals for the Seventh Circuit, which reached the same conclusion as the district court.

Like the *Gaines* court, the Seventh Circuit rejected the notion that the NCAA's eligibility rules were subject to the antitrust laws. According to the majority opinion in *Banks,* "none of the NCAA rules affecting college football eligibility restrain trade in the market for college players because the NCAA does not exist as a minor league training ground for future NFL players but rather to provide an opportunity for competition among amateur students pursuing a collegiate education."[146] Reinforcing this point, the majority articulated the traditional view of college sports as extracurricular activities for students whose primary goal was to obtain an undergraduate education. "We consider college football players as student-athletes simultaneously pursuing academic degrees that will prepare them to enter the employment market in non-athletic occupations," the majority opinion observed, "and hold that the regulations of the NCAA are designed to preserve the honesty and integrity of intercollegiate athletics and foster fair competition among the participating amateur college students."[147] Thus, the Seventh Circuit affirmed the district court's dismissal of Banks's case, concluding that "Banks's failure to allege an anti-competitive impact on a discernible market justified the district court's dismissal for failure to state a claim upon which relief can be granted."[148]

But the most interesting aspect of the Seventh Circuit's decision in *Banks* was the contrast between the majority opinion and the partial dissent written by Judge Joel M. Flaum, concerning their respective portrayals of big-time college sports. According to Judge Flaum, Braxton Banks's complaint "define[d] a market and describe[d] how the NCAA rules harm[ed] competition in that market."[149] Unlike the majority, Judge Flaum was receptive to Banks's claim that the no-draft and no-agent rules served a commercial purpose and hence should be subject to the antitrust laws. He wrote that the no-draft rule "permit[ted] colleges to squeeze out of their players one or two more years of service, years the colleges might have lost had the ability to enter the draft without consequence to eligibility been the subject of bargaining between athletes and colleges."[150] Therefore, it was "anticompetitive because it constitute[d] an agreement among colleges to eliminate an element of competition in the college football labor market."[151]

Under these circumstances, Judge Flaum reasoned, Banks had "properly alleged an anticompetitive effect in a relevant market and ha[d] demonstrated antitrust injury," so the district court erred in dismissing his lawsuit.[152] He acknowledged, however, that "[t]o ultimately prevail, Banks [would have to] demonstrate, under the rule of reason, that the no-agent and no-draft rules . . . [we]re not justifiable means of fostering competition among amateur athletic teams and therefore procompetitive on the whole."[153] He also conceded that even if Banks had a full opportunity to challenge the no-draft and no-agent rules at trial, he might still lose based on the court's determination that those rules "are essential to the survival of college football as a distinct and viable product."[154] Judge Flaum's view did not command a majority, though, so Banks would not have that opportunity.

Still, the point of Judge Flaum's dissent was that college sports *were* a product, which the NCAA preserved and enhanced with eligibility rules grounded at least as much in commerce as in education. "The NCAA would have us believe," he wrote, "that intercollegiate athletic contests are about spirit, competition, camaraderie, sportsmanship, hard work (which they certainly are) . . . and nothing else. Players play for the fun of it, colleges get a kick out of entertaining the student body and alumni, but the relationship between players and colleges is positively noncommercial."[155] That was a misleading picture, he added, noting that because of the no-draft and no-agent rules, "[t]he pros get a free farm system that supplies them with well-trained, much-publicized employees," and "[t]he colleges get to keep their players the equivalent of barefoot and pregnant."[156]

Despite NCAA victories in both cases, the *Gaines* and *Banks* decisions reflect the tug-of-war between commerce and higher education that has characterized big-time college sports in the years since *NCAA v. Regents.* The decisions by counsel for both plaintiffs to challenge the no-draft and no-agent rules on antitrust grounds would have been unthinkable in an earlier day, but they seem eminently reasonable in the post-*Regents* era of enormous athletic budgets, corporate sponsorships of bowl games, and an NCAA grown wealthy from selling the rights to televise its annual men's basketball tournament.[157] Moreover, the *Gaines* court recognized the close ties between commerce and higher education, acknowledging that "the NCAA, with its multimillion dollar annual budget, is engaged in a business venture and is not entitled to a *total* exemption from antitrust regulation."[158] Accordingly, it reasoned that "by holding that the eligibility Rules challenged by Gaines are not subject to antitrust analysis, this Court is by no means creating a total exemption, but rather a very narrow one," namely, for NCAA rules lacking a primarily commercial aim.[159]

The *Banks* court endorsed and adopted this narrow exception from antitrust scrutiny for noncommercial NCAA rules, thereby implicitly acknowledging the hybrid nature of both big-time college sports and NCAA rules. But even this exception proved controversial in *Banks*, as Judge Flaum argued that the no-draft and no-agent rules, which are mostly about eligibility, are "commercial" and can be challenged on antitrust grounds for restricting the free flow of athletes from college to pro teams, thereby enabling college teams to retain their revenue-producing volunteer workforce for as long as possible. In an earlier era, it would have been unthinkable to consider college players a "workforce" or to equate them, as Judge Flaum did, with women kept "barefoot and pregnant" by controlling husbands and rigid social mores. Today, though, with some institutions, many coaches, and the NCAA profiting handsomely from the players' efforts, the players look increasingly like a grossly underpaid workforce, and even rules that could benefit them by keeping them in school longer seem designed instead to prolong their subservience to the college sports industry. In this atmosphere, the concept of "players playing for the fun of it" appears to be as outdated as the flying wedge and the leather helmet, at least in Division I-A, and antitrust challenges to NCAA rules have become "a cost of doing business" for the NCAA.

The next major antitrust challenge to an NCAA rule came not from players, though, but from their coaches. In *Law v. NCAA* the plaintiffs were a class of restricted-earnings coaches (RECs) in college basketball, whose salaries had been drastically reduced by the NCAA's adoption in 1992 of two rules designed to reduce costs in college sports.[160] One rule limited basketball coaching staffs at Division I colleges to four members, including a head coach, two assistants, and one REC, whose position would replace the previous positions of part-time assistant coach, graduate assistant coach, and volunteer coach.[161] The second rule restricted the compensation of RECs in all Division I sports except football to a total of $12,000 for the academic year and $4,000 for the summer months, which was roughly equivalent to the stipends previously paid to graduate assistant coaches.[162] The plaintiffs, who had been RECs in men's basketball during the 1992–93 school year, challenged these rules under the Sherman Antitrust Act.[163] A federal district court in Kansas had permanently enjoined the NCAA from enforcing or attempting to enforce the "REC rule," and the NCAA appealed to the United States Court of Appeals for the Tenth Circuit.[164]

The Tenth Circuit began its analysis by reiterating the familiar standard to be used when examining an antitrust claim under the rule of reason. First, the plaintiff must show that the challenged policy had "a substantially adverse effect on competition."[165] If the plaintiff (i.e., the coaches) satisfies this burden, then "the burden shifts to the defendant [i.e., the NCAA] to come forward with evidence of the procompetitive virtues of the alleged wrongful conduct."[166] If the defendant can demonstrate a procompetitive effect, "the plaintiff then must prove that the challenged conduct is not reasonably necessary to achieve the legitimate objectives or that those objectives can be achieved in a substantially less restrictive manner."[167] In this case, the appellate court observed, "the undisputed evidence support[ed] a finding of anticompetitive effect," because the coaches showed that (1) the NCAA member colleges had agreed to "fix prices" for one category of coaches, the RECs; (2) the agreement was effective; and (3) the price it set for the RECs was "more favorable to the [NCAA] than otherwise would have resulted from the operation of market forces."[168] In other words, the REC rule artificially lowered the price for coaching services.

Turning to the NCAA's justifications for the REC rule, the appellate court noted that such justifications "may be considered only to the extent that they tend to show that, on balance, the challenged restraint enhances competition."[169] The NCAA offered three justifications for the challenged salary restrictions, including retaining entry-level coaching positions, reducing costs, and maintaining competitive equity among the members of Division I.[170] But the court quickly disposed of the first justification, noting that the NCAA had not presented any evidence showing that entry-level applicants filled the REC positions or that the challenged rules would, over time, achieve that end.[171]

The NCAA's second justification was that these rules would enable colleges to reduce the costs of athletic competition. The court rejected this argument, too, stating that "cost-cutting by itself is not a valid procompetitive justification."[172] Moreover, the court continued, the NCAA had presented no evidence indicating that limiting the salaries of the RECs would reduce athletic departments' budget deficits, "let alone that such reductions were necessary to save college basketball."[173] "There is no reason to think," the court observed, "that the money saved by a school on a salary of a restricted earnings coach will not be put into another aspect of the school's basketball program, such as equipment or even another coach's salary, thereby increasing inequity in that area."[174]

The NCAA's third and final justification fared no better. The court rejected the NCAA's argument that the REC rule would "help to maintain competitive equity by preventing wealthier schools from placing a more experienced, higher-priced coach in the position of restricted-earnings coach."[175] The court reasoned that "[w]hile the REC Rule will equalize the salaries paid to entry-level coaches in Division I schools, it is not clear that the REC Rule will equalize the experience level of such coaches."[176] "Nowhere does the NCAA prove," the court added, "that the salary restrictions enhance competition."[177] Having dismissed all of the NCAA's justifications for the challenged rules, the Tenth Circuit then affirmed the district court's order granting the coaches a permanent injunction that barred the NCAA from reenacting compensation limits such as those included in the REC rule.[178]

Like *Gaines* and *Banks, Law* is symptomatic of modern college sports, which retain important ties to educational institutions but nonetheless operate in a commercially aggressive manner that invites antitrust scrutiny by the federal courts. That scrutiny proved fatal to the REC rule, which was hopelessly incapable of achieving its stated goals to cut costs, provide more job opportunities for entry-level coaches, and enhance competitive equity in Division I. In retrospect, the rule seems to have been designed to give the appearance of addressing budget deficits without actually doing so. Addressing budget deficits would have required cutting or eliminating athletic scholarships and reducing the number of regular-season games. But those changes would have threatened revenues, which the NCAA was loath to do, so it singled out the RECs instead. They were the easiest targets because of their lowly position at the bottom of the pecking order in college basketball. They won, though, because the commercial nature of the REC rule attracted a degree of antitrust scrutiny that the rule could not survive.

More recently, the NCAA faced a different type of antitrust challenge in *Worldwide Basketball and Sport Tours, Inc. et al. v. NCAA*.[179] The facts of this case were unique because the plaintiffs were not NCAA member institutions but, rather, promoters of college basketball tournaments who sought to prevent the NCAA from enforcing its "two-in-four rule."[180] That rule pertained to "exempt" tournaments, such as the Great Alaska Shootout, the Coaches vs. Cancer Classic, the Maui Invitational, and the

Las Vegas Invitational, which occurred before and during the regular college basketball season.[181] The term *exempt* meant that a team's participation in one of these tournaments counted as only a single game on its 28-game regular-season schedule, even if it played three or four games in the tournament.[182] In 1999 the NCAA changed its rules to prohibit college basketball teams from participating in more than two exempt tournaments every four years.[183]

A federal district court in Ohio granted the promoters' request for a permanent injunction barring the NCAA from enforcing the two-in-four rule.[184] It noted that under antitrust law, the NCAA had to show that the challenged rule, which had resulted in 72 fewer exempt games having been played in 2002–3 than in 2001–2, served a procompetitive end that justified retaining it.[185] Nobody disputed that the new rule had shrunk the market for exempt tournaments; the number of exempt tournaments declined from 26 the year after its adoption to 17 just three years later.[186] But the NCAA claimed that the rule was justified because it limited the number of games played per season out of concern for student welfare and gave less visible teams more opportunities to play in desirable tournaments.[187]

The district court rejected both justifications. Regarding the NCAA's claim that the rule served "student welfare," the court wrote that "if the NCAA truly had the best interests of athletes as students in mind, it would limit the number of games being played while school is in session, such as during the well-known NCAA Tournament, which takes place during the spring college semester."[188] The two-in-four rule, the court observed, affected "at most 5% of the total games played by Division I teams"; therefore, "if student welfare were the justification, to be effective, the rule would certainly have to regulate the other 95% of games played."[189] Besides, the court added, "at the same time as the passage of the Two in Four Rule, the NCAA actually *raised* the number of games, from 27 to 28, which a team may play each season."[190] As a result, despite the decline in the number of games played in exempt tournaments, the total number of games played per year in Division I since the adoption of the challenged rule had increased from 4,911 in 1999–2000 to 4,974 in 2002–3. Thus, the evidence belied the NCAA's claim that the two-in-four rule served student welfare.

The evidence also belied the NCAA's claim that the two-in-four rule enhanced competitive equity by offering less prestigious teams more chances to play in exempt tournaments than they would otherwise have. The court explained that "the teams which the NCAA claims it intended to benefit —

the lesser known, non-power conference teams—played in substantially fewer exempt games in 2002–03 than in the previous years."[191] "In view of this evidence," the court concluded, "the goal of competitive equity is hardly being achieved."[192] The district court therefore granted the injunction sought by the promoters.

But the NCAA appealed to the United States Court of Appeals for the Sixth Circuit, which reversed the district court's decision, thereby preserving the two-in-four rule. The NCAA dodged a bullet in the appellate court, winning a ruling in its favor despite its flimsy justifications for the two-in-four rule. The flimsiness of those justifications did not matter because the promoters failed to prove that the challenged rule unreasonably restrained trade in a relevant market.[193] The promoters' failure to meet their burden of proof prevented the court from assessing the effect of the two-in-four rule on the consumers (i.e., fans) of college basketball.[194] The Sixth Circuit observed,

> The burden is on the antitrust plaintiff to define the relevant market within which the alleged anticompetitive effects of the defendant's actions occur. Failure to identify a relevant market is a proper ground for dismissing a Sherman Act claim.[195]

Thus, the appellate court was left with "insufficient information to reach the question of whether the promoters suffered an antitrust injury—that is, an injury resulting from interference with the economic freedom of participants in the relevant market."[196] It therefore reversed the district court's decision, leaving the two-in-four rule in effect.

Worldwide Basketball is reminiscent of *Law*, even though the NCAA won the former and lost the latter. Both cases present the schizophrenic nature of college sports vividly, showing colleges grappling with the burgeoning costs of maintaining semiprofessional sports enterprises while also trying to limit the academic consequences of demanding travel schedules and to address the need for the competitive equity necessary to retain the fans' interest. Both cases also show feeble attempts by the NCAA to remedy these problems; the two-in-four rule did not promote "student welfare" or competitive equity any more effectively than the REC rule held down costs or expanded career opportunities for young coaches. Finally, both cases show that even the NCAA's feeble attempts at economic regulation, which merely nibble around the edges of the problems facing college sports, are subject to expensive and distracting antitrust challenges. One need not be clairvoyant to anticipate how expensive and distracting the likely antitrust challenge to a rule limiting coaches' salaries or shortening the regular season would be.

Moreover, when *Gaines, Banks, Law,* and *Worldwide Basketball* are viewed collectively, they reveal the need for a mechanism by which the NCAA could enact rules designed to make college sports more educationally compatible and less commercially driven without repeatedly having to defend itself against antitrust lawsuits. The lawsuits, like the commercialism that spawns them, are part of the legacy of the Supreme Court's invalidation of the NCAA's Football Television Plan in *NCAA v. Regents*. Chapter 8 presents a mechanism aimed at blunting the impact of the Supreme Court's decision, namely, an antitrust exemption for NCAA rules having a demonstrable connection to reasonable educational objectives. Under this exemption, for example, the NCAA could adopt a rule prohibiting college basketball games from starting later than 7:30 p.m. on weeknights, so as to minimize the likelihood of late arrivals home and missed classes the next morning.[197] If Congress adopts this proposal for an educationally based antitrust exemption, antitrust law will no longer prevent the NCAA from treating schizophrenia in the college sports industry or offer it an excuse for inertia.

Before turning to solutions, though, it is necessary to examine another Supreme Court decision that has affected college sports adversely, namely, *NCAA v. Tarkanian*, which the Court decided in 1988.[198] The origins of the *Tarkanian* decision are the focus of chapter 5.

Chapter 5

HUNTING THE SHARK
The Road to *NCAA v. Tarkanian*

The House That Enforcement Built

Two forces—television and enforcement—transformed the NCAA into the wealthy, powerful regulatory body that it is today. But both forces are the subjects of continuing controversy. Although commercialization, facilitated by television, has made the NCAA wealthy, it is also largely responsible for the academic fraud and the financial excesses that have plagued college sports for decades. Although the enforcement program has made the NCAA powerful, it has also painted a public image of the NCAA as tyrannical, inflexible, and vindictive. Thus, the NCAA has obtained its wealth and power at a high price.

The NCAA established its first enforcement program in 1948 in order to correct recruiting abuses. The program featured a Constitutional Compliance Committee, which was responsible for interpreting rules and investigating alleged violations. In 1951 the Committee on Infractions (COI) replaced the Constitutional Compliance Committee. The COI enjoyed broader investigative powers than its predecessor had.[1] The COI's first major target was the University of Kentucky's men's basketball team, which had been implicated in a gambling scandal. Former NCAA employee and later Big 10 commissioner Wayne Duke recalled, "With [executive director] Walter Byers principally behind the effort, [the NCAA] suspended the University of Kentucky basketball team for a full year."[2] Duke added, "I think the Kentucky action just indelibly stamped on the public that the NCAA meant business. It was the first thing out of the box, so to speak, and it gave the NCAA clout."[3] Similarly, former Pacific-10 Conference commissioner Wiles Hallock observed, "Before the NCAA was involved in an enforcement program, it didn't have any power. It was a scheduling organization. [It] conducted a few championships. But as far as the power was concerned, it wasn't there until Walter [Byers] started working enforcement."[4]

In 1973 the NCAA's in-house staff assumed the investigative duties, and the COI took charge of enforcement hearings. This arrangement enabled the NCAA to achieve a high "conviction" rate in enforcement proceedings, but it also led critics to charge that the NCAA had in those proceedings an unfair "home-court advantage" that made guilt a foregone conclusion. One commentator said of the relationship between the enforcement staff and the COI, "The same people who investigate cases serve as staff support for the committee that must eventually rule on the quality and outcome of those investigations. It's as if the police officer [who] arrested you also clerked for the judge [who] tried you."[5] This relationship deviates sharply from the relationship between police officers and prosecutors in the criminal justice system. Police officers and prosecutors may work closely together, but judges and juries are independent of them and hence can be a check on sloppy police work or malicious prosecutions. No such healthy separation exists in the NCAA enforcement process.

Thus, in the words of one commentator, "there are no external checks on the NCAA to ensure [the] accuracy and fairness of findings and penalties imposed on private citizens."[6] Consequently, a coach or other university employee can lose a livelihood and suffer damage to his or her professional reputation, and an athlete can lose a scholarship and suffer damage to his or her reputation, but the NCAA has retained an enforcement process that is neither as accurate nor as fair as its high stakes require. The unfairness in this process is a continuing source of criticism of the NCAA, even though much of the Association's power derives from its enforcement role.

Undue Process

Current deficiencies in the enforcement process, while real and significant, are not the subject of this chapter. This chapter is concerned with NCAA enforcement during the 1970s and 1980s, when it involved Jerry "Tark the Shark" Tarkanian, who coached the highly successful men's basketball team at the University of Nevada, Las Vegas. The NCAA enforcement process that Jerry Tarkanian faced operated under the "cooperative principle," which envisioned the enforcement staff and the institution working together to determine the validity of allegations that the institution violated NCAA rules.[7] The enforcement process consisted of six components, including (1) a preliminary inquiry; (2) an official inquiry; (3) a hearing conducted by the COI; (4) a report of findings by the COI; (5) an assignment of penalties, if warranted; and (6) a right of appeal to the NCAA Council.[8]

If the alleged violations were serious and plausible, the enforcement staff initiated a preliminary inquiry, in which case the NCAA sent a letter to the accused institution, notifying it that members of the enforcement staff would visit the campus in the near future to investigate alleged rules infractions.[9] But the letter would not specify the nature of the allegations. If the institution requested additional information, the NCAA would reveal when and where the alleged violations occurred and the institutional personnel who were supposedly involved in them, but it would not reveal the source of the allegations.[10] At the conclusion of the preliminary inquiry, if the enforcement staff concluded that the allegations were likely valid, the NCAA could either resolve the matter by means of a summary procedure before the COI or, in the case of more substantial allegations, initiate an official inquiry.

The COI was responsible for authorizing an official inquiry, based on the results of the preliminary inquiry. The official inquiry triggered a second letter to the institution, identifying a list of specific infractions and directing the institution, as a condition of its NCAA membership, to conduct its own investigation immediately. The institution had 60 days to respond, although the COI frequently granted extensions.[11]

An official inquiry had three parts: the overture, the allegations, and the coda. The overture consisted of four questions seeking information about how the accused institution's athletic programs were organized and administered. The allegations included the specific charges involved, the NCAA rules allegedly violated, and the persons believed to be responsible for the violations. One or more allegations could exist, and the responsible parties identified could be athletes, potential recruits, coaches, alumni, or "boosters" (i.e., fans of and donors to the accused institution's athletic department).[12] The coda was directed to the president of the accused institution. Beginning in 1974, the NCAA required the president of each member institution to certify, through a signed statement, that the institution was complying with Association rules.[13] Beginning in 1975, the NCAA required all staffers in the athletic departments of its member institutions to sign statements indicating that they had reported their knowledge of and involvement in any violation of NCAA rules. These institutional and departmental certifications of compliance comprised the coda.[14]

After completing its own investigation of the NCAA's charges, an institution was required to draft a response, which could be several hundred pages long, and transmit it to NCAA headquarters and to the COI.[15] Once the COI had reviewed the response, the COI scheduled a hearing at NCAA headquarters in Kansas, at least until 1979, when the Association began experimenting with prehearing conferences. By 1984, prehearing conferences had become standard operating procedure in NCAA enforcement cases.[16] During the conferences, enforcement staff met with representatives of the accused institutions to review institutional responses, allegation by allegation. The conferences were designed to identify undisputed issues and to prevent surprises at the hearing. According to a former chair of the COI, conferences also apprised institutions of additional evidence to gather and review regarding disputed issues.[17]

The subsequent hearing was closed and confidential; the only participants were members of the COI, a delegation representing the accused institution, and members of the NCAA's enforcement staff.[18] A hearing began with opening statements, first by a spokesperson for the institution, who was usually an attorney, and then by a spokesperson for the enforcement staff. These opening statements provided an overview of the respective positions of the accused institution and the NCAA enforcement staff.[19]

But the heart of the proceeding was a review of the allegations, which included determining which ones were disputed. The enforcement staff presented all of its evidence regarding each allegation, whether or not that evidence supported the allegation.[20] When the enforcement staff had finished presenting evidence, the institution's spokesperson responded, sometimes referring exclusively to the written response already submitted but sometimes supplementing the written response with additional comments. The procedure was informal, providing for frequent verbal exchanges between members of the COI, institutional representatives, and the enforcement staff.[21] The strict evidentiary rules governing courtroom proceedings did not apply. A hearing could last several days in order to address every allegation.[22]

After all of the allegations were aired and discussed, both the institution and the enforcement staff could make closing statements if they wished. The chair of the COI advised the accused institution of the remaining steps in the process, including the right of the institution to appeal to the NCAA Council if dissatisfied with the COI's findings, the penalty it imposed, or both. Then the hearing adjourned.[23]

After adjournment, members of the COI deliberated about the allegations and made their findings. The NCAA charged the COI to base its findings on information it determined to be "credible, persuasive, and of a kind on which reasonably prudent persons rely in the conduct of serious affairs."[24] When the members of the COI reached a consensus, they compiled all their findings into a confidential report, which they sent to the president of the institution involved.[25]

If penalties were imposed, the final report identified them. They could include prohibiting an institution's team(s) from performing on television or participating in postseason play and reducing the institution's customary allotment of athletic scholarships in a particular sport.[26] These penalties flowed from the COI's decision to place the institution "on probation." Coaches of offending teams faced the possibility of having their salaries frozen, their expense accounts reduced, and their travel for recruiting purposes restricted.[27]

Institutions found guilty by the COI could appeal to the NCAA Council, which heard the appeal de novo, meaning that it did not rely on factual findings by the COI but instead considered the evidence anew. The council sat atop the NCAA hierarchy and operated like a board of directors. It was comprised of the Association's president, its secretary-treasurer, and 44 institutional representatives selected by the delegates to the NCAA's annual convention.[28] The council could affirm, reverse, expand, contract, or change completely the finding of the COI.[29]

Once the council announced its decision, the NCAA issued a press release identifying the allegations found to be true and specifying the penalties imposed.[30] Until then, the Association operated under a gag rule, refusing even to acknowledge the existence of an investigation unless it felt compelled to respond to information released by the accused institution.[31] The gag rule bound only the NCAA, not the institution.[32] Still, it may have made institutions reluctant to disclose much information for fear of angering the NCAA.

Unfortunately for the targets of NCAA investigations, the "cooperative principle" was not nearly as benign in practice as it was in theory. Burton Brody, a professor of law at the University of Denver who served as his institution's faculty athletic representative to the NCAA, told a congressional subcommittee investigating the NCAA's enforcement process in 1978 that NCAA investigations were "cooperative only in the same sense ancient Rome's system of capital punishment was cooperative—the condemned is expected to carry his cross to the crucifixion."[33] Professor Brody, whose institution had been the subject of a NCAA investigation some years before, added,

It is at best a burlesque of fairness. No evidence was presented; only the conclusions of staff members. No witnesses were called. The only "testimony" was by the enforcement staff member, without oath, stating the rankest sort of mixture of hearsay and opinion as part of his prosecutorial arguments.[34]

North Carolina State University basketball coach Norman Sloan echoed Professor Brody's theme that the NCAA demanded cooperation from institutions under investigation but offered only intimidation, not cooperation, in exchange. Regarding his reluctance to testify for fear of reprisal by NCAA staff, Coach Sloan told the subcommittee,

They are very powerful, as you know, and they have a great deal of influence on my life or the life of any other coach of a major institution. I just do not think it is a healthy situation to have those people upset at you.[35]

Later, he added, "I just—I just don't want to get involved in a situation whereby I may be appearing to be testifying against the NCAA."[36]

Professor Brody and Coach Sloan were not alone in their criticisms and fears of the NCAA. Indeed, the impetus for the hearings during which both men testified was a letter signed by 68 members of the House and sent to subcommittee chair John Moss (D-CA) urging him to convene hearings about the NCAA's enforcement process.[37] The first signature on the letter belonged to James Santini (R-NV), then Nevada's lone member of the House, whose interest stemmed from the NCAA's dogged pursuit of Jerry Tarkanian.[38] That letter spawned a nationwide investigation by Mr. Moss's Subcommittee on Oversight and Investigations of the House Commerce Committee, including 10 days of hearings during a 10-month period, 41 witnesses, thousands of documents, and hundreds of interviews.[39]

The subcommittee's overarching conclusion was that self-reform by the NCAA was "possible and preferable"; therefore, it recommended that for the time being, Congress merely monitor the enforcement process. The subcommittee specifically rejected requiring the NCAA to adopt guarantees of procedural fairness (e.g., a right to call friendly witnesses and to cross-examine hostile ones) comparable to those applicable in criminal cases and proceedings involving administrative agencies.[40]

That is not to say that the lawmakers found the enforcement process to be satisfactory. On the contrary, the majority report included several findings highly critical of the process. Perhaps the subcommittee's most damning finding was "the appearance of an 'inescapable relationship' between the NCAA enforcement staff and the Committee on Infractions members, providing the prosecutorial staff an 'unbeatable home court advantage.'"[41] Exacerbating that cozy relationship was the absence of a statute of limitations, which enabled the NCAA to prosecute stale infractions allegedly committed by persons who were no longer enrolled or employed at the accused institution.[42]

Based on its findings, the subcommittee made several recommendations for change. One recommendation was that the NCAA create a "new collegial body" to supervise the enforcement (i.e., investigative) staff, establish and administer policy guidelines for the staff, and take responsibility for authorizing official inquiries. Under this arrangement, the enforcement staff and the COI would be separate and distinct, with the former no longer serving as the investigative arm of the latter. The COI would remain an adjudicative body and, outside of hearings, would have no contact with the investigators.[43] The NCAA should give the COI whatever staff assistance it might need to compensate for the loss of the enforcement staff's services.[44] The subcommittee specified, "The Committee on Infractions should have its own staff as needed, reporting directly and only to the Committee."[45]

Another recommendation concerning the COI was that it should have "a fulltime clerk, preferably a lawyer," whose job would be to draft the equivalent of a judicial opinion explaining the result of each infractions case. The opinion would have "an independent statement of the facts as they appear[ed] to the Infractions Committee after the hearing, a discussion of the evidence and how it was perceived by the Infractions Committee (not how it was presented by the staff), and the reasoning employed by the Committee in reaching its decision."[46] Still another recommendation concerned the NCAA's "practice of not affording member institutions a complete transcript of infractions hearing proceedings," which the subcommittee concluded was "fatally defective to the fundamental fairness of the appeals system" that was a part of the NCAA enforcement process.[47] The subcommittee recommended that the NCAA furnish accused institutions with printed transcripts of COI hearings.[48]

According to the subcommittee, the NCAA should also establish "evidentiary standards" by which the accuracy and the significance of information presented during enforcement hearings could be evaluated. These standards "[s]hould specify whether affidavits, statements and the like are acceptable and if so, what weight they will have."[49] The evidentiary standards should be published and should specify that the burden of proof in enforcement proceedings was on the NCAA, not the accused institution. In other words, the institution must be regarded as innocent until the NCAA proved it guilty.[50]

Closely related to its recommendation regarding an evidentiary standard was the subcommittee's criticism of the NCAA's habit of "conducting and later making evidentiary use of *ex parte* interviews with sources of allegations against individuals and member institutions."[51] Ex parte interviews were conducted between an investigator from the NCAA and the source, without a representative of the institution present and without a recording or written transcript being made. "More often than not," the majority report noted, "the identity of such sources is revealed to the accused member institution for the first time at the infractions hearing, when it is simply too late to prepare a defense, or to enable the institution to properly question the circumstances and context of the interview, or the interrogative techniques of the interviewer."[52] Accordingly, the subcommittee recommended that ex parte interviews conducted by either the NCAA or the accused institution be recorded, transcribed, and admitted as evidence at enforcement hearings.[53]

Moreover, those hearings should be open not only to accused institutions but to "anyone who stands in any sort of even remote jeopardy in the proceeding."[54] That category would include current athletes, former athletes, and boosters, all of whom, the subcommittee believed, "ha[d] too much to lose in the process not to be afforded access to it."[55] These individuals should have the right to be represented by counsel if they wished and should be able to present evidence and "know to a reasonable moral certainty that it will be judged on the basis of some sort of discernible, which is to say predictable, standard."[56] In contrast, the existing NCAA rules prohibited boosters from participating in hearings before the COI, but if the COI found that a booster had violated its rules, it could force the accused institution to ban the booster from additional involvement in the athletic program, despite that person's inability to be heard before the NCAA.[57] The subcommittee also concluded that the NCAA must initiate prosecutions of alleged infractions within four years of their occurrence.

Next, the subcommittee recommended that the NCAA's appeal procedure be narrowed from a complete rehearing of the evidence to just a consideration of possible errors by the COI, either in determining guilt or in imposing a penalty.[58] That would make it more like an appeal filed in a civil or a criminal court, because appellate courts do not reconsider the evidence already heard by a trial court. Instead, they determine whether the trial court made a legal error, such as admitting illegally seized evidence or giving prejudicial or incorrect instructions to the jurors before their deliberations.

Finally, the subcommittee addressed the relationship between the NCAA and the individuals who were subject to its considerable power. The majority report explained that the NCAA was "an association of institutions, not individuals," hence its jurisdiction was limited to college and university athletic departments and to athletic conferences comprised of member institutions.[59] The majority report noted, though, that despite lacking formal jurisdiction over individuals, the NCAA controlled coaches, athletic directors, athletes, and boosters, "often with awesome ferocity," by requiring its member institutions "to perform the unpleasant task of imposing punishment on individuals, many of whom have not to this point been allowed to participate in the process."[60]

Accordingly, the subcommittee recommended that the NCAA abandon the fiction that only member institutions could suspend a coach or declare an athlete ineligible for collegiate competition. "Ineligibility should be declared, if at all," the majority report stated, "by the NCAA itself, whose philosophy may or may not allow it to do so without extending membership privileges to (and therefore jurisdiction over) student athletes."[61] The subcommittee also recommended that the NCAA abandon Section 10 of its enforcement regulations, "allowing for retributive sanctions against member institutions or individuals if and when court actions are ultimately resolved in favor of the NCAA."[62] In the lawmakers' view, Section 10 was "a dangerous and unacceptable inhibition on citizens of the United States seeking access to the courts," which the NCAA should repeal, leaving the original penalties in place even when the Association prevailed in court.[63]

Thus, although the subcommittee did not seek to reform the NCAA enforcement process by legislation, it recognized the principal deficiencies in that process and made numerous recommendations for increasing the fairness of NCAA disciplinary proceedings to institutions and individuals alike. The majority report concluded by expressing the hope that the subcommittee's investigation, findings, and recommendations would spur the NCAA to reform the process itself so that "federal action can be avoided."[64]

Unfortunately, the NCAA did not adopt the subcommittee's major recommendations. Hence the enforcement staff remained cozy with the COI, and accused institutions and individuals continued to be denied access to printed transcripts of COI hearings.[65] At the 1979 NCAA Convention, Professor Brody moved for the adoption of proposals to (1) establish a committee to oversee the enforcement staff, (2) adopt an official policy of presuming accused institutions and individuals were innocent until proved guilty, and (3) provide transcripts of hearings to interested parties; but they were defeated.[66] The delegates did, however, adopt proposals to let persons accused of infractions be represented by counsel at hearings before the COI, establish evidentiary standards for those hearings, and set a time limit for reviewing alleged violations (i.e., a statute of limitations).[67]

Still, the NCAA rejected more of the lawmakers' recommendations than it adopted, so the enforcement process remained subject to criticism long after the subcommittee hearings ended. In a commentary published in a law journal in 1991, scholar of sports law C. Peter Goplerud recommended that when major violations are alleged, the NCAA should provide procedures akin to those followed by federal agencies under the Administrative Procedure Act. Such procedures would apply in a hearing seeking to determine a person's continued eligibility for social security disability benefits or veterans' educational benefits. Under those procedures,

1. a letter of official inquiry would clearly identify specific allegations, evidence, and witnesses;
2. witness interviews would be conducted in a "deposition-like setting," meaning that counsel for the accused institution (and accused individuals) would be present along with the NCAA investigator, witnesses would be questioned under oath, and interviews would be recorded or transcribed;
3. accused parties would receive a recording and a transcript of all such interviews;
4. these interviews would be completed before the COI hearing took place;
5. the COI hearing would be open to the public;
6. it would include the cross-examination of witnesses;
7. the COI would be expected to follow stare decisis, that is, to honor its past decisions and use them as a guide in reaching decisions in current cases;
8. a panel of "judges," comprised of law professors and sitting or retired judges and practicing attorneys, would preside at COI hearings and during appeals;

9. "judges" and enforcement staff could not have contact with each other without counsel for the accused parties present;

10. accused parties would have a right to counsel throughout the investigation; and

11. as in proceedings involving administrative agencies, the formal rules of evidence used in courtrooms would not necessarily apply.[68]

Don Yeager, whose 1991 book was highly critical of the NCAA's enforcement process, reached similar conclusions, although he made several recommendations that were not part of Professor Goplerud's commentary. For example, Yeager recommended that the NCAA honor its so-called cooperative principle by conducting a joint investigation with the accused institution.[69] In his view, the NCAA investigator and an institutional representative should interview witnesses jointly, thereby saving time and probably reducing disagreement between them about what each witness said.[70]

Yeager also recommended that the NCAA "overhaul" its appeal process, principally by removing jurisdiction over appeals from the NCAA Council, which not only heard appeals but also appointed the members of the COI, from whose decisions appeals originated. Yeager noted that it was highly unlikely that the council would overturn a decision of the COI, because doing so "would seem to be questioning the judgment of the people it appointed."[71] Yeager also advocated ending the practice of hearing appeals de novo. Instead, the accused institution "should be able to select the points that it believes the infractions committee misunderstood or ignored and appeal only those points."[72]

Finally, Yeager advised the NCAA to stop using its lack of subpoena power to justify its refusal to record witness interviews. The NCAA claimed that if it sought to record witnesses' statements while it lacked subpoena power, the witnesses would cease to cooperate and investigations would fail. He recommended that the NCAA seek subpoena power from the state legislatures in states where investigations were in progress. Subpoenas would compel witnesses to cooperate.[73]

The Goplerud and Yeager critiques of the NCAA enforcement process appeared three years after the Supreme Court decided *NCAA v. Tarkanian*. The procedural shortcomings discussed in those critiques were evident in the years between 1973, when the NCAA began investigating Jerry Tarkanian and his UNLV Runnin' Rebels, and 1988, when the litigation resulting from that investigation reached the United States Supreme Court. Indeed, the shortcomings of the NCAA enforcement process were the subject of that litigation, an epic, David-and-Goliath battle that is focus of the rest of this chapter.

Hot Pursuit

The NCAA's investigation of Jerry Tarkanian began during his employment at California State University, Long Beach (Long Beach State), between 1968 and 1973. While Tarkanian was the head basketball coach at Long Beach State, where his teams won 116 games and lost just 17 (an outstanding .872 winning percentage),[74] the NCAA began investigating the 49ers for alleged recruiting violations.[75] In March 1973, when Tarkanian left Long Beach for the University of Nevada, Las Vegas, he narrowly escaped the three-year probation the NCAA imposed on Long Beach State for various rules violations.[76] But he did not escape the NCAA's attention for long, as he transformed a mediocre 14–14 team into a 29–3 juggernaut (and third-place finisher in the NCAA Tournament) four years later.[77] Indeed, the Association had begun investigating UNLV in 1972, the year before Tarkanian's arrival, but it did not notify UNLV of an official inquiry until after his appointment as head coach of the Runnin' Rebels. Thus, the investigation of UNLV was personal as well as institutional. NCAA records that later became public revealed that the NCAA, which had designated the UNLV investigation "inactive" before Tarkanian became the men's basketball coach, reactivated it on March 29, 1973, six days after he became the Runnin' Rebels' coach.[78]

Initially, the NCAA charged UNLV with 78 rules violations. But in 1977, after a four-year investigation, it reduced the number of charges to 38, of which 10 allegedly involved Tarkanian.[79] The charges against him were as follows:

1. Violation of the principles governing expenses, extra benefits, and financial aid to student-athletes [NCAA Constitution, Articles 3-1-(g)-5, 3-1-(g)-(6), and 3-4-(a)].

The NCAA charged that Tarkanian arranged for free air travel for two players in 1973 and 1974, respectively; free housing in a UNLV booster's home for a player in 1973–74 and 1974–75; free clothing purchases for two players at a Las Vegas clothing store; and free meals for a player at a Las Vegas hotel.[80]

2. Violation of the principles governing ethical conduct [NCAA Constitution, Article 3-6-(a)].

The NCAA charged that Tarkanian's "involvement in various violations in this case demonstrate[d] a knowing and willful effort . . . to operate [UNLV's] intercollegiate basketball program contrary to NCAA legislation."[81]

3. Violation of principles governing ethical conduct and the cooperative principles governing the NCAA enforcement program [NCAA Constitution, Article 3-6-(a), Bylaw 7-5-(d), and the opening statement of the Official Procedure Governing the NCAA Enforcement Program].

The NCAA charged that "during [its] investigation into the athletic policies and practices of [UNLV's] intercollegiate basketball program, Jerry Tarkanian contacted and arranged for other individuals to contact principals involved in the case in an effort to discourage them from reporting information related to violations of NCAA regulations when contacted by members of the NCAA enforcement staff, and in an effort to cause them to give untruthful information to [UNLV]."[82]

4. Violation of the principles governing eligibility of student-athletes, and the provisions governing recruiting and institutional eligibility for championship events [NCAA Constitution, Article 3-9-(e); Bylaws 1-1-(a) and 4-6-(b)].

The NCAA charged that in 1973–74, Tarkanian asked Harvey Munford, a UNLV booster, to help a prospective basketball player by cosigning a promissory note enabling the player to buy furniture at a Las Vegas furniture store and by paying $400 from his (Munford's) personal funds to retire the note.[83] The NCAA also charged that in 1973–74, Tarkanian arranged for Munford, who was a part-time instructor at UNLV, to give a basketball player a B in a course Munford taught, with the understanding that the player would not attend classes or do any coursework.[84] The NCAA charged further that Tarkanian permitted a prospective player to participate in basketball practice during a monthlong "mini semester" in 1973–74 during which he was not enrolled at UNLV.[85]

5. Violation of the provisions governing recruiting [NCAA Bylaws 1-1-(a) and 1-5-(b)].

The NCAA charged that a booster whose help Tarkanian had enlisted in recruiting two players from Kansas had paid a friend of one of the players $10 for driving the players from Hutchinson to Wichita, a distance of 40 miles one way, to meet the booster.[86]

6. Violation of the provisions governing recruiting [NCAA Bylaws 1-1-(a), 1-5-(e), 1-5-(e)-(3), 1-5-(f), and 1-5-(I)].

The NCAA charged that Tarkanian paid for the booster referred to by item 5 to accompany the two players from Kansas on a recruiting visit to UNLV and to be housed, fed, and entertained. A related charge was that Tarkanian also gave the man $300 in cash and paid for his one-way flight from Las Vegas to New York.[87]

7. Violation of the provisions governing recruiting [NCAA Bylaws 1-1-(a) and 1-5-(f)].

The NCAA charged that Tarkanian's assistant coach, Tony Morrocco, provided a car to a prospective basketball player who made a recruiting visit to UNLV in April 1973.[88]

8. Violation of the provisions governing recruiting [NCAA Bylaws 1-1-(a) and 1-6-(a)].

The NCAA charged that Tarkanian arranged for a basketball player to fly from Pittsburgh to Las Vegas and to live in Las Vegas rent-free for a month during the summer. The Association also charged that assistant coach Tony Morrocco arranged for a U-Haul to move a basketball player's household goods from Tulsa to Las Vegas.[89]

9. Violation of the provisions governing certification of compliance with NCAA legislation [NCAA Bylaw 4-6-(d)].

The NCAA charged that although Tarkanian knew the UNLV basketball program was not in compliance with NCAA rules, he "failed to report to

University officials during an institutional review conducted in conjunction with the University's May 21, 1974, certification of compliance with NCAA legislation, his knowledge of and involvement in any violations of NCAA legislation."[90]

10. Questionable practice in light of NCAA requirements [NCAA By-laws 4-6-(d) and 4-6-(d)-(4)].

This is essentially the same allegation as item 9. The NCAA charged that although Tarkanian knew UNLV's basketball program was not complying with NCAA rules, he "attested to the chief executive officer of the University on a statement filed in conjunction with the University's June 25, 1975, certification of compliance with NCAA regulations, that he had reported his knowledge of and involvement in any violations of NCAA legislation involving the institution." This was the only allegation against Tarkanian on which the COI did not find he had violated NCAA rules.[91]

In retrospect, the NCAA's dogged pursuit of Jerry Tarkanian appears to have been driven at least as much by personal animus as by evidence against him or his players. To be sure, Tarkanian fueled the NCAA's fire by repeatedly chastising it for punishing less visible, low-budget teams, such as Long Beach State, for minor rules violations, while refusing to even investigate "marquee programs," such as UCLA and the University of Kentucky, for more serious transgressions. Tarkanian argued that the NCAA did not investigate institutions such as UCLA and Kentucky because they and comparable schools had made the NCAA wealthy from the televising of its annual men's basketball tournament.

Emblematic of Tarkanian's critique of the NCAA's double standard of enforcement was his often-quoted quip that "in the late 1980s the NCAA was so mad at Kentucky [that it] gave Cleveland State two more years of probation."[92] He had held that view ever since the early 1970s, when, he maintains, UCLA athletic director J. D. Morgan reported alleged rules violations at Long Beach State to the NCAA. Tarkanian, instead of acquiescing to the Association's investigators, told them that "far worse things were happening at UCLA," where the recruiting budget was much larger and the boosters were far wealthier.[93] In Tarkanian's view, that comment began what would become his more than 20-year feud with the NCAA.[94]

Whatever the NCAA's motivation to pursue Jerry Tarkanian was, its investigators were relentless, searching every nook and cranny of the UNLV men's basketball program for two-and-a-half years before sending the university notice of an official inquiry on February 25, 1976. In keeping with NCAA rules, UNLV conducted its own investigation of the allegations. More precisely, the office of the Nevada attorney general investigated at UNLV's request, after which UNLV sent its response to the COI, supported by two boxes full of affidavits, sworn statements, and other evidence contradictory to the NCAA's allegations.[95] UNLV's response ensured that the COI hearing would be lengthy; indeed, it lasted for four days.[96]

The testimony of the NCAA enforcement staff consisted of the investigators' recollection of interviews with sources and included memoranda of those interviews, some memoranda written after the interviews had ended.[97] The interviewees verified the accuracy of the memoranda, but with respect to Jerry Tarkanian, the NCAA's allegations conflicted with the evidence the Nevada attorney general's office had obtained from its investigation.[98] Indeed, during the first trial in Tarkanian's subsequent lawsuit against the NCAA, he would obtain an injunction blocking his suspension from coaching based partly on the testimony of a staff attorney from the attorney general's office. According to the testimony, the investigation conducted by that office "found no factual basis for the NCAA charges" against Tarkanian.[99]

The COI found UNLV guilty of 38 violations of NCAA rules, with Coach Tarkanian implicated in 10 of them.[100] The COI placed UNLV on probation, which included a two-year ban on postseason play and television appearances by Tarkanian's basketball team.[101] In an unprecedented move reflecting the NCAA's desire to punish Tarkanian, the COI directed UNLV to show cause why it should not be penalized if it failed to suspend him from its athletic department for two years.[102]

In May 1977 UNLV appealed the COI's findings to the NCAA Council, which, on August 15, 1977, upheld all of the findings reached and penalties imposed by the COI.[103] On August 26 the NCAA issued a press release announcing that, based on the COI's findings, it would place UNLV on probation. After its appeal failed, UNLV conducted an internal hearing to determine whether it should suspend Tarkanian from coaching, as the NCAA had directed it to do.[104] UNLV president Donald Baepler appointed Brock Dixon, a vice president at the university, to review the case and identify UNLV's options regarding its controversial coach.[105] When the in-house hearing was complete, Dixon wrote a report stating that the facts supporting the NCAA's charges were "clearly in doubt" and that the NCAA's "standards of proof and due process were inferior to what we might expect."[106] "In almost every factual situation delineated by the NCAA," the report observed, "the university's own investigation has been able to find a substantial body of conflicting evidence, some of which has been heard and considered by the NCAA and some of which has been brushed aside."[107]

For example, to support the charge that Coach Tarkanian had asked Harvey Munford to give a basketball player a B in a course for which the athlete had done no work, the NCAA relied on investigator Hale McMenamin's "recollection" of his conversation with Munford.[108] According to McMenamin, Munford stated that Tarkanian had asked him to give the athlete a B and that Munford had complied with the request, even though the athlete had not attended any classes or completed any assignments in the course.[109] But UNLV had countered the NCAA's charge by producing (1) a sworn affidavit signed by Munford stating he had not done any of the things alleged by the NCAA, (2) a sworn affidavit signed by the athlete denying that Coach Tarkanian had arranged for him to take the course and stating that he had attended classes and completed the required assignments, (3) sworn statements from five students who remembered the athlete's regular attendance in the class, (4) the sworn statement of a typist who remembered typing a paper for the athlete for this class, and (5) positive results of both polygraph and voice analysis tests of Harvey Munford.[110]

Still, Brock Dixon was well aware that UNLV's NCAA membership required it to accede to the directive to suspend Coach Tarkanian, even if the NCAA's investigative procedures and evidentiary standards were deficient. "In this instance," he wrote to President Baepler, "we could wish for standards of due process and evidence far superior to that which we have observed, but given the terms of our adherence to the NCAA we cannot substitute—biased as we must be—our own judgment on the credibility of witnesses for that of the infractions committee and the Council."[111] Dixon then presented Baepler with alternative courses of action, including (1) refusing to suspend Tarkanian and taking the risk that the NCAA would impose additional sanctions on UNLV as a result, (2) recognizing the NCAA's authority in this matter and suspending Tarkanian despite believing the Association was wrong in this case, or (3) withdrawing UNLV from membership in the NCAA. Dixon concluded that the second option was the best of a bad lot.[112] Agreeing with Dixon's conclusion, President Baepler suspended Jerry Tarkanian from coaching for two years, as the NCAA had directed.

"The University is left without alternatives," Baepler wrote to Tarkanian in a September 1977 letter informing the coach of his suspension.[113]

On September 8, 1977, the day before his suspension was due to begin, Jerry Tarkanian sued UNLV in a Nevada trial court. He asked the court, first, to declare that UNLV, by suspending him based on the NCAA's findings, had violated his constitutional rights to liberty and property without due process of law and, second, to enjoin (i.e., bar) the university from imposing the suspension.[114] In Tarkanian's view, UNLV had violated Section 1983 of Title 42 of the United States Code, which prohibits state officials from abridging individual rights guaranteed by the United States Constitution.[115]

The trial court sided with Tarkanian; after a trial, it issued an order permanently enjoining UNLV from carrying out the suspension, because the process by which the coach was suspended had violated Section 1983.[116] UNLV appealed to the Nevada Supreme Court. The NCAA, which was not a party to Tarkanian's suit against UNLV, filed an amicus curiae brief in the case, arguing that the Nevada Supreme Court should order the trial court to dismiss the suit because no actual controversy existed between Tarkanian and UNLV.[117] If an actual controversy justifying a lawsuit existed, the NCAA maintained, it was between the NCAA and Coach Tarkanian, hence the court should add the Association as a party if the case were to proceed.[118]

The Nevada Supreme Court agreed with the NCAA. It held that the NCAA was a necessary party to the case because the NCAA had "initiated and controlled the proceedings which led to Tarkanian's suspension" and had "made the factual findings upon which Tarkanian's suspension was based."[119] To hold otherwise would be to prevent Tarkanian from making constitutional claims against the NCAA to which he might be entitled.[120] Therefore, in May 1979 the Nevada Supreme Court reversed the trial court's order barring UNLV from suspending Tarkanian and returned the case to the trial court, with instructions to add the NCAA as a party and to hold a second trial.[121] Thus began a legal battle between Jerry Tarkanian and the NCAA that would last for two decades and include a trip to the United States Supreme Court.

Full-Court Press

While Coach Tarkanian's lawsuit was pending, the federal courts changed their minds about the legal status of the NCAA in a way that would affect him adversely. During the 1970s, federal courts had held consistently that the NCAA was a "state actor," meaning it had to provide "due process" to institutions and individuals whom it investigated and punished for rules violations.[122] Due process takes one of two alternative forms, namely, procedural or substantive. The former refers to the procedural protections necessary to ensure fairness when government imposes criminal penalties or administrative sanctions on individuals. The latter refers to the requirement that government action not be arbitrary and capricious or infringe on certain "fundamental" rights, such as the rights to marry, have children, and make basic decisions about their upbringing.[123] Procedural due process lay at the heart of *Tarkanian v. NCAA*.

To succeed, a plaintiff who alleges the denial of procedural due process must show that (1) state or federal governmental action is involved, (2) the aggrieved party is a person, and (3) the governmental action infringed on the plaintiff's constitutionally protected interest in life, liberty, or property. When a constitutionally protected interest is at stake and fair procedures are required, just what process is due is determined by striking a balance between (a) the private interest that will be affected by the official action; (b) the risk of an erroneous deprivation of that interest through the procedures used and the probable value, if any, of additional or substitute procedural safeguards; and (c) the government's interest, including the function involved and the financial and administrative burdens likely to result from additional or substitute procedures.[124]

Jerry Tarkanian's right to live was not at stake in his battle with the NCAA, but both his liberty interest in preserving his reputation and his property interest in retaining his coaching job were.[125] Under the NCAA's enforcement mechanism, the NCAA, a private association, could force a public university, such as UNLV, which unquestionably was a governmental entity required to observe due process, to penalize a private citizen, such as Coach Tarkanian.[126] In these circumstances, the university was required to provide due process, but the procedures governing the outcome were the NCAA's procedures, not the university's. Scrupulous adherence to due process by the university would not ensure fairness to accused persons if the NCAA's procedures were arbitrary and capricious. Thus, Jerry Tarkanian's chances for success in his lawsuit depended on the courts holding that the NCAA, despite its private character, was sufficiently linked to public colleges and universities or performed a sufficiently regulatory function that it was a "state actor" within the meaning of the Fourteenth Amendment to the

Constitution and Section 1983 and, hence, had to observe due process in its investigations and hearings.

In the earliest cases in which plaintiffs, who usually were athletes declared ineligible for collegiate competition, challenged the fairness of NCAA enforcement procedures, courts held that the NCAA was indeed a state actor required to provide due process. For example, in *Buckton v. NCAA,* the court held that the NCAA was a state actor when it denied eligibility for collegiate ice hockey to Canadian athletes who had played Junior A hockey in Canada, which the NCAA considered to be professional sport.[127] The *Buckton* court reasoned that the NCAA was a state actor because public institutions comprised half of its member institutions; the court even found the private institution involved in the *Buckton* case, Boston University, to be a state actor because it received state and federal funds.[128] This view prevailed in a series of cases decided through 1982; therefore, when the *Tarkanian* litigation began, the prevailing judicial view was that NCAA action was state action.[129]

But showing that a private entity had behaved as a state actor became significantly more difficult after the United States Supreme Court's 1982 decisions in *Rendell-Baker v. Kohn, Blum v. Yaretsky,* and *Lugar v. Edmonson Oil Company.*[130] In *Buckton* and other early cases featuring due process challenges to the NCAA, courts had relied, wholly or in part, on "public function" analysis in concluding that the NCAA behaved as a state actor when enforcing its rules. Under this legal doctrine, a private entity was a state actor for due process purposes if it acted in ways and in pursuit of aims typically associated with governmental functions.[131] But in *Rendell-Baker* and *Blum,* both of which arose outside the context of college sports, the Supreme Court announced a more restrictive interpretation of public function analysis: state involvement in the challenged action had to be much more overt than under previous interpretations in order to find state action by a private entity, and courts would resolve ambiguous cases by concluding that the private entity was not a state actor.[132]

For example, in *Rendell-Baker,* the Court held that employees discharged by a nominally private school were not entitled to due process because the school was not a state actor. The Court reached that decision even though the federal government supplied 90 percent of the school's operating budget, the school was subject to extensive state regulation, and it served a public function by educating students whom the public schools had been unable to educate.[133] In the Court's view, even if the school, as the plaintiffs alleged, had fired them for exercising their First Amendment rights to criticize school governance procedures and form a union, respectively, their terminations were not state action because a private board managed the school and because the state had little involvement in personnel matters, such as hiring and firing teachers.[134] Similarly, in *Blum v. Yaretsky,* the Court held that a private nursing home was not a state actor when it transferred or discharged Medicaid patients, thereby reducing their federal benefits, without notice or a hearing.[135] The Court reasoned that decisions to transfer or discharge patients were the responsibility of physicians and nursing home administrators, who were private parties, and the Court found no evidence indicating that the state's desire to reduce its Medicaid expenses had influenced those decisions.[136]

In 1984 college sports felt the impact of *Rendell-Baker* and *Blum* when the United States Court of Appeals for the Fourth Circuit held, in *Arlosoroff v. NCAA,* that the NCAA was not a state actor because (1) no state agency had ordered or caused it to issue the challenged regulation (a declaration of ineligibility against a Duke University tennis player) and (2) the governance of college sports was not a function traditionally reserved to the state.[137] *Arlosoroff* involved an Israeli citizen who, after his discharge from the Israeli Army in March 1979 at the age of 22, played in 17 amateur tennis tournaments and was a member of Israel's Davis Cup team before enrolling at Duke in August 1981.[138] As a freshman, Arlosoroff played the number one singles position on Duke's tennis team, but afterward the NCAA declared him ineligible based on its rule stating that "organized competition in a sport during each twelve-month period after the student's 20th birthday and prior to matriculation with a member institution should count as one year of varsity competition in that sport."[139] Although this rule included an exception for athletic competition occurring during military service, the exception did not apply to Arlosoroff, because he had participated in organized tennis for three years after his discharge from the Israeli Army and before his enrollment at Duke. Thus, he was entitled to just one year of collegiate eligibility, which he had used as a freshman.[140]

Arlosoroff first filed suit in a state court, which granted a temporary restraining order in his favor. Duke and the NCAA then removed the case to federal court, where Arlosoroff obtained a preliminary injunction barring the NCAA from enforcing its eligibility rule against him.[141] The federal trial court that issued the injunction treated the NCAA's actions against Arlosoroff as state action under the Fourteenth Amendment.[142] That decision triggered an appeal by the NCAA to the Fourth Circuit, which reversed the trial court's ruling because the NCAA was not a state actor.

The appellate court acknowledged that in prior cases, most courts considering whether the NCAA was a state actor had concluded that it was.[143] The appellate court pointed out that courts in the earlier cases had found that the Fourteenth Amendment bound the NCAA because (1) the NCAA performed a public function in regulating college sports, (2) a substantial interdependence existed between the NCAA and the public institutions that comprised approximately half its membership, and (3) the public institutions played a key role in funding the NCAA and in its decision making.[144] Moreover, the earlier cases had "rested upon the notion that indirect involvement of state governments could convert what otherwise would be considered private conduct into state action."[145] But "that notion has now been rejected by the Supreme Court," the appellate court observed in *Arlosoroff*, "and [the Supreme Court's] decisions require a different conclusion."[146]

The Fourth Circuit noted in *Arlosoroff* that although "the NCAA may be said to perform a public function as the overseer of the nation's intercollegiate athletics," the regulation of intercollegiate athletics was not a function traditionally reserved exclusively to the state.[147] Therefore, even though a public benefit resulted from NCAA regulation of college sports, that benefit was not sufficient to support a finding of state action by the NCAA based on a public function analysis.[148] Neither did the presence of public institutions in the NCAA change its basic character as a voluntary association comprised of both public and private institutions. Besides, no evidence existed to indicate that the public institutions were more influential than the private institutions belonging to the NCAA in the adoption of the rule to which Arlosoroff objected.[149]

Thus, in *Arlosoroff* the Fourth Circuit applied the view of public function analysis articulated by the Supreme Court in *Rendell-Baker* and *Blum* to the college sports context. "It is not enough," the judges reasoned, "that an institution is highly regulated and subsidized by the state."[150] They explained, "If the state in its regulatory or subsidizing function does not order or cause the action complained of, and the function is not one traditionally reserved to the state, there is no state action."[151] Accordingly, *Arlosoroff* held that the NCAA's adoption of its eligibility rule was purely private action not subject to the Fourteenth Amendment, and it vacated the injunction the trial court had issued in the plaintiff's favor.[152] His collegiate tennis career was over after just one year.

After *Arlosoroff* every federal court asked to decide whether the NCAA was a state actor held that it was not.[153] As a result, athletes and employees of institutions participating in college sports could not successfully challenge the fairness of NCAA enforcement proceedings on due process grounds; the NCAA, as a private actor, was not required to meet the due process standards of the Fourteenth Amendment.[154] In other words, persons whom the NCAA investigated would have to rely on the Association itself for procedural fairness, because judicial review of due process challenges was no longer available.

Happily for Jerry Tarkanian, though, an exception to this rule existed in Nevada, where the judicial tide had turned against the NCAA on this issue. After the Nevada Supreme Court ordered the trial court to add the NCAA as a party to the *Tarkanian* lawsuit, the coach filed an amended complaint, which named both the NCAA and UNLV as defendants in the case.[155] Four years of delays followed, during which Jerry Tarkanian remained head coach of the men's basketball team at UNLV, because the trial court issued a preliminary injunction barring his suspension pending the outcome of a trial.[156] In 1984 a "bench trial" (with a judge but no jury) occurred, which Tarkanian won, as the court held that the NCAA's conduct was state action. The court also held that the NCAA had violated Tarkanian's right to procedural due process, by denying him an "opportunity to be heard at a meaningful time and in a meaningful manner,"[157] and his right to substantive due process, by arbitrarily and capriciously suspending him from coaching, thereby depriving him of constitutionally protected liberty and property interests.[158] As a result, the court permanently enjoined UNLV and the NCAA from carrying out the suspension.[159] Thereafter, the coach petitioned to recoup his attorney's fees, and the trial court ordered the NCAA to reimburse him for those fees in the amount of $196,000.[160] UNLV did not appeal from the trial court's decision, but the NCAA appealed to the Nevada Supreme Court.[161]

In 1987, ten long years after Jerry Tarkanian first filed suit, the Nevada Supreme Court upheld both the trial court's grant of a permanent injunction against suspending the coach and its award to him of attorney's fees. The only aspect of the trial court's decision the appellate court reversed was the amount of the attorney's fees, which the appellate court ordered the trial court to reconsider.[162] In finding for Tarkanian, the Nevada Supreme Court rejected the NCAA's argument that *Rendell-Baker v. Kohn, Blum v. Yaretsky,* and *Lugar v. Edmonson Oil Company* required the Nevada court to conclude that the NCAA was not a state actor.[163] On the contrary, the Nevada court explained, both *Rendell-Baker* and *Blum* had acknowledged that state action may exist "if the private entity has exercised powers that are traditionally the exclusive prerogative of the state."[164] In this case, UNLV was a public institution existing by virtue of Section 4 of Article 11 of the Nevada Constitution.[165] Therefore, Jerry Tarkanian was a public employee, and, the Court reasoned, "The right to discipline public employees is traditionally the exclusive prerogative of the state."[166] Accordingly, "UNLV [could] not escape responsibility for disciplinary action against employees by delegating that duty to a private entity," namely, the NCAA.[167] *Arlosoroff* and the cases following it in which courts held that NCAA regulatory action was not state action did not control here because they did not address the enforcement of NCAA rules against a state employee.[168]

The Nevada Supreme Court added that even the two-part test the United States Supreme Court articulated in *Lugar v. Edmonson Oil Company* required a finding of state action in this case. The first part of the test required that the deprivation of rights alleged by the plaintiff result from a third party's exercise of a right or privilege created by the state, by a rule of conduct imposed by the state, or by a person for whom the state was responsible.[169] This part of the test was met in *Tarkanian* because the "third party" (the NCAA) could not have punished Coach Tarkanian, a "state university employee," unless UNLV had bestowed on it the right or privilege to do so.[170] The second part of the *Lugar* test for state action requires that the third party act jointly with the public entity, to the extent that both could be considered state actors.[171] The Nevada Supreme Court concluded that this part of the test was also met in the *Tarkanian* case. "By delegating authority to the NCAA over athletic personnel decisions and by imposing the NCAA sanctions against Tarkanian," the Court reasoned, "UNLV acted jointly with the NCAA."[172] Thus, despite the U.S. Supreme Court's stringent standard for finding state action by nominally private entities and despite the Fourth Circuit's application of that standard to the NCAA in *Arlosoroff,* the Nevada Supreme Court held in *Tarkanian v. NCAA* that the NCAA was a state actor bound by the due process requirements of the Fourteenth Amendment.

Having reached that threshold decision, the Nevada Court proceeded to reject the NCAA's argument that Coach Tarkanian did not possess a constitutionally protected property or liberty interest triggering due process protections.[173] "In our view," the Court observed, "Tarkanian's contractual relationship with UNLV establishes a property interest in continued employment."[174] The NCAA argued that Tarkanian was not deprived of a property interest because his suspension affected only his coaching duties, not his position as a tenured professor of physical education.[175] But the Nevada Supreme Court rejected that argument because in 1977, when he filed suit, Jerry Tarkanian had been a head basketball coach for 28 years, including four years at UNLV. Therefore, the Court wrote, "[c]ontinued employment only as a professor of physical education would be a drastic change from his previous assignment."[176] Thus, Jerry Tarkanian had a constitutionally protected property interest in retaining his coaching job at UNLV.

He also had a constitutionally protected liberty interest in maintaining his professional reputation.[177] To demonstrate a liberty interest, Tarkanian had to show that a right or status he had enjoyed, which state law recognized, "was distinctly altered or extinguished" and that, as a result, he had suffered injury to his reputation.[178] This is known as the "stigma plus" test; the "stigma" is an injury to one's reputation, and the "plus" is a change in one's previous status.[179] In the employment context, the stigma satisfying this test prevented a plaintiff from taking advantage of other employment opportunities. For example, termination on grounds of immorality or dishonesty would satisfy the stigma component of the stigma plus test.[180] The Nevada Supreme Court reasoned that the grounds on which Coach Tarkanian's suspension was based met this standard because they involved allegations of dishonesty.[181] Tarkanian also satisfied the plus portion of the stigma plus test because of the change in status represented by a shift in employment from head men's basketball coach to physical education professor.[182] Thus, the Nevada Supreme Court concluded that Jerry Tarkanian possessed a constitutionally protected liberty interest triggering the due process requirements of the Fourteenth Amendment. The Court wrote,

> Tarkanian's suspension likely would have ended his near-thirty-year career as a head coach and permanently tarnished his reputation. He no doubt possessed a significant interest in the outcome of the NCAA proceedings, an interest which cannot be taken lightly.[183]

Having determined that the NCAA was a state actor and that Jerry Tarkanian possessed liberty and property interests worthy of due process, the Court considered whether the NCAA had denied Tarkanian the procedural due process to which he was entitled under the Fourteenth Amendment. The Court noted that the NCAA investigation of UNLV took two-and-a-half years to complete and produced 58 typed pages of information, including 78 alleged infractions.[184] It added that "Tarkanian not only denied the allegations" but "produced numerous sworn statements directly contradicting the testimony of the NCAA's investigators."[185] Under these circumstances, the Court reasoned, the NCAA's practice of basing factual findings on what the Court termed "predigested information," namely, the investigators' recollections of witness interviews, created "serious due process problems."[186] "The lengthy and far-reaching scope of the NCAA's investigation in this case," the opinion observed, "creates the danger that the enforcement staff may not remember the precise nature of interviews."[187] The opinion continued, "This increases the likelihood that investigators, no matter how pure their intentions, will gloss their testimony with an 'unconscious subjective coloring.'"[188] Even though the NCAA envisioned the investigative process as cooperative, the opinion explained that the process became adversarial in this case, which "enhance[d] the likelihood that predigested information [would] be presented in a fashion favorable to the investigator-witness's position."[189]

To make matters worse, the NCAA relied on its investigators' recollections of witness interviews even though alternative methods were available to ensure due process for Coach Tarkanian. The Court held that "[a]t a minimum, the NCAA should be required to produce written affidavits of persons interviewed by the enforcement staff," so as to mitigate the problem of investigators subjectively coloring the facts.[190] Thus, the Nevada Supreme Court concluded that the NCAA had deprived Jerry Tarkanian of his property interest in continued employment as a basketball coach and of his liberty interest in maintaining his professional reputation, without due process of law, in violation of the Fourteenth Amendment.

Finally, the Court held that although Coach Tarkanian was entitled to recover attorney's fees under 42 U.S.C. § 1988 because state authorities had deprived him of federal constitutional rights, the trial court had erred by awarding him attorney's fees for a phase of the litigation that he had not won.[191] Noting that 42 U.S.C. § 1988 permits only victorious parties to recover attorney's fees, the Court pointed out that Tarkanian had been unsuccessful in his first trial; indeed, the Nevada Supreme Court itself had reversed the decision in the first trial because the NCAA had not been a party to the case.[192] The trial court had also erred in awarding Tarkanian $5,000 more in attorney's fees than the billing records submitted to the trial court supported.[193] Thus, in a minor "victory" for the NCAA, the Nevada Supreme Court sent the *Tarkanian* case back to the trial court for a recalculation of the coach's award of attorney's fees.[194]

Otherwise, *Tarkanian v. NCAA* was a rout in Jerry Tarkanian's favor. Not only would he keep his coaching job at UNLV (much to the NCAA's chagrin) and recover a substantial portion of his legal fees at the Association's expense, but he could take pride in exposing the deficiencies of its enforcement process, exposure that might lead to reforms that would benefit another accused coach in the future. But Tarkanian's victory was short-lived, as the NCAA quickly appealed the Nevada Supreme Court's decision to the United States Supreme Court, which agreed to hear the case. The appeal reached Washington, D.C., in 1988, 15 years after the NCAA investigation of UNLV began.[195] The United States Supreme Court's decision is the subject of chapter 6.

Chapter 6

TAMING THE SHARK

The Supreme Court Decides *NCAA v. Tarkanian*

State Action or No State Action?

When the Supreme Court accepted the *Tarkanian* case, it agreed to determine only whether the NCAA was a "state actor" within the meaning of the Fourteenth Amendment to the United States Constitution. The Court's decision would not determine whether the NCAA's allegations against Coach Tarkanian were true or whether the punishment levied against him was warranted. Other courts would have to answer those questions.

That the question of state action was central to the NCAA's appeal was evident in the brief the Association filed in the Supreme Court. The brief identified the "question presented" in the appeal as "[w]hether the action of the NCAA, in directing one of its members, a state university, to show cause why it should not temporarily suspend an employee from his duties relating to intercollegiate athletics for violating the Association's rules, constitutes state action, where the member university, in compliance with NCAA rules, suspends the coach from coaching."[1] The NCAA's answer to this question, of course, was an emphatic no.

The NCAA used the two-part test for state action articulated in *Lugar v. Edmonson Oil Company* as the basis for its argument.[2] It explained that, under the test, the primary inquiry was whether the private conduct that allegedly caused the deprivation of a constitutional right was "fairly attributable to the State."[3] To complete that inquiry, it was necessary to determine whether (1) the claimed deprivation of a constitutional right resulted from the exercise of a right or privilege that derived from state authority and (2) the actor(s) who perpetrated the violation could be appropriately characterized as state actors.[4]

Accordingly, the NCAA argued in its brief, the Court must "first ask whether the challenged conduct results from state law, such as a statute or regulation, or from a private source."[5] If the source of the conduct was private, then no state action took place.[6] But when the source of the constitutional deprivation was state authority, the NCAA continued, the Court must focus on whether the private party "has acted together with or has obtained significant aid from state officials, or [whether the private party's] conduct is otherwise chargeable to the State."[7] Absent a sufficient "nexus" between the private actor and the state, the Court's inquiry must end because no state action exists.[8]

That nexus is difficult to establish, the NCAA continued, citing several cases after *Arlosoroff v. NCAA*[9] in which federal courts held that the NCAA was not a state actor.[10] According to the NCAA, one could not establish the nexus merely by showing that an existing state statutory scheme permitted the action the private party had taken.[11] Nor could one establish the nexus just by showing that the state acquiesced in the private actor's conduct.[12] Instead, the NCAA argued, for the nexus to exist, "the state must, by its statutes, customs or decisions, order or compel the offending conduct."[13]

Returning to the *Lugar* framework, the NCAA argued that its suspension of Coach Tarkanian was not state action because the suspension did not result from the exercise of a right or privilege flowing from state authority. Specifically, the NCAA contended that the rules UNLV violated, which violations precipitated the Association's punishment of both the university and Coach Tarkanian, were not UNLV's rules or governmental rules but, rather, the rules of a private, voluntary association (i.e., the NCAA) that existed to govern the Association and its members only. Accordingly, Tarkanian's claim that the NCAA's recommendation to UNLV to suspend him amounted to state action failed the first prong of the *Lugar* framework.[14]

Then the NCAA proceeded to the second prong of the *Lugar* framework, arguing that the Association could not be held liable for violating Coach Tarkanian's constitutional rights because he could not appropriately characterize it as a state actor.[15] Therefore, in the NCAA's view, Tarkanian's claim failed the second prong of the *Lugar* test, too. The Association observed that in *Lugar* the Court identified four tests under which it has determined whether a private party is a state actor, namely, the "public function" test, the "state compulsion" test, the "nexus" test, and the "joint action" test.[16] According to the NCAA's brief, the Nevada Supreme Court had held that the NCAA was a state actor under the public function and nexus tests, respectively.[17]

The brief then argued that the NCAA does not perform a "public function" because the governance of college sports is not a traditional governmental function.[18] Moreover, the brief continued, the Nevada Supreme Court erred in holding that the NCAA had disciplined a public employee in this case, because the NCAA "has no authority to compel a member to comply with its rules, or to hire or fire a university employee."[19] Instead, the NCAA maintained, it "simply determines the conditions under which a member may continue to participate in full standing in NCAA activities."[20] Under these circumstances, the Association concluded, the Court could not reasonably find that it had performed a public function just because UNLV responded to its finding that Coach Tarkanian had violated Association rules by suspending him from his coaching position.[21]

The NCAA argued that it was not a state actor under the nexus theory either. It noted that "[s]tate action will not be ascribed to private conduct unless the government has compelled the private decision."[22] The pertinent inquiry is whether a sufficiently close nexus exists between the state and the decision of the private entity to warrant treating the latter's action as that of the state.[23] In the NCAA's view, a nexus was not established merely because, as the Association acknowledged, its membership included "numerous public institutions, which supply at least some of its financial support."[24] Neither those institutions nor their funds, the NCAA emphasized, had compelled its adoption of the rules Coach Tarkanian allegedly violated or the decision by the Committee on Infractions that he had violated them.[25]

Besides, the brief continued, NCAA member institutions themselves, not the Association, were primarily responsible for administering and monitoring their athletic programs and for disciplining their athletic department employees when necessary.[26] "At most," the NCAA argued, "the University 'reacted' to the Committee's decision by independently deciding to suspend Tarkanian."[27] In the NCAA's view, the university's reaction did not establish a nexus between the state of Nevada and the Association's conclusion that UNLV should suspend Tarkanian from his coaching position.[28] Indeed, the NCAA reminded the Court, *Rendell-Baker v. Kohn* and *Blum v. Yaretsky* had established that even regulatory and financial relationships between governmental and private entities do not necessarily establish the nexus making the latter state actors. A private entity becomes a state actor only when "the government regulation or subsidy compels the action taken [by the private entity]."[29]

Thus, the NCAA's brief concluded that (1) the Association's supervision of college sports does not occur under a rule imposed or a privilege granted by the state and (2) such supervision is not sufficiently connected with the state to render the NCAA a state actor.[30] Therefore, the NCAA asked the United States Supreme Court to reverse the Nevada Supreme Court's decision and to dissolve the injunctions the trial court had issued preventing UNLV from enforcing the NCAA's suspension order against Jerry Tarkanian.[31]

For his part, Tarkanian also relied on the *Lugar* decision, but his brief reached a dramatically different conclusion than the NCAA's brief had reached. According to the coach, *Lugar* held that when private parties use state procedures with the "overt, significant assistance of state officials," a court may find state action occurred.[32] In this case, Tarkanian's brief argued, "the State's involvement [wa]s not merely significant, substantial, and pervasive, it [wa]s essential to enforcement of the NCAA's determination and directive that Tarkanian be suspended."[33] That was because the NCAA's bylaws prevented it from suspending Coach Tarkanian directly, so it used a state official, namely, President Donald Baepler of UNLV, to discipline Tarkanian, a state employee who worked in intercollegiate athletics. The NCAA's use of President Baepler to enforce its directive made the NCAA a joint participant in state action.[34]

Coach Tarkanian's brief explained that the "joint participation" (aka "joint action") theory on which it relied differed from the nexus theory often cited by the Supreme Court, in which the question that arose when the plaintiff challenged the action of a private party was whether a nexus existed between that action and the state sufficient to make the private action state action.[35] In *Blum* and *Rendell-Baker*, for example, the plaintiffs challenged the actions of private parties, and the question for the Court was whether a sufficient nexus existed between the state and the private action to make the private parties' action state action.[36] In this case, however, state action was evident because UNLV suspended Coach Tarkanian from coaching. The issue, then, was not whether state action had occurred but whether, in light of the NCAA's use of both state officials and Nevada's authority over its public employees to enforce the NCAA's ostensibly private suspension order, the Association participated jointly in state action, thereby becoming a state actor.[37] Coach Tarkanian's brief, of course, concluded that the NCAA's use of state officials to enforce its directive against a public employee surely made the NCAA a state actor in this case.

The Tarkanian brief also argued that "joint participation" lay in the state of Nevada's delegation to the NCAA of power to discipline public employees and in the state's obligation (through UNLV) to impose on the coach the NCAA's directive suspending him from coaching. According to Tarkanian,

the power to hire, fire, and suspend state employees in Nevada is traditionally the exclusive prerogative of the state.[38] Yet the NCAA Constitution, despite endorsing the principle of "institutional control of intercollegiate athletics," requires that control to be exercised in conformity with the NCAA
Constitution and the Association's bylaws.[39] Moreover, the NCAA Constitution obligates member institutions to "apply and enforce" NCAA "legislation" and threatens to penalize any institution that fails to do so.[40] The Association's bylaws obligate member institutions to comply with its
enforcement system.[41] Therefore, state institutions had to adopt NCAA
standards, procedures, and decisions when disciplining state employees
working in intercollegiate athletics. In this case, the brief concluded,
UNLV's adoption of the NCAA's "standards, procedures, and determina-
tions" when disciplining Coach Tarkanian made the NCAA a "joint participant in the State's suspension of Tarkanian."[42]

Finally, Coach Tarkanian's brief argued that the state of Nevada and the
NCAA were joint participants in his suspension because of the "mutual de-
pendency" that characterized their relationship in this case.[43] In the coach's
view, UNLV depended on the NCAA for the privilege of participating in
"big-time" college sports, and the NCAA depended on member institutions, including UNLV, to enforce its disciplinary rules.[44] In this instance,
the NCAA required UNLV to suspend Coach Tarkanian, and UNLV acquiesced in order to retain its NCAA membership.[45] These circumstances
illustrated that the NCAA's authority in disciplining state employees working in college sports was "decisive, not just advisory"; therefore, in Tarkanian's view, "fundamental fairness demand[ed] that the NCAA give State employees connected with intercollegiate athletics the same due process rights
as the State must give to all other State employees."[46] "Otherwise," Tarkanian's brief argued, "the State would be free to simply evade its Fourteenth
Amendment obligations by transferring its responsibilities to private parties like the NCAA."[47]

According to Tarkanian, the best evidence that the NCAA's authority in
this case was decisive, not advisory, was the amicus curiae brief the NCAA
had filed in the Nevada Supreme Court in 1979 arguing that the Court
should add the Association to Tarkanian's suit against UNLV because (1) it
was an "indispensable party" to the suit concerning UNLV's right to suspend
him and (2) the trial court's injunction against the suspension had effectively
invalidated the NCAA's enforcement proceedings and its suspension order
against the coach.[48] In Coach Tarkanian's view, the "symbiotic relationship"

between the NCAA and UNLV made the NCAA a joint participant in his suspension by UNLV, hence a state actor. Accordingly, the Supreme Court should affirm the Nevada Supreme Court's decision that the NCAA was a state actor in this case.[49]

The NCAA exercised its prerogative to file a reply brief challenging the arguments made in Coach Tarkanian's brief. Specifically, the reply brief sought to rebut the coach's claim that UNLV and the NCAA had participated jointly in his suspension. It contended that under the first prong of the *Lugar* test, state action does not occur merely because a private party "participates" in an activity of the state. Instead, state action occurs only when the private party's participation occurred under the authority of the state.[50] In this case, the NCAA noted, neither Nevada nor any other state influenced or coerced the adoption of the NCAA's rules or its decision that UNLV and Coach Tarkanian had violated them. On the contrary, the rules were the results of votes by members of the Association, and the Association itself enforces them. Therefore, the NCAA did not act under the authority of state law in suspending Jerry Tarkanian.[51]

The reply brief then argued that Coach Tarkanian's claims also failed to satisfy the second prong of the *Lugar* test, because he could not show that the NCAA behaved as a state actor in this case. According to the NCAA, it did not discipline the employees of its member institutions. Instead, in the words of the reply brief, the NCAA "sets minimum standards for the conduct of intercollegiate athletic programs for members wishing to remain in good standing with the Association, and recommends to member institutions appropriate corrective action when athletic personnel fail to comply with those standards."[52] The NCAA is a voluntary association, the reply brief added, so "the decision to accept or reject a recommendation rests exclusively with the member [institution]."[53]

In other words, the NCAA argued, UNLV did not delegate to it authority to discipline UNLV employees; rather, UNLV "reacted" to the NCAA's decision by suspending Coach Tarkanian.[54] After all, the governance of college sports is not a function traditionally or exclusively reserved to government. In this case, as in *Blum*, the NCAA contended, just because the state responds to NCAA action by disciplining an employee does not mean that the NCAA itself has performed a state function.[55] Thus, the reply brief asked the Supreme Court to reverse the decision of the Nevada Supreme Court and dissolve the injunctions preventing the suspension of Coach Tarkanian.[56]

The Supreme Court heard oral arguments in *NCAA v. Tarkanian* on October 5, 1988.[57] The NCAA's advocate was Rex Lee, the dean of the Brigham Young University Law School and formerly solicitor general of the United States. Early on in his argument, one of the justices commented to Lee that it was "a little strange" that the NCAA, which had argued in 1979 that it was an "indispensable party" in this case, was arguing in 1988 that it was not a state actor.[58] The questioner asked, "Is there any tension there?"[59] The question echoed an observation Coach Tarkanian's brief had made, namely, the NCAA's status as an indispensable party in this case reflected its joint action, along with UNLV, in disciplining Tarkanian.

But Rex Lee answered that no tension existed between the NCAA's status as an indispensable party in this case and its claim that its directive to UNLV to suspend Coach Tarkanian was not state action under the Fourteenth Amendment. In Lee's view, the first part of the *Lugar* test "is that you look to the substantive rule that is being enforced in the particular case and inquire into whether that rule has its source in some State authority."[60] The NCAA was an indispensable party in this case because the integrity of its disciplinary rules was at stake, but those rules derived from a purely private source—namely, the membership of the NCAA—not from state statutes or regulations. Therefore, the NCAA could be an indispensable party to this case without being a state actor.

Continuing his argument, Lee analogized this case to *Blum v. Yaretsky.* In *Blum,* he observed, doctors had decided to transfer patients from a medical facility offering them more care to one offering less care, thereby affecting the patients' Medicaid status. Then he noted that in *Blum,* the Supreme Court held that the transfers were not state action because, when the government changed the patients' Medicaid status, it merely responded to the doctors' private decisions. The same thing happened in this case, he concluded; the NCAA, like the doctors in *Blum,* engaged in a private action to which UNLV, like the government in *Blum,* reacted. This action-reaction scenario did not make the NCAA a state actor in this case any more than it had made the doctors state actors in *Blum.*[61]

Las Vegas attorney Samuel Lionel, arguing for Coach Tarkanian, countered that the NCAA was a state actor because UNLV had delegated to it the right to establish and enforce disciplinary rules, as the NCAA had done in this case.[62] More important, for the purposes of this case, UNLV had delegated to the NCAA the right to establish disciplinary standards for state employees working in college sports and to penalize the employees for violating those standards.[63] That was evident, Lionel noted, in President Bae-pler's letter to Coach Tarkanian in September 1977 notifying the coach that UNLV had no choice but to suspend him because neither one of the alternatives—namely, defying the NCAA or resigning from it—was a viable option for the university.[64]

That point prompted a question from the bench. The question hypothesized that United Airlines informed the management of O'Hare Airport that its planes would no longer land there because of safety deficiencies at the airport, which prompted the airport to fire its CEO because it could not continue to function without United's business. The question then asked whether such economic power would make United Airlines a state actor with respect to the firing of the airport manager.[65] Mr. Lionel responded that the hypothetical revealed a "gray area" between a private party exerting pressure on a public entity, which would not make the pressuring party a state actor, and a private party having the capacity to put a public entity "out of business," which might well make the private party a state actor.[66] The NCAA, he noted, could put a university that defied it out of the business of big-time college sports because the NCAA controlled college sports at their most competitive level.[67]

When Mr. Lionel's allotted time ended, Rex Lee strode to the lectern for the several minutes of rebuttal time he had reserved earlier. As counsel for the petitioner, Lee was entitled to make a rebuttal because he was the first lawyer to argue. Lee countered Lionel's claim that UNLV had delegated disciplinary authority over UNLV's athletes and athletic department employees to the NCAA, arguing instead that the university had agreed to abide by NCAA rules but not to delegate the disciplining of state employees or any other governmental function to the NCAA.[68] The best indication of such agreement, Lee asserted, was that if President Baepler had refused to suspend Coach Tarkanian, the NCAA could not have required the suspension; it would have had to consider other sanctions against UNLV instead.[69] Thus, Lee concluded, "All that happened here was a response by a governmental entity to a non-governmental entity."[70]

No State Action

The Supreme Court issued its decision in *NCAA v. Tarkanian* on December 12, 1988. The vote was 5–4, with Chief Justice Rehnquist and Justices Stevens, Blackmun, Scalia, and Kennedy in the majority and Justices White,

Brennan, Marshall, and O'Connor dissenting.[71] The majority concluded that the NCAA was not a state actor; therefore, the Association did not violate Coach Tarkanian's right to due process because, as a private entity, it was not required to provide him with due process of law.

Writing for the majority, Justice John Paul Stevens observed that the Supreme Court could affirm the decisions of the Nevada courts only if the NCAA's involvement in the events leading to Coach Tarkanian's suspension by UNLV amounted to "state action." In other words, the issue in this case was whether UNLV's actions in complying with NCAA rules and recommendations turned the NCAA's conduct into state action. Justice Stevens and the majority concluded that the answer was no.

Justice Stevens began his analysis of the *Tarkanian* case by noting that American law draws a major distinction between "state action," which is subject to judicial scrutiny under the due process clause of the Fourteenth Amendment, and private conduct, which is not subject to such scrutiny no matter how unfair it might be.[72] Quoting one of the Court's own precedents, Stevens observed that in general the protections of the Fourteenth Amendment do not apply to "private conduct abridging individual rights."[73] As a practical matter, this meant that a private entity could discipline violators of its rules without giving them notice of the claims against them or a chance to present their "side of the story," which are the minimal requirements of due process. State actors, in contrast, must provide due process, although the process due could vary from notice and a brief hearing, in the case of a student who is suspended from school for a short time, to the full panoply of procedures attendant to a criminal prosecution.

In Justice Stevens's view, the distinction between private action and state action was necessary in a country like the United States, which adhered to the principles of limited government and individual freedom. Justice Stevens observed that this distinction preserves individual freedom by "limiting the reach of federal law" and by refusing to assign to government responsibility for conduct it cannot control.[74] That, he noted, is why Congress limited liability under 42 U.S.C. § 1983 (the portion of the Civil Rights Act of 1871 providing a remedy for the violations of civil rights) to violators who acted "under color of state law," namely, persons who occupied their positions under state authority and who represented a state (or municipality, school district, etc.) in some official capacity.[75]

In this case, Stevens noted, Coach Tarkanian argued that UNLV delegated its own functions to the NCAA, clothing the Association with the au-

thority to both adopt rules governing UNLV's athletic programs and enforce those rules on behalf of UNLV.[76] Stevens also noted the Nevada
Supreme Court holding that UNLV had delegated its authority over personnel decisions to the NCAA; hence the Association and the university
had acted jointly to deprive Tarkanian of liberty and property interests,
thereby making them both "state actors" within the meaning of the Fourteenth Amendment.[77] Under these circumstances, Justice Stevens continued, this case was "the mirror image of the traditional state action case,
where a private party has taken the decisive step that harmed the plaintiff,
and the question is whether the State was sufficiently involved to treat that
decisive conduct as state action."[78] Stevens observed that in the traditional
state action case, the private party's decision could be state action if "the
State create[d] a legal framework governing the conduct, delegate[d] its authority to the private actor, or knowingly accept[ed] the benefits derived
from unconstitutional behavior."[79] In other words, Justice Stevens reasoned,
the question for a court in the customary state action case is whether the
state "provided a mantle of authority that enhanced the power of the harm-
causing individual actor."[80]

But in this case, the state actor, UNLV, suspended Coach Tarkanian.
Therefore, according to Justice Stevens, the question for the justices here
was not whether UNLV had participated to a substantial degree in NCAA
activities but, instead, whether UNLV's suspension of Coach Tarkanian,
carried out in compliance with NCAA rules, converted the NCAA's conduct
into state action.[81] The NCAA was a private entity, Stevens emphasized, because "the source of the legislation adopted by the NCAA is not Nevada,
but the collective membership, speaking through an organization that is independent of any particular State."[82]

Stevens acknowledged that the NCAA could be a state actor if UNLV,
by embracing the NCAA's rules, transformed them into the rules of the state
of Nevada. But, he hastened to add, that transformation did not occur here
because UNLV had the right either to cancel its membership in the NCAA
and free itself from the Association's rules or to remain a member but use
the Association's legislative process to change the rules it opposed.[83] As a result, Stevens concluded, "[n]either UNLV's decision to adopt the NCAA's
standards nor its minor role in their formulation is a sufficient reason for
concluding that the NCAA was acting under color of Nevada law when it
promulgated standards governing athlete recruitment, eligibility, and academic performance."[84] Besides, he added, UNLV did not delegate to the

NCAA the authority to punish Jerry Tarkanian. Only UNLV could punish the coach, and if it failed to do so in accordance with the NCAA's directive, UNLV itself, not Coach Tarkanian, would be subject to NCAA sanctions.[85]

Moreover, Justice Stevens noted, UNLV and the NCAA could hardly be characterized as partners in the Tarkanian matter. "During the several years that the NCAA investigated the alleged violations" by Tarkanian, he wrote, "the NCAA and UNLV acted much more like adversaries than like partners engaged in a dispassionate search for the truth."[86] Therefore, in Stevens's view, the NCAA was not an "agent" of UNLV in the Tarkanian investigation but was "more correctly characterized as an agent of its remaining members which, as competitors of UNLV, had an interest in the effective and even-handed enforcement of the NCAA's recruitment standards."[87] In support of that conclusion, he pointed out that the NCAA lacked the authority to discipline directly Jerry Tarkanian or any other UNLV employee and that the confidential report Brock Dixon submitted to UNLV president Donald Baepler had presented options other than suspending the coach.[88] "UNLV could have retained Tarkanian and risked additional sanctions, perhaps even expulsion from the NCAA," Stevens wrote, "or it could have withdrawn voluntarily from the Association."[89]

Then, perhaps anticipating the criticism that those choices amounted to no choice at all, Justice Stevens added that even if the NCAA's power were so great UNLV felt obliged to obey the Association's orders and suspend Tarkanian, "it does not follow that such a private party is therefore acting under color of state law."[90] Indeed, that conclusion would be "ironic," he observed, considering UNLV had "steadfastly opposed" the NCAA's decision to suspend Coach Tarkanian and had insisted suspension was unwarranted.[91] Thus, Justice Stevens rejected Tarkanian's contention that the NCAA had acted under color of state law in suspending him, reasoning instead that "[i]t would be more appropriate to conclude that UNLV has conducted its athletic program under color of the policies adopted by the NCAA, rather than that those policies were developed and enforced under color of Nevada law."[92]

Based on this reasoning, the Supreme Court majority determined that the NCAA was not a state actor in this case and hence was not required to provide Jerry Tarkanian with due process during its investigation of his basketball program. Accordingly, the Court reversed the decision of the Nevada Supreme Court and remanded (i.e., returned) the case to that court for further proceedings.

Joint Action as State Action

Justice Byron White, writing for the four dissenters, accepted the majority's conclusion that this case was different from many previous state action cases the Court had decided, because in this instance, unlike in the prior cases, "the final act that caused the harm to Tarkanian was committed, not by a private party, but by a party [UNLV] conceded to be a state actor."[93] But that was where White's agreement with the Stevens opinion ended, as was reflected in White's framing of the question posed by the *Tarkanian* case. "The question here," Justice White wrote, "is whether the NCAA acted jointly with UNLV in suspending Tarkanian, and thereby also became a state actor. I would hold that it did."[94] Despite conceding that this case was different, White observed that it was not unique: in two prior cases, *Adickes v. S. H. Kress & Co.*[95] and *Dennis v. Sparks,*[96] the Court had answered the question whether a private party could be a state actor even though the final or decisive act that injured the plaintiff was the act of a state official.[97] "In both cases," Justice White wrote, "we held that the private parties could be found to be state actors if they were 'jointly engaged with state officials in the challenged action.'"[98]

In the *Dennis* case, White noted, a state trial judge enjoined the extraction of minerals from oil leases owned by the plaintiff. The plaintiff appealed, and the appellate court dissolved the injunction, which it concluded the trial judge had issued illegally. The plaintiff then filed another suit under 42 U.S.C. § 1983, alleging that the trial judge had conspired with (i.e., taken a bribe from) the private corporation that had sought the original, illegal injunction so as to deprive the plaintiff of property (two years of oil production) without due process.[99] White recalled the Supreme Court's unanimous holding that the private parties involved—namely, the corporation and its individual owner—were state actors in this episode because they were "willful participant[s] in joint action with the State or its agents" (i.e., the trial judge).[100]

Similarly, White recounted that in *Adickes* the Court had held that relief was warranted for a plaintiff under 42 U.S.C. § 1983 if she could show that a private party and a police officer had "reached an understanding" to cause her arrest on illegitimate grounds.[101] The plaintiff in *Adickes* was a white teacher who had attempted to patronize a department store lunch counter in Hattiesburg, Mississippi, with her black students. The white store owner prohibited the teacher from sitting with her students because Mississippi law at that time prohibited whites and blacks from sitting together in restaurants and other public accommodations. Later, when the teacher left the store, a police officer arrested her on a vagrancy charge. She alleged that the store owner conspired with the police officer to arrest her.

Applying the rule of *Dennis* and *Adickes* to the present case, Justice White determined that "the NCAA acted jointly with UNLV in suspending Tarkanian."[102] He based this determination on three separate facts. First, UNLV suspended Coach Tarkanian for violating NCAA rules, which UNLV had adopted when it joined the NCAA.[103] Second, as a condition of its NCAA membership, UNLV had agreed that the Association would conduct the enforcement hearings arising out of the alleged violation of its rules. Therefore, the NCAA had conducted the hearings that the Nevada Supreme Court concluded had violated Tarkanian's due process rights.[104]

Third, UNLV and the NCAA had agreed that the findings of fact the NCAA (in the form of its Committee on Infractions, or COI) made at its hearings would bind UNLV. This agreement was reflected in the report UNLV vice president Brock Dixon sent to president Donald Baepler after conducting an internal hearing to determine whether the university should follow the NCAA's directive to suspend Coach Tarkanian. Justice White noted Mr. Dixon's statement in his report to President Baepler that by accepting NCAA membership, UNLV had agreed to accept the NCAA's "findings of fact as in some way superior to [its] own."[105] "By the terms of UNLV's membership in the NCAA," White observed, "the NCAA's findings were final and not subject to further review by any other body, and it was for that reason that UNLV suspended Tarkanian, despite concluding that many of those findings were wrong."[106] "In short," he continued, "it was the NCAA's findings that Tarkanian had violated NCAA rules, made at NCAA-conducted hearings, all of which were agreed to by UNLV in its membership agreement with the NCAA, that resulted in Tarkanian's suspension by UNLV."[107] Under these circumstances, Justice White concluded, the NCAA and UNLV were jointly responsible for the suspension of Jerry Tarkanian, hence the NCAA was a state actor in this instance.[108]

In reaching this conclusion, White rejected the majority's reliance on the NCAA's lack of power to punish the coach directly as indicative that the Association had not behaved as a state actor here. Returning to the *Dennis* analogy, he noted similar circumstances existing in that case because "the private parties did not have any power to issue an injunction against the plaintiff."[109] Instead, "[o]nly the trial judge, using his authority granted under state law, could impose the injunction."[110] Nevertheless, the Court had held unanimously in *Dennis* that the private parties involved were state actors because their joint action with the trial judge produced the unauthorized injunction imposed on the plaintiff.

White also rejected as irrelevant Justice Stevens's contention that UNLV was free to withdraw from the NCAA instead of obeying the Association's directive to suspend Tarkanian. Rather than argue that withdrawal was so unrealistic as to not be a viable option, White noted that UNLV did not withdraw from the NCAA and hence was required to honor the latter's directive to suspend Tarkanian.[111] For the same reason, he also rejected Stevens's argument that UNLV and the NCAA could not have acted jointly in this matter because they behaved more like adversaries than partners throughout the litigation. In White's view, UNLV's reluctance to suspend its highly successful basketball coach and its belief that the facts did not warrant his suspension were irrelevant because, in the final analysis, UNLV agreed to follow the NCAA's directive to suspend Tarkanian, thereby insuring joint action between the university and the Association against the coach.[112]

Justice White illustrated his point by reasoning that if UNLV had refused to suspend Tarkanian and the NCAA had reacted by imposing sanctions on UNLV, "it would be hard indeed to find any state action that harmed Tarkanian."[113] But then he observed that the preceding scenario was not what occurred here. Instead, UNLV suspended Tarkanian "because it embraced the NCAA rules governing conduct of its athletic program and adopted the results of the hearings conducted by the NCAA concerning Tarkanian, as it had agreed that it would."[114] Consequently, Justice White concluded, "the NCAA acted jointly with UNLV, and therefore is a state actor."[115] Thus, at least in this case, which featured a public university, Byron White would have required the NCAA to provide Jerry Tarkanian with due process during its investigation of his basketball program.

Had this view commanded a majority of the Court, the NCAA would have been bound by the requirements of due process when drafting its rules and enforcing them against public universities. The rules would have to be rational; they could not be arbitrary or capricious in substance, and the process for enforcing them would have to include notice of the violations alleged and a hearing in which to challenge the allegations. Legally, the NCAA would have had to honor these requirements only when dealing with public colleges. Practically, though, it would have had to honor them in dealing with its private members, too, or face an outcry that would have threatened its continued existence. But Justice Stevens's view prevailed, and the NCAA's enforcement program is free from constitutional restrictions.

Justice Stevens's view reflected a trend begun during the chief justiceship of Warren Burger (1969–86) and continued during the chief justiceship of William Rehnquist (1986–2005), namely, to significantly restrict the number and scope of private decisions deemed to be "state action" that were subject to constitutional protections and, hence, judicial scrutiny. That trend coincided with the conservative judicial philosophy espoused by both the Burger Court and the Rehnquist Court. The Burger Court sought to reduce the sphere of state action by reinterpreting both the public function theory and the nexus theory of state action.[116]

Recall from chapter 5 that public function theory treats private entities performing essentially public, or governmental, functions as state actors for due process purposes.[117] Under this theory, as interpreted by federal courts before the *Arlosoroff* decision in 1984 (see chapter 5), the NCAA could be a state actor because it regulated intercollegiate athletics, a function that, without the Association, would likely fall to government to perform. Nexus theory, however, imposes due process requirements on private entities when sufficient "points of contact" exist between the private entity and the state to justify treating the former as a state actor.[118] Under this theory, as interpreted prior to *Arlosoroff,* the NCAA could be a state actor because approximately half of the member institutions it regulated were public. But the Supreme Court limited the reach of both theories during the 1970s and the 1980s. It restricted the public function theory to traditional public functions historically reserved exclusively to government and required some form of affirmative action or coercion of a private entity by the state to find a nexus between the two.[119]

In 1974 the Court reduced the scope of public function theory by holding that a private entity can be a state actor only when it exercises "powers traditionally exclusively reserved to the states."[120] Four years later, the Court cut the nexus theory down to size, holding that a state is responsible for the act of a private entity only when the state compels an unconstitutional act. Mere acquiescence by the state in a private act does not convert that act into state action.[121] These decisions set the stage for *Rendell-Baker v. Kohn* and *Blum v. Yaretsky* in 1982 (see chapter 5).[122] Taken together, *Rendell-Baker* and *Blum* stand for the proposition that state financial support of a private entity, without some other state coercion or encouragement to commit an objectionable act, does not constitute the state involvement necessary to convert the private action to state action.[123]

The Supreme Court's restricted view of the public function and nexus theories was evident in Justice Stevens's majority opinion in *Tarkanian*. Using the public function theory, he reasoned that UNLV had not delegated any governmental powers to the NCAA. Indeed, the only power the NCAA possessed was the power to impose sanctions on UNLV if UNLV did not honor the NCAA's directive to suspend Coach Tarkanian. The power to suspend Tarkanian belonged solely to UNLV because NCAA rules prohibited the Association from taking direct disciplinary action against a coach or any other employee of a member institution.[124] UNLV could defy the NCAA by retaining Tarkanian, although by doing so it would risk incurring heavier penalties from the Association. Because UNLV had not delegated any governmental powers to the NCAA, Justice Stevens concluded, the NCAA did not possess powers traditionally reserved exclusively to a state, hence it was not a state actor under the public function theory.[125] Using the nexus theory, Justice Stevens reasoned that UNLV and the NCAA were not sufficiently intertwined in the suspension of Coach Tarkanian to make the NCAA's action state action. UNLV's persistent opposition to the suspension throughout the protracted litigation meant that the interests of the university and the Association were too adverse for a nexus to have existed between them.[126]

But the Stevens view was hardly an inevitable conclusion, as evidenced by the 5–4 vote in the case. Precedents also supported Justice White's view, which was grounded in the "joint participant" (aka "joint action" or "symbiotic relationship") theory, an offspring of the nexus theory. Under the joint participant theory, courts can find private parties to be state actors when those private parties engage jointly with state officials in actions the Constitution prohibits.[127] The crucial determinant of state action under this theory is the degree to which the state's action is linked with that of the private party; by acting jointly with the state, the private party becomes a state actor.

The triumph of the Stevens view is unfortunate because Justice White's view reflects a better understanding of the NCAA's power in rule making and rule enforcement. Justice White recognized that the NCAA calls the tune and that colleges dance to it because without NCAA membership they cannot reap the psychic or the financial rewards associated with athletic commerce. Therefore, he knew it was naive, if not disingenuous, to claim that UNLV had acted alone in suspending Coach Tarkanian and that the

NCAA's conduct was not attributable to the state of Nevada. Put another way, he understood that UNLV had suspended Tarkanian at the NCAA's insistence for fear of sacrificing its good standing as a member and that this joint action warranted treating the NCAA as a state actor. Thus, UNLV's opposition, throughout the litigation, to suspending Tarkanian did not make UNLV and the NCAA too adverse to be partners in the suspension decision. Instead, as Justice White recognized, UNLV's opposition was powerful evidence of the NCAA's power to compel UNLV, however grudgingly, to follow orders.

Dancing to the NCAA's Tune

As a result of the *Tarkanian* decision, colleges still dance to the NCAA's tune, and their students and employees continue to be denied sufficient legal protections in the enforcement process. That was a consistent theme in law review commentaries about *Tarkanian* published within several years after the decision. For example, one commentary noted that in *Tarkanian,* the Supreme Court "affirmed the NCAA's broad regulatory power, while taking away the individual's constitutional protections."[128] Striking a similar theme, another commentary observed that after Tarkanian "it seems the creature [i.e., the NCAA] does control its masters [i.e., the member institutions]."[129]

That accretion of power to the NCAA was regrettable, another post-*Tarkanian* commentary noted, because individuals and institutions under investigation by the NCAA had several liberty interests at stake. After *Tarkanian* the NCAA could direct a member institution to terminate a coach or suspend a student and hence could deprive that institution of a liberty interest in freedom of association without due process.[130] A coach who was terminated or suspended in connection with an NCAA investigation had a liberty interest triggered by the stigma associated with termination or suspension, which stigma could limit or even eliminate future employment options in coaching.[131] An athlete whom the NCAA declared ineligible to compete arguably had a liberty interest in engaging in a significant human activity or in attempting to pursue a career in professional sports, which pursuit, at least in football and basketball, usually requires college-level participation.[132]

Property interests could also be at stake for institutions and individuals targeted by NCAA investigations. For institutions, the likely property interest to be affected was revenues from television appearances by their athletic teams, most notably, their football and men's basketball teams. For coaches, the likely deprivation of property would be the loss of a livelihood, including the future income from that livelihood, whereas for athletes, the presumed deprivation would be the loss of an athletic scholarship (i.e., a free college education) or a future career in professional sports.[133]

Despite the weighty interests, the *Tarkanian* majority absolved the NCAA of responsibility for providing due process to the targets of its investigations. In the view of a third critical commentary, this absolution for the NCAA resulted from the majority's failure to conduct "the pertinent inquiry" in the *Tarkanian* case.[134] That inquiry was, "How much did the NCAA participate in UNLV's suspension of [Coach] Tarkanian"?[135] The author answered this question by first agreeing with the Court majority that the NCAA could not have suspended the coach without the participation of UNLV, because the NCAA, acting alone, was powerless to suspend him. But instead of inferring from this premise that UNLV acted alone in suspending Tarkanian, as the Court majority had done, the author concluded that UNLV and the NCAA acted jointly in suspending Jerry Tarkanian from coaching.[136]

According to this commentary, the *Tarkanian* majority "manipulated" the public function theory. The majority conceded that a state may delegate authority to a private party, making the latter a state actor. Yet it found that UNLV had made no such delegation, even though the parties agreed that by joining the NCAA, UNLV had delegated to the NCAA its authority to investigate alleged rules violations and to make findings resulting from those investigations. By joining the NCAA, UNLV had also agreed to be bound by and to enforce NCAA findings and directives.[137] The author added that besides misapplying the public function theory, the *Tarkanian* majority erred in its use of the nexus theory. Specifically, the majority evaluated the nexus between UNLV and the NCAA in the context of UNLV's decision to join the NCAA, reasoning that as one institution, UNLV had played such a minor role in creating NCAA rules that no nexus existed between the state of Nevada and the NCAA. Instead, this commentary concluded, the majority should have examined "the nexus between [UNLV and the NCAA] with regard to UNLV's suspension of Tarkanian."[138]

Another commentary challenged the majority's reasoning that because both UNLV and the Nevada attorney general's office opposed the suspension, it was unreasonable to conclude that the NCAA's directive to suspend Tarkanian was "state action."[139] Even if UNLV and the NCAA were adversaries in this litigation, the commentary observed, they had agreed that the latter would have authority over enforcement proceedings against UNLV employees, who were also employees of the state of Nevada.[140] Most important, UNLV had executed the NCAA's directive to suspend Jerry Tarkanian.[141] This commentary also challenged the Court majority's reasoning that UNLV could have withdrawn from the NCAA rather than suspend Tarkanian. According to the author, UNLV's ability to withdraw from the NCAA was irrelevant because UNLV did not do so, choosing instead to enforce the NCAA's directive.[142] Thus, he concluded that after *Tarkanian*, the NCAA was the master rather than the servant of the member institutions that created it.[143]

Other commentaries also focused on the adversary status of UNLV and the NCAA during the *Tarkanian* litigation, but unlike the Court majority, which inferred that UNLV had acted alone in suspending the coach, the commentaries concluded that this "adversariness" demonstrated "UNLV's delegation of authority to the NCAA."[144] According to one commentary, "The only reason that UNLV suspended Tarkanian was its reluctant acknowledgment that it had delegated to the NCAA the power to act as the ultimate arbiter of the matter."[145] Another commentary agreed, noting that the Court majority had focused on the wrong target in relying on the adversary status of UNLV and the NCAA during the *Tarkanian* litigation. In so doing, this commentary noted, the Court missed the key point in the case, namely, that "ultimately, UNLV, a state actor, agreed to take the action the NCAA wanted by suspending Tarkanian."[146] In other words, UNLV had danced to the NCAA's tune in suspending Coach Tarkanian, thereby making the NCAA's action in ordering the suspension state action.

Still another commentary on the *Tarkanian* decision strayed from the decision itself to examine the NCAA's enforcement procedures as of 1992. It posited that despite the Supreme Court's decision in *Tarkanian*, individuals and institutions under investigation by the NCAA have several liberty and property interests at stake during those investigations.[147] Therefore, the author argued that NCAA enforcement proceedings should provide due process as reflected in a list of procedures Judge Henry Friendly of the United States Court of Appeals for the Second Circuit had identified in a 1975 article as necessary for fair administrative hearings.[148] These procedures included

1. an unbiased tribunal;
2. notice of the proposed action and the grounds asserted for it;

3. an opportunity to present reasons why the proposed action should not be taken;
4. the right to present evidence, including calling witnesses;
5. the right to know the opposing evidence;
6. the right to cross-examine witnesses;
7. a decision based exclusively on the evidence presented;
8. an opportunity to be represented by counsel;
9. a requirement that the tribunal prepare a record of the evidence presented;
10. a requirement that the tribunal prepare a record of written findings of fact and the reasons for its decision;
11. an open hearing (i.e., attendance by the public permitted).[149]

According to the author of the 1992 commentary, the NCAA's enforcement regulations at that time satisfied six of Judge Friendly's requirements for due process in an administrative proceeding: (1) notice of the proposed action and the grounds asserted for it, (2) an opportunity to present reasons why the proposed action should not be taken, (3) the right to know opposing evidence, (4) a decision based exclusively on the evidence presented, (5) representation by counsel, and (6) a requirement that the tribunal prepare written findings of fact and the reasons for its decision.[150] The five components of Judge Friendly's list that NCAA regulations did not include were (1) an unbiased tribunal, (2) the right to call witnesses on one's behalf, (3) the right to cross-examine witnesses called by the opponent, (4) a requirement that the tribunal prepare a record of the evidence presented, and (5) an open hearing.[151] The author recommended that the NCAA adopt items 1, 2, and 4, respectively.

According to the author, the NCAA should replace the members of the Committee on Infractions and the Infractions Appeals Committee (IAC) with impartial judges, "[b]ecause it is likely that challenges to NCAA regulations would dramatically decrease if it appeared that subjects under investigation were treated fairly."[152] Accordingly, the author continued, "the NCAA should incur the increased administrative costs and create an unbiased tribunal."[153] Also recommended were changes giving parties to NCAA enforcement proceedings a chance to call all relevant witnesses and requiring the NCAA to provide a transcript of the enforcement hearing to the accused institution. In the author's view, "[T]hese investigative procedures will increase the fairness of the investigative proceedings without creating substantial administrative problems."[154]

But the author declined to recommend permitting cross-examination or attendance by the public at NCAA hearings. Cross-examination would be difficult to achieve because the NCAA lacked the authority to subpoena unwilling witnesses, and it would be ill-advised because lawyers could use it as a delaying tactic.[155] Open hearings would be a mistake because of the considerable public interest and media attention that sometimes surround NCAA hearings. The author wrote, in this regard,

> NCAA investigations often involve high-profile sports programs that are frequently featured in newspaper and television stories, capturing the public's attention. This disproportionate amount of publicity surrounding NCAA proceedings enhances the negative effects of open hearings, distinguishing them from most other administrative proceedings.[156]

Interestingly, this commentary's rejection of open NCAA enforcement hearings conflicted with the conclusion reached by a commission the Association had appointed in 1991 to examine its enforcement process. The Lee Committee (named for its chair, former solicitor general Rex Lee, who had argued for the NCAA against Jerry Tarkanian in the Supreme Court) had proposed opening NCAA hearings to the public.[157] The Lee Committee was the brainchild of NCAA executive director Dick Schultz and a response to the criticism the NCAA had received because of revelations about its enforcement process that surfaced during and after the *Tarkanian* litigation.[158]

To its credit, the NCAA adopted some of the Lee Committee's recommendations for ensuring due process, such as by establishing (1) a preliminary notice of impending investigation (NOI); (2) a summary disposition procedure in certain cases of major rules violations; (3) an appellate body, the IAC; (4) a mechanism for expanded public reporting of COI decisions; and (5) a conflict-of-interest policy for members of the NCAA's enforcement staff.[159] But the NCAA did not adopt all of the Lee Committee's recommendations. The major recommendations that it rejected had urged it to (1) establish a group of former judges to act as hearing officers who would resolve factual disputes in enforcement cases before the COI imposed penalties and (2) open up COI hearings to the public except when highly confidential information was being presented.[160]

Thus, even after the Supreme Court, in *Tarkanian,* had absolved the NCAA of any duty to provide due process in its enforcement proceedings, the Association continued to feel pressure from several quarters to enhance the fairness of those proceedings voluntarily. That pressure continued through the 1990s and into the new millennium, and it included a hearing held by the House Judiciary Committee's Subcommittee on the Constitution in September 2004. The opening remarks of the subcommittee's chair, Representative Steve Chabot (R-OH), reflected the concern of some lawmakers that despite having made progress toward due process in enforcement proceedings, the NCAA had not gone far enough to achieve it. Mr. Chabot noted that in the wake of the Lee Committee's report, the Association had "strengthened its appellate system for infractions, providing more protections for schools, athletes, and coaches."[161] But, he added, it had not adopted "the 1991 study's recommendations to hire independent judges to hear infractions cases and to open infractions hearings to the public."[162]

Representative Spencer Bachus (R-AL) delivered perhaps the most significant opening statement of the hearing. It reflected the frustration with the NCAA's enhanced clout and diminished need for accountability after *Tarkanian* that was evident in the law review commentaries described earlier. Representative Bachus stated,

> I think that anybody that has studied the NCAA readily realizes that the athletes are not members nor are they invited to be members, but the greatest number of decisions affect more athletes than anyone else. Athletes are not members, and they have no input, but they are controlled.[163]

He might have added that coaches are not members of the Association either.

Frustration with the NCAA's enforcement process was also the theme of the testimony of B. David Ridpath, who, in 2004, was a professor of sports administration at Mississippi State University. In 2001 Ridpath had lost his job as assistant athletic director for compliance and student services at Marshall University. Marshall reassigned him to another post as a "corrective action" in response to an NCAA investigation of the university's employment program for athletes, which violated Association rules (see chapter 1). Ridpath's reassignment resulted not from any wrongdoing by him but, instead, from Marshall's eagerness to convince the NCAA that it was contrite and determined to mend its ways. His subsequent lawsuit against Marshall alleged that although he was not involved in any violations of NCAA rules and was unaware of the employment scheme, "he became a convenient scapegoat for MU when his vigorous defense of the University [which counsel for Marshall had encouraged him to present] . . . [angered] the NCAA Committee on Infractions."[164]

In response to a question from Chairman Chabot, Dr. Ridpath offered several suggestions for changing the NCAA's enforcement process. One suggestion was "opening up the infractions and hearing process to the public, making those hearing transcripts public, letting the media participate in that."[165] Dr. Ridpath's other suggestions were "an independent Committee on Infractions, [excluding] anybody from [NCAA] member institutions" and "[d]ue process for everyone involved in an NCAA investigation," including a university employee whose employer might use the employee as a scapegoat for wrongdoing by superiors.[166]

Gary Roberts, then a professor at Tulane University Law School, who also testified before the subcommittee, agreed with Dr. Ridpath's call for more independence among the decision makers in the NCAA's enforcement process. Regarding the staffers who investigate alleged violations, he observed, "Were there to be a substantially larger and more stable and highly paid professional staff of experienced investigators, the likelihood of detecting violations would be greater, the confidence of everyone in the thoroughness and reliability of investigations would be greater, and the need to rely on 'rats,' to cut corners, and to employ questionable tactics would be greatly diminished."[167] Regarding the committees that decide NCAA infractions cases, Professor Roberts stated, "I believe that both the Committee on Infractions and the Infractions Appeals Committee in Division I should be composed of paid professional jurists—not necessarily current or former public judges, but highly respected individuals with training in law and dispute resolution whose motives, knowledge, and skill could not possibly be doubted."[168] He added that these "judges" would have more time than the current, volunteer members of the COI have to conduct hearings, so the hearings would not have to be as "streamlined" as they must be when conducted by volunteers.[169]

Professor Roberts acknowledged that implementing his suggested change would require a financial investment by the NCAA. "But with billions of dollars flowing through Division I college athletics," he continued, "the level of expenditure needed to upgrade the enforcement process to an appropriate level would be a relatively tiny investment in order to achieve fairness, justice, and public confidence in the system."[170] Therefore, he recommended that Congress "urge and even pressure the NCAA to invest far greater resources in its enforcement process" in order to expand the size and improve the compensation of the enforcement staff and establish "a 'judiciary' of paid and properly trained 'judges.'"[171] Finally, Professor Roberts told the lawmakers,

> I believe Congress should fully explore and structure a mechanism for the NCAA enforcement staff to obtain search warrants and subpoenas from federal courts, which would enable it to obtain evidence and compel testimony from reluctant or unwilling individuals under penalty of perjury. . . . [Then the NCAA could compel witnesses to testify and] witnesses would not have to be coddled with promises of being insulated from exposure or cross-examination.[172]

Thus, the Supreme Court's decision in *NCAA v. Tarkanian* was hardly the last word on due process in NCAA enforcement proceedings. After *Tarkanian*, courts could not require the NCAA to observe due process during those proceedings, but advocates for due process in NCAA proceedings nevertheless pursued that goal vigorously in academic journals and congressional testimony. Therefore, despite its disappointing result for the cause of fairness in NCAA enforcement cases, the *Tarkanian* decision has been valuable in clarifying the concept of due process and in stimulating considerable commentary about what process should be due in the NCAA disciplinary context. Chapter 7 presents a model of due process for the NCAA to follow and recommends that Congress enact legislation requiring the NCAA to implement it.

Chapter 7

WHAT PROCESS IS DUE?

The Implications of *NCAA v. Tarkanian*

Winning the Battle, Losing the War

A New Investigation Begins

Jerry Tarkanian lost his war with the NCAA in the United States Supreme Court, but he won the battle to keep his job at UNLV. After the High Court ruled, the case returned to a state trial court in Nevada, which vacated its previous ruling enjoining the NCAA from forcing UNLV to suspend Tarkanian. Still, the Nevada trial court left its injunction against UNLV intact, because UNLV was a state actor required to observe due process but had suspended Tarkanian without doing so.[1] The injunction prevented UNLV from suspending the coach, which, of course, UNLV did not want to do anyway. As for the NCAA, it was free from the strictures of due process, but its determined effort to banish Jerry Tarkanian from college basketball had failed. He would remain the men's basketball coach at UNLV for several more years.

Meanwhile, the NCAA was not finished investigating Tarkanian and his Runnin' Rebels. In 1987, after a talented but troubled basketball recruit named Lloyd Daniels, whom one of Tarkanian's assistant coaches had adopted as his ward, was arrested in a North Las Vegas crack house, the NCAA initiated a new investigation of the UNLV men's basketball program.[2] In December 1990, after spending three years investigating UNLV, the NCAA alleged that the men's basketball program had committed 22 violations of Association rules and had engaged in seven instances of "unethical conduct," the most serious charge the NCAA can level against an institution.[3] Still, according to journalist Don Yeager, Jerry Tarkanian survived the "Daniels episode" because "there was enough doubt about what [UNLV] President Robert Maxson knew and had approved and what the NCAA knew and had approved about the guardianship situation that this one couldn't be laid entirely at Tarkanian's feet."[4]

What the crack house could not accomplish, however, the hot tub did. The beginning of the end for Jerry Tarkanian at UNLV came on May 26, 1991, when the *Las Vegas Review-Journal* published a picture in which three young men who had played on UNLV's 1990 national championship team were drinking beer, sitting in a hot tub, and playing two-on-two pickup basketball with a man the players knew as "Sam" Perry. "Sam" was actually Richard "the Fixer" Perry, who had served a prison sentence for "fixing" the outcome of horse races during the mid-1970s.[5] Perry had also been the "brains" behind a point-shaving scandal in 1978–79 featuring members of the Boston College men's basketball team; in exchange for his guilty plea, Perry received one year of probation and a $5,000 fine.[6]

The players' association with Perry proved to be Tarkanian's undoing at UNLV. In light of Perry's past, his friendship with UNLV players was too unsavory to bear, even for a gambling town where unsavory pasts are routinely discarded, like clothes that no longer fit. This time, responsibility fell directly at Coach Tarkanian's feet, because the players were in his charge and gamblers were considered a constant threat to the integrity of college sports. He resigned at UNLV effective at the end of the 1991–92 basketball season.[7] After leaving UNLV, Tarkanian coached briefly in the National Basketball Association, then returned to the college game in 1995, becoming head coach of the men's basketball team at his alma mater, California State University, Fresno (Fresno State). He retired from coaching in 2002, at the age of 71, having won 778 games in the NCAA's Division I, then one of the top ten records in the history of college basketball.[8]

Despite Coach Tarkanian's resignation from UNLV in 1991, the NCAA proceeded with the case it had brought against the university late in 1990. The Association scheduled a hearing before the COI regarding the recruitment of Lloyd Daniels. But before the hearing could occur, several UNLV employees who were targets of the investigation (including Tarkanian) demanded that the Association forgo its customary procedures and instead comply with a recently enacted Nevada law calling for due process in NCAA investigations of Nevada colleges.[9] The NCAA replied that it could not follow the Nevada law without violating its established enforcement procedures, which applied to its members in every other state. The result would be that the Association could not enforce its rules uniformly nationwide in the future. Thus, the NCAA sued, seeking an injunction sparing it from having to honor the Nevada due process law in its enforcement action against UNLV.[10]

States Respond to the *Tarkanian* Decision

Nevada and several other states responded to the Supreme Court's decision in *NCAA v. Tarkanian* by enacting a statute requiring due process in NCAA investigations of colleges located within their respective borders. The Nevada statute, which the NCAA challenged in federal court in Nevada in November 1991, required "national collegiate athletic associations" (principally, the NCAA) to follow "minimum procedural standards," which it proceeded to identify.[11] They included (1) notice of the time, place, and nature of hearings; the governing rules; the violations alleged; and the factual basis for each violation; (2) discovery at least 30 days beforehand of all evidence to be used at the hearing; (3) an impartial presiding officer who was prohibited from having ex parte contact with any party to the proceeding; (4) the rights to be represented by counsel, call witnesses, and cross-examine hostile witnesses, respectively; (5) a record of the proceedings, including all the evidence considered, all findings of fact, and the decision of the COI; (6) the establishment of violations of NCAA rules by means of the "preponderance-of-the-evidence" standard; and (7) judicial review of NCAA decisions in the same manner in which decisions by state agencies are reviewed, with plaintiffs being eligible for compensatory damages for losses suffered as a result of penalties imposed in violation of the statute.[12]

The NCAA Fights Back: The *Miller* Case

Those provisions were front and center in *NCAA v. Miller,* the NCAA's lawsuit challenging the Nevada due process statute. Governor Robert F. Miller was the principal defendant in the case, to which Jerry Tarkanian and his wife, Lois, were also parties.[13] The federal district court that tried the lawsuit held that Sections 155–255 of Chapter 398 of the Nevada Revised Statutes, the sections which imposed the aforementioned due process requirements on "interstate national collegiate athletic associations," violated the United States Constitution's commerce clause (Article I, Section 8, Clause 3) and contract clause (Article I, Section 10, Clause 1). Accordingly, the trial court enjoined the state of Nevada from enforcing this statute.[14] Governor Miller and others, including the Tarkanians, appealed the trial court's decision to the United States Court of Appeals for the Ninth Circuit, which hears appeals from decisions by federal district courts in Nevada and other western states.

The Ninth Circuit affirmed the trial court's decision based on the commerce clause only; it did not address whether the Nevada law also violated the contract clause.[15] It began its analysis by noting that courts had "consistently held" the NCAA to be engaged in interstate commerce in governing college sports, because the games transcend state boundaries. "The NCAA schedules events that call for transportation of teams across state lines," the court observed, "and it governs nationwide amateur athlete recruiting and controls bids for lucrative national and regional television broadcasting of college athletics."[16] "Thus," the court continued, "the Statute regulates only interstate organizations which are engaged in interstate commerce, and it does so directly."[17]

Because the Nevada law regulated interstate commerce directly, the Ninth Circuit reasoned, the NCAA would have to follow that law whenever it investigated a college located in Nevada. Therefore, in order for the Association to comply with Nevada law while maintaining the uniform enforcement procedures necessary to govern institutions located nationwide, it would have to apply the Nevada law to enforcement proceedings that it conducted anywhere in the United States.[18] That arrangement would violate the commerce clause, the court reasoned, because it would give the Nevada law an "extraterritorial effect" forbidden by that clause. Besides, if the Nevada law enjoyed an extraterritorial effect, conflict with similar statutes enacted in other states would occur if the NCAA tried to follow the Nevada law when investigating an institution whose home state had an athletic due process statute of its own.[19] Therefore, the Nevada law would disrupt the NCAA's enforcement programs, just as "changes in train length at each state's border would disrupt a railroad."[20] Thus, the Ninth Circuit affirmed the district court's decision invalidating the Nevada statute.

In *NCAA v. Roberts* in 1994, a federal district court in Florida relied on the reasoning of both the Ninth Circuit and the federal district court in Nevada that originally heard *Miller* to conclude that Florida's athletic due process statute violated both the commerce clause and the contract clause of the Constitution.[21] After the *Miller* and *Roberts* decisions, most states in which similar legislation had been introduced abandoned it. The Illinois and Nebraska statutes remain in effect, but no one has sought to apply them to an NCAA enforcement proceeding.[22]

Ironically, by the time *Miller* was decided, the investigation of UNLV that followed the Lloyd Daniels episode was over. In July 1990 the NCAA accepted UNLV's position that the injunction issued by the state trial court in Nevada prevented UNLV from suspending Jerry Tarkanian from coaching. To resolve the suspension issue, the COI imposed an alternative penalty, barring UNLV from postseason competition in 1991, thereby preventing the Runnin' Rebels from defending the national championship they had won in 1990.[23]

A Softer Approach: The Lee Committee

Challenging the Nevada due process statute in court was not the NCAA's only response to state laws designed to govern its enforcement process. The Association also established a special committee to examine that process. The Lee Committee, chaired by Rex Lee, who had argued the NCAA's case before the Supreme Court in *NCAA v. Board of Regents* in 1984, met five times and presented its final report, including a list of recommendations, at a press conference held on October 28, 1991.[24]

The recommendation representing the biggest change from the Association's existing procedures was that "in cases involving charges of major violations not resolved by the summary disposition procedure, a hearing officer be used to review stipulated facts, resolve factual issues that are in dispute and recommend an appropriate disposition to the infractions committee."[25] The COI would no longer conduct hearings; it could reject a finding by a hearing officer, but only after concluding that the finding was "clearly erroneous."[26] Otherwise, the COI would be restricted to supervising the summary disposition process (i.e., reviewing penalty agreements between the NCAA and rule violators), considering appeals of findings by hearing officers, and imposing penalties. Accordingly, the NCAA should select and maintain a pool of hearing officers.[27]

Another important change recommended by the Lee Committee was that COI hearings (although not deliberations among COI members) should, ordinarily, be open to the public. An exception would govern, though, when the hearing officer concluded that part or all of a hearing should be kept confidential for "good cause," such as when the evidence included test scores, drug use, or medical records.[28] Still another big change advocated by the Lee Committee was that tapes or transcripts of open enforcement hearings should be "sent upon request to parties named in the case and to the involved institutions under circumstances providing protection of confidentiality of appropriate information."[29] The committee recommended further that when the enforcement process was finished, anyone who wished to could buy a tape or a transcript of the hearing.[30]

The NCAA membership rejected these proposals. Still, at its 1993 national convention, the Association adopted several proposals that either had been recommended by the Lee Committee or were milder versions of Lee Committee recommendations. These included

- expanding the COI to include two members from the general public;
- creating a five-member Infractions Appeals Committee to hear appeals from decisions of the COI;
- expanding the amount of information the NCAA was required to provide when notifying accused institutions they were under investigation; future notice would include, among other things, (1) the sport involved, (2) the approximate time period when the alleged violations occurred, (3) the individuals involved, (4) the approximate time frame of the investigation, and (5) a statement indicating that the institution and involved individuals could have legal representation throughout the enforcement proceedings;
- prohibiting any member of the NCAA enforcement staff who had a conflict of interest regarding a particular investigation from participating in that investigation;
- approving the use of tape recorders by NCAA investigators when interviewing witnesses; and
- requiring NCAA investigators to provide to the member institution and the involved individuals "reasonable access to pertinent information, including tape recordings of interviews and documentary evidence."[31]

Congress Enters the Game

The NCAA did not act fast enough or go far enough in altering its enforcement process for some members of Congress. The *Tarkanian* decision troubled these lawmakers, who wished to enact legislation that would overrule it and force the NCAA to adopt stronger due process protections. Edolphus Towns, a Democratic congressman from New York City, introduced H.R. 2157, the Coach and Athlete's Bill of Rights, in the House of Representatives in May 1991, nearly six months before the Lee Committee presented its final report.[32] If Congress had enacted it, this bill would have reversed the *Tarkanian* decision by requiring the NCAA to provide due process protection to any institution, coach, or athlete whom it investigated for allegedly violating Association rules.[33] In the bill's words, the Association was a state actor "when the final or decisive act of suspending or reprimanding a coach, player, or institution of higher education is carried out as a result of sanctions imposed, or the threat of sanctions, by the NCAA upon such coach, player, or institution."[34]

Representative Tom McMillen, a Democrat from Maryland, introduced a similar but more ambitious bill called the Collegiate Athletics Reform Act, also in 1991.[35] McMillen's bill addressed not only due process but also the other main focus of this book, namely, the commercialization of college sports via television. The Collegiate Athletics Reform Act would have given the NCAA a five-year exemption from the antitrust laws, during which time the NCAA could negotiate and execute, with anyone, a contract involving (1) the use or sale of the logo of a commercial sponsor in association with a postseason amateur athletic event in which one or more of its member institutions participated, (2) the sale of the right to telecast an amateur athletic event in which one or more of its member institutions participated, or (3) both of those activities.[36] In other words, during the period of the exemption, the McMillen bill would have effectively overruled the Supreme Court's decision in *NCAA v. Board of Regents*.

In return for freeing the NCAA from the antitrust laws, the McMillen bill would have required the Association to honor the constitutional guarantee of due process before suspending or reprimanding a coach or player from a member institution, prohibiting a member institution from participating in an amateur athletic event, or suspending a member institution's right to televise athletic events featuring its teams.[37] Thus, like Congressman Towns's bill, Congressman McMillen's bill would have effectively overruled the Supreme Court's decision in *NCAA v. Tarkanian*.[38] Neither bill became law.

The *Tarkanian* Legacy

Meanwhile, the underlying dispute between Jerry Tarkanian and the NCAA continued apace. In November 1992 Tarkanian and his wife, Lois, filed a new lawsuit against the NCAA in a state court in Nevada, seeking damages for economic injuries allegedly suffered as a result of the Association's efforts to suspend Jerry from coaching and for the intentional infliction of emotional distress.[39] A scheduled trial date of May 1997 came and went, even though the lawyers had by then deposed all the witnesses and produced the necessary documents.[40]

The NCAA filed a motion in the United States District Court for the District of Nevada asking the court to enjoin the relitigation of issues the

Association claimed Tarkanian should have raised in his 1977 suit.[41] When that court refused to issue an injunction, the NCAA appealed to the United States Court of Appeals for the Ninth Circuit in January 1998. Two months later, the mediation clerk for the appellate court contacted the parties and suggested they mediate their dispute. Mediation began on March 29, 1998, and on April 1, the legal marathon between the NCAA and Jerry Tarkanian finally ended in a settlement.[42] Under the agreement, the NCAA would pay the Tarkanians $2.5 million, and the parties would release each other from all claims relating to the pending lawsuit.[43] Neither party would admit liability, and the court would dismiss the lawsuit.[44]

That agreement had no effect on the Supreme Court's decision a decade earlier holding that the NCAA is not a state actor and hence is not bound to honor due process guarantees in its enforcement proceedings. *NCAA v. Tarkanian* is still the law today, as it was in 2001, when the Supreme Court noted its continued vitality in *Brentwood Academy v. Tennessee Secondary School Athletic Association.*[45] The question before the Court in *Brentwood Academy* was whether a state high school athletic association, the Tennessee Secondary School Athletic Association (TSSAA), had engaged in state action when enforcing a rule against a member school and hence was bound by due process requirements.

In 1997 the TSSAA brought an enforcement proceeding against Brentwood Academy, a private, parochial high school that was a member of the association, for violating a rule prohibiting "undue influence" in recruiting athletes, by writing a letter to incoming students and their parents notifying them about spring football practice.[46] The TSSAA placed Brentwood Academy's athletic program on probation for four years, declared its football and boys' basketball teams ineligible for postseason playoffs for two years, and fined the school $3,000.[47] All of the voting members of the TSSAA's governing board, which imposed these penalties, were public school administrators.[48]

In response to the probation order, Brentwood Academy sued the TSSAA under 42 U.S.C. § 1983, the same statute on which Jerry Tarkanian had based his original suit against the NCAA. The academy's lawsuit charged that enforcement of the rule against "undue influence" was state action and that the TSSAA had sought to enforce it without providing Brentwood Academy the due process the Fourteenth Amendment requires under such circumstances.[49] A federal district court granted "summary judgment" for Brentwood Academy, meaning the school prevailed without need of a trial.[50] The TSSAA appealed to the United States Court of Appeals for the

Sixth Circuit, which reversed, whereupon Brentwood Academy appealed to the Supreme Court.[51]

In reversing the Sixth Circuit and holding that the TSSAA was a state actor, Justice David Souter, writing for the majority, anticipated the likely criticism that this case was similar to *Tarkanian;* hence, if the NCAA was not a state actor, then neither was the similarly private TSSAA. Responding to this expected critique, Justice Souter wrote that in *Tarkanian* "the NCAA's policies were shaped not by the University of Nevada alone, but by several hundred member institutions, most of them having no connection with Nevada, and exhibiting no color of Nevada law."[52] In other words, Justice Souter continued, the NCAA was a collection of member institutions from around the country, not a "surrogate for one State"; therefore, the Court concluded that the NCAA's connection with Nevada was "too insubstantial" to be state action.[53] But in *Brentwood,* Justice Souter noted, "the record indicate[d] that half the . . . meetings [held by the TSSAA regarding enforcement of the "undue influence" rule] documented . . . were held during official school hours, and that public schools have largely provided for the [TSSAA's] financial support."[54] "There would be no recognizable [TSSAA], legal or tangible," he added, "without the public school officials, who do not merely control but overwhelmingly perform all but the purely ministerial acts by which the [TSSAA] exists and functions in practical terms."[55]

Invoking a word the Supreme Court had not used in a state action case for decades, Justice Souter concluded that the "entwinement" between the Tennessee State Board of Education and the TSSAA was so significant as to turn the action of the nominally private TSSAA into state action. "Entwinement" had last been the basis for a finding of state action in a Supreme Court opinion in the 1966 case *Evans v. Newton,* which concerned whether the nominally private ownership of a municipally managed park authorized the continuance of racial segregation in the park.[56] In *Evans* the Court stated, "Conduct that is formally 'private' may become so entwined with governmental policies or so impregnated with a governmental character as to become subject to the constitutional limits placed upon state action."[57] Similarly, in *Brentwood Academy* Justice Souter wrote, "Entwinement will support a conclusion that an ostensibly private organization ought to be charged with a public character and judged by constitutional standards; entwinement to the degree shown here requires it."[58] Accordingly, the Supreme Court reversed the Sixth Circuit's decision and remanded the case to the trial court for a trial to determine whether the TSSAA had furnished

Brentwood Academy with due process when investigating the latter's recruitment of athletes.[59]

Today, a decade after *Brentwood Academy*, it is unclear whether the Supreme Court's use of the entwinement concept in that case marked a return to an old theory of state action or the adoption of a new one. It is also unclear, as Justice Clarence Thomas noted in his dissent in *Brentwood Academy*, what the term *entwinement* means in the state action context.[60] Whether it is separate and distinct from the more established nexus and joint participant theories and whether the Court will continue to use it to resolve future state action cases also remain to be determined.

These uncertainties have prompted the authors of one commentary to argue, in light of *Brentwood Academy*, that the aims and operations of state high school athletic associations and the NCAA are sufficiently similar that if the former are state actors for purposes of due process, the latter should be, too. According to these authors,

> The dichotomy created by *Tarkanian* and *Brentwood* is unsustainable. Not only are purpose, structure, and operations of the NCAA and high school athletic associations similar, with state schools critically involved in both associations, but in the 20 years since *Tarkanian*, state involvement in the NCAA has only deepened with the expanding role played by Division I members due to the popularity of college basketball and football.[61]

Still, as of late 2011, courts have shown no sign of abandoning *Tarkanian* or of using *Brentwood* as a lever for weakening *Tarkanian* on the ground that the similarities between state high school athletic associations and the NCAA are so great that the law should treat both entities as state actors.[62] After *Tarkanian, Miller,* and *Brentwood*, then, judicial review of the NCAA enforcement process, at either the federal or the state level, is highly unlikely.[63] One prominent sports law textbook summed up this situation well by observing, "It would appear that only a challenge to the procedures utilized in a particular investigation under the laws of private associations would have a chance for success."[64]

Thus, although Jerry Tarkanian won the battle to keep his job at UNLV, he lost the war to extend the due process requirements of the Fourteenth Amendment to NCAA enforcement proceedings. The NCAA won the biggest prize in the *Tarkanian* case, namely, retention of its status as a private entity unbound by the strictures of due process. Absent federal legislation imposing those strictures in NCAA enforcement proceedings, only the NCAA's own version of due process will constrain it.[65] Unfortunately, despite improvements over the years, that version is still less protective of individuals than necessary, considering the high stakes involved for coaches, athletes, and others in NCAA investigations.

More Process Is Due: NCAA Enforcement Procedures Today

Continuity and Change

The NCAA enforcement process needs further improvement, but it is more protective of the rights of individuals and institutions than it was in the 1970s, when it focused on Jerry Tarkanian. Current due process protections include

> notice of an inquiry and notice of specific allegations;
> a right to be represented by counsel for both individuals and institutions;
> the tape-recording of witness interviews unless the interviewee objects;
> a four-year statute of limitations (subject to exceptions), meaning that any alleged violation presented to the COI must have occurred within four years before notification that an investigation has begun;
> notice of the witnesses and the information on which the NCAA staff will rely during the hearing;
> a prohibition on the consideration of information from confidential sources;
> recording and transcription of the COI hearing;
> a burden of proof resting with the NCAA; and
> the opportunity for an appeal.[66]

The most significant improvements since Jerry Tarkanian's day are the tape-recording of witness interviews and the notice to accused individuals and institutions of the witnesses and information on which the NCAA investigative staff will rely. Tarkanian was entitled to a lawyer and an appeal, but neither one could overcome the extraordinary advantage the NCAA enjoyed because it controlled the flow of information during the enforcement process. Tarkanian did not know what evidence the NCAA staff would present against him, and much of that evidence was the investigators' recollections, from handwritten notes, of their interviews with witnesses. Tarkanian did not have access to those notes.

One thing that has remained the same since Coach Tarkanian's day, though, is that NCAA investigations customarily result from tips provided by high school and college coaches or from investigative reports published in newspapers or magazines or broadcast on television. Less often, an athlete will report a violation, or an institution will self-report.[67] An investigation begins when the president of an NCAA member institution receives a notice of inquiry advising that the enforcement staff (20 "assistant directors," or field investigators, supervised by six directors, who report to the vice president for enforcement services) plans to investigate the institution for possible rules violations.[68] Then the enforcement staff investigates to determine whether sufficient information exists to indicate that "major violations" have occurred. Major violations are defined partly by what they are not, namely, isolated or inadvertent, and partly by their result, namely, "an extensive recruiting or competitive advantage" for the offending institution.[69] If sufficient evidence of major violations exists, the institution's president will receive a notice of allegations from the NCAA.[70]

Accusation and Response

The notice of allegations will notify the accused institution and all involved parties of the alleged violations of NCAA rules uncovered by the enforcement staff. The cover letter accompanying the notice will

- inform the president or chancellor (CEO) of the matter being investigated, request institutional cooperation in obtaining all pertinent facts, and provide specific information on how the accused institution should investigate the allegation(s);
- ask the CEO to respond and to provide all relevant information the institution has or may reasonably obtain, including evidence of new violations;
- ask the CEO or another institutional staff member to appear before the COI at a time and place determined by the committee;
- inform the CEO that if the institution fails to appear after having been asked to do so, it may not appeal the COI's findings or the penalty;
- require the institution to give any present or former employee named in an allegation and any present or former athlete with eligibility re-

maining whose eligibility could be affected based on involvement in an alleged violation a chance to submit in writing any information the person wishes to submit that is relevant to the investigation; and

- inform the CEO that the enforcement staff's primary investigator in the case will be available to discuss the institution's development of its response and to assist the institution in locating persons who have or might have important information about the allegations.[71]

The institution and accused individuals will have 90 days in which to respond.[72]

After the enforcement staff files the notice of allegations, the accused institution must respond in writing, whether or not it disputes the charges. Indeed, the institution's response can range from a denial of all charges to an admission of all charges, in which case the NCAA and the institution will likely settle the matter by "summary disposition."[73] Ordinarily, the institutional response admits the truth of some facts or allegations and disputes others. It will probably make one or more of the following claims: (1) the evidence is insufficient to support the facts alleged; (2) the undisputed facts do not amount to a rule violation; (3) the violation alleged is secondary, not major; and (4) the cumulative violations do not reflect "a loss of institutional control" over the athletic program.[74]

After the institution responds, the parties attend a prehearing conference to identify the issues to be addressed at the COI hearing, which occurs between four and six weeks after the conference.[75] The conference sometimes occurs by telephone, but whether it occurs by telephone or in person, its participants are representatives of the accused institution and members of the NCAA enforcement staff, and its purpose is to (1) clarify the issues to be discussed during the hearing, (2) suggest that the institution investigate further or conduct additional interviews, and (3) identify allegations that the enforcement staff intends to withdraw.[76] Once the issues have been joined, the NCAA enforcement staff prepares a memorandum called the "enforcement staff case summary," which summarizes the case for the COI.[77]

Summary Disposition

An accused institution may choose not to contest the charges against it, opting instead for "summary disposition," which is available under Operating Bylaw 19.5.2.3.1 as long as the institution is not a "repeat violator," having two major violations within the past five years.[78] Summary disposition is akin to a plea bargain in a criminal prosecution, because the accused accepts responsibility for the offense in return for a shortened proceeding and, usually, a reduced penalty.[79] But in the NCAA enforcement process, unlike in the criminal justice process, the offender "cops a plea" by agreeing to the charges, not to the penalty.[80]

An institution choosing summary disposition works with the NCAA enforcement staff to produce a written report including (1) proposed, agreed-on findings of fact; (2) a summary of the information on which those findings are based; (3) a stipulation, agreed to by both the enforcement staff and the institution, that the proposed findings are substantially correct; (4) a stipulation that the findings establish one or more violations of NCAA legislation; and, if applicable, (5) a statement of unresolved issues the parties do not consider important enough to affect the outcome of the case.[81] But the report does not include an agreed-on stipulation of the penalty. Instead, the accused institution and individuals submit proposed penalties, within the guidelines established by the penalty structure in the NCAA bylaws, rather like attorneys submit proposed jury instructions to a judge at the end of a trial.[82] In this instance, though, only one side submits proposed penalties for consideration; the NCAA enforcement staff does not do so.[83]

The COI reviews the joint report and reaches one of three possible conclusions. If it accepts the agreed-on findings and the proposed penalties, the COI prepares its own written report, provides a copy to the institution, and then announces publicly the matter's resolution.[84] If the COI rejects the agreed-on findings, the matter is removed from summary disposition, and a COI hearing follows.[85] If the COI accepts the agreed-on findings but rejects the penalties the institution proposed, the accused institution and individuals can participate, if they wish, in an expedited hearing, during which the only issue considered will be the penalties to be imposed.[86] An institution that participates in the expedited hearing but disagrees with the penalties imposed there may appeal those penalties to the Infractions Appeals Committee (IAC).[87]

COI Hearings

Enforcement matters not resolved by summary disposition proceed to a hearing before the COI, which meets approximately six times a year, for two or three days each time, usually during a weekend.[88] During hearings, the COI considers allegations brought by the enforcement staff, reviews documentary evidence and recordings of witness testimony, makes factual findings, and imposes penalties if it concludes that violations have occurred.[89] Hearings are scheduled in half-day or whole-day blocks; all hearings are tape-recorded, and a certified court reporter is present to transcribe a written record.[90]

COI hearings differ from criminal trials in several respects. First, in a COI hearing, the cooperative principle not only requires the "prosecutor" (the NCAA) to disclose all information regarding each allegation, whether that information helps or hurts the accused institution's case, but also obligates the accused to do the same.[91] That is because NCAA proceedings do not recognize the protection against compelled self-incrimination provided by the Fifth Amendment to the United States Constitution. Accordingly, if an institution or one of its staff members fails to self-report fully any violation that the staff member knew about or should have known about and that the enforcement staff subsequently verifies, that failure is considered a breach of the cooperative principle, which can increase the penalty eventually imposed.[92]

Second, in a COI hearing, an institution can be "convicted" of an offense that is not part of the original charges included in the notice of allegations.[93] In other words, the COI may find a violation based on information either discussed for the first time or developed at the hearing.[94] At first blush, the power to punish for an offense of which the accused lacked notice seems like a prescription for unfairness. But the IAC has blunted the potential unfairness in this arrangement by holding that an accused institution must receive notice of and a meaningful opportunity to be heard on all charges, including those first raised during a COI hearing. Specifically, the IAC has held that if the COI decides, based on evidence presented during the hearing, that additional findings not included in the notice of allegations or the enforcement staff case summary may be appropriate, the COI must give the accused institution and individual(s) a chance to respond in writing and to present their responses at another hearing, if an accused so requests.[95] Therefore, although the enforcement staff can base an amendment of the charges on evidence first discussed during the hearing, the COI is obligated to ensure that an accused institution or individual has sufficient time to mount a defense to the new charge(s).[96]

A COI hearing begins with opening statements by representatives of the accused institution, involved individuals, and the NCAA enforcement staff, respectively. These statements are generally limited to 15 minutes each in length and are designed to provide only general information about the nature of the dispute and the position of each party. They are not supposed to present specific evidence to be reviewed during the consideration of particular allegations.[97]

In a COI hearing, as in a civil or criminal trial, the presentation of evidence follows the opening statements. For each allegation, the enforcement staff generally describes the allegation and identifies the information that it believes supports a finding that a violation has occurred.[98] The accused institution then has a chance to respond, as do any "involved individuals" named in that particular allegation.[99] During the discussion of allegations, COI members may ask questions at any time, and they may question an institutional representative or an involved individual about any relevant issue.[100] If, however, counsel for the institution, counsel for an individual, or even a member of the enforcement staff wishes to ask a question of another party, hearing procedures specify that the "question should be directed to the [COI], which will then decide if the question is appropriate and will direct it to the appropriate individual."[101]

If the institution or an involved individual opposes procedures followed by the enforcement staff before the hearing or by the COI during the hearing, that institution or individual must object during the hearing and identify the resulting prejudice to its case, even if it already did so in prior written submissions. Failure to object during the hearing prevents the objection from entering the hearing "record," which in turn precludes raising it on appeal.[102] The same rule governs in civil and criminal courts. Unlike in a criminal proceeding, though, an accused party at a COI hearing cannot confront or cross-examine hostile witnesses. Indeed, few witnesses other than the accused individuals attend COI hearings, and when they do, the COI members ask all the questions.[103] The institution may ask the COI to ask a member of the enforcement staff or another witness certain questions, but the institution cannot question witnesses directly.[104]

Once the evidence has been presented, the parties make their respective closing statements, with the institution going first, followed by each involved individual who wishes to make such a statement and then by a representative of the enforcement staff.[105] Like opening statements, closing statements do not address the details of specific allegations, and the COI admonishes parties not to use closing statements to review evidence. Although parties may include in their closing statements "thoughts not discussed during the hearing," they are generally expected to summarize earlier discussions and offer a brief overview of the case.[106] The closing statements conclude the hearing.

Posthearing Deliberations

After the hearing, members of the COI meet privately to resolve disputed facts and to determine whether the facts, as found, constitute violations of NCAA rules.[107] During its deliberations, the COI may decide that additional evidence is needed and may request it from the parties.[108] If the COI finds that a violation has occurred, it imposes the proposed penalty. If the COI finds that a staff member of an athletic department has been involved in a major violation, it can require, as it sought to do in Jerry Tarkanian's case, that the institution suspend or eliminate that person's "athletically related duties" at the institution.[109] Similarly, if the COI finds that a booster was involved in a major violation, the COI may require the institution to "show cause" why it should not disassociate that person from its athletic programs.[110]

Appeals

A unanimous vote is not required for the COI to impose a penalty. Only a simple majority is needed, unless fewer than eight members are present and voting.[111] After a vote is taken and a penalty imposed, the COI follows procedures prescribed in NCAA bylaws for notifying the institution and the public of its decision.

The institution or individual found to have violated NCAA rules may appeal to the IAC. Each party may appeal regardless of whether the other one does. Moreover, although each party may accept the COI's finding that a violation has occurred, each may still appeal the penalty or even appeal one part of the penalty while accepting the others.[112] The IAC may hear an appeal in person or by means of a written submission only. Like appellate tribunals generally, it defers to the factual findings of the tribunal below—in this case, the COI. The IAC will not reverse the COI's findings of fact and of violations unless the appealing party can show that (1) the finding is clearly contrary to the evidence presented, (2) the facts the COI found do not constitute a violation of NCAA rules, or (3) a procedural error occurred without which the COI would not have found a violation.[113] Similarly, the IAC will not set aside on appeal a penalty imposed by the COI unless the appealing party can show that the penalty is excessive, thereby constituting an "abuse of discretion" by the COI.[114]

The party who intends to appeal a decision by the COI must file a written notice of appeal (NOA) with the NCAA president no later than 15 calendar days from the date of the public release of the COI's report.[115] The NOA must identify the specific findings or penalties being appealed. The NCAA will reply by letter, acknowledging receipt of the NOA; the appealing party then has 30 days from the date of the acknowledgment letter to file a written appeal. Failure to file the written materials will cause the IAC to dismiss the appeal.[116]

After filing the NOA, an appealing party will have access to a custodial file of key documents in the case, thanks to a "Web-based custodian" system established by the NCAA in 2008.[117] Absent technical difficulties, this arrangement gives the appealing party access to the case file on the party's own computer, thereby eliminating the need to travel to NCAA headquarters or to a "neutral site," such as a nearby law office, to view the file. The portions of the appellate record accessible only through the custodial arrangement include the official transcript of the COI hearing, the COI's response to the written appeal (explained shortly), and any additional materials the IAC has authorized to become part of the record on appeal. The contents of the custodial file may not be copied, and only the appealing party and that party's counsel may review them.[118]

Within 30 days from the date of the NCAA's letter acknowledging receipt of a written appeal, the COI must file a response with the IAC. The COI's response must include

>   a statement of the origins of the case;
>   the violation(s) found;
>   the disciplinary or corrective action taken by the institution or its conference;
>   the COI's proposed penalties;
>   the issue(s) raised in the appeal;
>   the COI's reply to the issue(s) raised on appeal; and
>   any additional information presented to the COI that it deems relevant to the appeal.[119]

The appealing party may submit a rebuttal to the COI's response within 14 days, but the rebuttal must be limited to matters discussed in the COI's response.[120]

If a hearing is held, the appealing party will make its oral presentation first, to be followed by a representative of the COI. A panel of at least three IAC members hears the arguments.[121] The enforcement staff may or may not make a presentation; if it does, its presentation will follow the one to which it wishes to respond.[122]

After the hearing, the IAC deliberates and decides by a majority vote of the members present and voting. According to Gary Roberts, the IAC, which was established in the early 1990s, has been "surprisingly independent and assertive in reversing some [COI] findings and reducing penalties, although it has never exonerated an institution that the [COI] has found to have committed one or more violations."[123] When determining whether penalties are excessive or inappropriate, the IAC considers (1) the nature, number, and seriousness of the violations; (2) the conduct and motives of the individuals involved in the violations; (3) the corrective action(s) taken by the institution; (4) the impact of the penalties on innocent athletes and coaches; and (5) NCAA policies regarding fairness in the resolution of infractions cases.[124] Accordingly, in decisions vacating or reducing penalties imposed by the COI, the IAC has noted facts such as that no current coaches or athletes were involved in the violations, that most of the violations did not result in a significant competitive or recruiting advantage to the offending institution, or that the violations were either self-reported or admitted.[125] Whatever the IAC decides and for whatever reason(s), its decision is final; no further review exists within the NCAA. The chair announces the IAC's decision to the public.[126]

The Need for Improvement

Although the current procedures used by the COI and the IAC represent a major improvement over their 1970s counterparts, the NCAA enforcement process needs further improvement. The stakes involved in NCAA investigations (i.e., loss of a livelihood, a free college education, or a chance to play professional sports) rival those involved in administrative agency adjudications and civil lawsuits, but the NCAA denies to its investigative targets a neutral decision maker and the right to confront and cross-examine hostile witnesses, which litigants in administrative adjudications and civil trials enjoy. Besides, as Professor Burton Brody noted in congressional testimony in 1991, because college sport "affects so many lives and molds the public perception of higher education," its enforcement procedures should be not only accurate but as fair as possible.[127] The following section presents recommendations designed to enhance fairness without reducing accuracy.

A Model of Due Process: Revamping NCAA Enforcement Procedures

The Administrative Analogy

The NCAA enforcement process is often compared to civil and criminal litigation, but proceedings involving administrative agencies offer a more appropriate analogy, because they are relatively informal, meaning that the rules of evidence governing civil and criminal trials do not apply. In "contested cases," administrative agencies play an adjudicatory role because, in the words of the United States Supreme Court, one or more persons are "exceptionally affected, in each case on individual grounds."[128] Agency adjudications resolve disputes in a wide array of matters, including, for example, the hiring and firing of permanent public employees (e.g., teachers, police, firefighters), the suspension or expulsion of public school students, the licensing of professionals, the disbursement of social security disability insurance, and the regulation of public utilities and public housing.[129] Thus, like NCAA enforcement proceedings, administrative agency adjudications often implicate individuals' interests in pursuing their livelihoods and preserving their reputations.

Besides the financial and reputational consequences institutions face in NCAA proceedings, coaches and other athletic department employees may face the loss of their livelihoods and irreparable damage to their reputations, which are constitutionally protected property and liberty interests relative to state actors. Athletes may not face the loss of a constitutionally protected interest, but they face the loss of athletic eligibility and an athletic scholarship, and losing the scholarship may mean sacrificing a college education and the chance for a career in professional sports. Thus, the stakes for individuals are as high in NCAA enforcement proceedings as in administrative agency adjudications; hence, the same measure of due process should apply in both settings. When determining that measure, it is necessary to remember that the "indispensable" elements of administrative due process are notice, disclosure of the agency's reasons for its proposed action, an opportunity for an individual to present evidence in rebuttal, and an unbiased decision maker.[130] These elements produce accurate, fair agency decisions based on rational choices rather than the personal preferences or prejudices of particular officials.[131]

Due process does not always require an oral hearing in the administrative context, and it would not always require such a hearing by the NCAA either.

Whether a party is entitled to an oral hearing depends on the issues to be considered. If the issues are factual, each party must have an opportunity to present its side of the story, call witnesses, and cross-examine those who testify counter to its position. But no need exists for a hearing when the key issues involve interpretations of test results or other scientific information; in those instances, participation may be limited to written submissions arguing opposing legal positions.[132] Similarly, hearings are only necessary in NCAA enforcement cases when the parties disagree about what happened; when the facts are undisputed, summary disposition is appropriate. This dichotomy already exists, so applying the agency adjudication model to NCAA enforcement proceedings would probably not increase or decrease the number of cases receiving hearings instead of summary disposition.

But when an oral hearing is required in NCAA proceedings, applying the agency adjudication model would require a major change from the present system, namely, substituting professional "hearing officers" or "administrative law judges" (ALJs) for the COI and the IAC. Although these officials are usually employees of the agencies for which they conduct hearings, they are required to be impartial and independent of agency employees who investigate or prosecute. For example, the federal Administrative Procedure Act (APA), which governs adjudications within federal agencies, states that an agency employee who presides at hearings may not "be responsible to or subject to the supervision or direction of an employee or agent engaged in the performance of investigative or prosecuting functions for an agency."[133] Another provision of the APA states that "[t]he functions of presiding employees . . . shall be conducted in an impartial manner."[134]

Both the APA and its state counterparts give ALJs authority to issue subpoenas to compel witnesses to appear at hearings and testify. For example, the Administrative Procedure Act in Indiana, the site of the NCAA headquarters, states that "an administrative law judge at the request of any party or an agency shall, and upon the administrative law judge's own motion, may, issue subpoenas" in the same way they are issued in civil courts.[135] The APA and its state counterparts also protect a right of cross-examination for the parties to a contested case. The APA states, "A party is entitled to present his case or defense by oral or documentary evidence, to submit rebuttal evidence, and to conduct such cross-examination as may be required for a full and true disclosure of the facts."[136] But to prevent duplicative questions or the use of cross-examination for purposes of delay, the APA also states that "the agency as a matter of policy shall provide for the exclusion of irrelevant, immaterial, or unduly repetitive evidence."[137] Similarly, under the Indiana statute, the ALJ "shall afford to all parties the opportunity to . . . conduct cross-examination,"[138] but the statute empowers the ALJ to "impose conditions upon a party necessary to avoid unreasonably burdensome presentations by the party," including limiting the party's use of cross-examination.[139] A unique feature of the Indiana statute is its offer to nonparties of an opportunity to present oral or written statements that will become part of the record of the proceedings and could affect the outcome. If the ALJ wishes to consider a statement by a nonparty, he or she must give all parties a chance to challenge that statement, and pursuant to a motion by any party, the ALJ must require that the statement be given under oath.[140]

Thus, the agency adjudication model features impartial decision makers with power to compel testimony and an ample opportunity for parties to challenge each other's evidence, tempered by authority in the decision maker to prohibit unnecessary, dilatory, or abusive cross-examination. A party disappointed in the outcome may appeal to an appellate panel within the agency and, if still dissatisfied, may seek judicial review of the agency's decision. In NCAA enforcement proceedings, however, the Association plays the roles of prosecutor (enforcement staff), judge (COI), jury (again, the COI), and appellate tribunal (IAC). No external checks exist to ensure the accuracy of the NCAA's findings or the fairness of the penalties it imposes.[141] To make matters worse, the absence of subpoena power and the lack of opportunity to confront and cross-examine opposing witnesses compromise accuracy and fairness in NCAA proceedings.

Applying the Administrative Model to the NCAA

The overarching remedy for these deficiencies is for the NCAA to use procedures akin to those required by the federal Administrative Procedure Act. Enforcement proceedings regarding alleged major violations of NCAA rules should include the following:

- A panel of "judges" to replace the COI and the IAC. The NCAA should create a pool of retired trial judges and ALJs from Indiana (and other states, if necessary) to replace the COI and a pool of retired appellate judges to replace the IAC. The "hearing judges" and the "appellate judges" should be independent contractors, and NCAA work should not be their principal source of income. Candidates with work experience in higher education generally or in college sports specifically would be especially welcome. They would conduct hearings and determine penalties, and they would be paid from a special fund supported by dues contributed by NCAA member institutions.

- A "discovery" process before every hearing, perhaps with a time limit enforced by the hearing judge, during which the NCAA enforcement staff and the accused parties would gather and exchange information pertinent to the hearing. This process would include the deposing of potential witnesses and the production of documents.

- The right to confront and cross-examine opposing witnesses at hearings. This change would discourage allegations motivated by spite or personal animosity, because the accuser would be subject to cross-examination. The judge would be authorized to issue subpoenas compelling the testimony of reluctant witnesses.

- Hearings and appellate proceedings open to the public unless either the accused institution or an accused individual objected. The only exception to this rule would be the posthearing deliberations of the three-member appellate panels, which would be closed. The accused parties are likely to benefit the most from open hearings, which would shine a bright light on any unfairness in the process, so these proceedings should be open to the public unless an accused party objects. To prevent disruptions caused by zealous fans of the accused institution, the NCAA could use the same methods the United States Supreme Court uses to maintain decorum: provide limited seating on a first-come, first-served basis, and require members of the public to submit to a security screening upon entering the building. The same special fund from which the judges are paid could also compensate the additional security staff these proceedings would require.[142]

The hiring of professional judges to replace the COI and IAC, respectively, is the most important recommendation. It will ensure impartiality and professionalism, thereby enhancing the legitimacy of the NCAA enforcement process in the eyes of skeptical member institutions. A training program for new judges, sponsored by the NCAA, will help to ensure that they have sufficient knowledge of college sports to determine penalties in addition to finding facts.

The presence of professional judges is also essential to implementation of the other changes advocated earlier. These judges would have the time necessary to oversee discovery, consider requests for and issue subpoenas, and preside at hearings featuring the direct examination and cross-examination of witnesses. As a result, the present rule permitting the COI to identify new charges during an enforcement hearing could (and should) be eliminated. Discovery would be sufficient to enable the enforcement staff to identify all pertinent allegations before the hearing. The new judges would also have the background necessary to accomplish their tasks in a timely and efficient manner. Finally, they would have the courtroom experience necessary to preside over public hearings, from which they might occasionally have to order a disruptive person removed.

Besides professional judges, discovery, confrontation and cross-examination, and open hearings, the NCAA enforcement process requires changes in the standards used to issue a notice of allegations and to evaluate evidence. Under current rules, the enforcement staff must issue a notice of allegations when it "believes there is sufficient information to conclude that the Committee on Infractions could make a finding" that a violation occurred.[143] A recent law review commentary correctly criticizes this standard as vague and as giving too much discretion to the enforcement staff. The authors recommend that the standard be changed to provide that the staff "may" issue a notice of allegations if it so believes.[144] Alternatively, the NCAA could retain the mandatory nature of the standard but only require the staff to issue the notice "when it discovers evidence that would cause a reasonable person to conclude that such evidence creates a substantial likelihood that the COI would make a finding."[145] Under the latter standard, which is used in securities regulation, only evidence strong enough to make a finding probable would justify issuance of the notice.

Also in need of change is the NCAA's standard for evaluating evidence presented at enforcement hearings. Indeed, the Association's bylaws do not identify a "burden of persuasion," that is, a standard by which the evidence presented by the enforcement staff can be evaluated as to whether it makes a finding of wrongdoing more likely than not. Instead, the bylaws merely require the COI to base its findings on information it "determines to be credible, persuasive and of a kind on which reasonably prudent persons rely in the conduct of serious affairs."[146] This guideline fails to identify a degree of probability the enforcement staff must satisfy to show that one or more violations occurred. In other words, it does not tell the COI how much "credible" and "persuasive" evidence the enforcement staff must present to establish that violations occurred.

Two potential alternatives exist. One would employ the customary standard used in civil court—namely, the preponderance of the evidence (e.g., 51 percent)—in every case. The other would apply that standard to all charges except unethical conduct; the latter "carry the most stigma and the harshest penalties."[147] The NCAA would have to prove its case regarding unethical conduct with "clear and convincing evidence."[148] The alternatives are preferable to the current situation; either one would require the NCAA to present and the judge to find more than "some" evidence showing that the alleged violations occurred.

Admittedly, imposing a civil court burden of persuasion on COI hearings represents a departure from the agency adjudication model generally followed here. Administrative procedure statutes typically only require "the exclusion of irrelevant, immaterial, or unduly repetitive evidence" and decisions supported by "reliable, probative, and substantial" evidence, which compares favorably with the NCAA's insistence on evidence that is credible, persuasive, and of a kind on which reasonably prudent persons rely.[149] But the high stakes involved in NCAA enforcement proceedings for institutions and individuals, the importance of college sports to the public image of higher education in the United States, and the long-standing mistrust of the NCAA by its members all support a more rigorous evidentiary standard for COI hearings.

The NCAA should make transcripts of hearings and appellate proceedings available to the public on its Web site once those hearings have concluded or at least when a final decision has been reached in a case. Confidential medical or academic information could be redacted to preserve personal privacy. This change would likely enhance the NCAA's reputation for fairness and professionalism without compromising its ability to combat wrongdoing or violating privacy rights.

Finally, the due process protections advocated here should apply to every person who is named in an NCAA investigation as having engaged in or enabled wrongdoing and who is subject to a loss of livelihood or educational opportunities or of damage to his or her reputation as a result of that investigation. The NCAA should be required to adopt the provision of Indiana's Administrative Procedure Act authorizing ALJs to give nonparties a chance to present oral or written statements at hearings, subject to rebuttal by the institution.[150] Beyond that, NCAA bylaws should be revised so that when an employee or booster is named in an NCAA investigation but is not a party to the case, member institutions may not fire or permanently reassign the employee or disassociate themselves from the booster until after the case has been resolved and the employee's or booster's role in it has been determined. This arrangement would prevent an institution from using innocent employees, such as Dr. David Ridpath (see chapter 1), or boosters as "scapegoats" to curry favor with the NCAA, by appearing to "put its house in order" without really addressing the behavior that prompted an NCAA investigation.

The foregoing changes would benefit both the NCAA and the targets of its enforcement probes. The Association would benefit because the increased fairness and public accessibility that these changes would bring to the enforcement process would likely enhance the Association's member support and public image. The accused parties, of course, would benefit from greater due process. Most important, these changes would protect the innocent without hindering the investigation, prosecution, or punishment of the guilty.

Beyond Due Process

These recommendations notwithstanding, Gary Roberts was correct when he testified in 2004 that the best possible change in the NCAA's enforcement process would be a significant reduction in cheating by member institutions, flowing from diminished commercial pressures on colleges to win at any cost. He stated, "In the final analysis, the most fundamental problem confronting the NCAA enforcement process is the inevitable one of trying to enforce a complex set of rules designed to preserve [NCAA] aspirations that are at odds with reality."[151] That reality, Roberts explained, is that "the market-driven commercial and psychic incentives for coaches, athletic administrators, boosters, and even university presidents and faculty to 'cheat' are enormous."[152]

The NCAA, with the limited resources of a private organization, faces an uphill battle against the powerful incentives to cheat in college sports. In Roberts's view "the one clear way to reduce the cheating" is to limit the power of those incentives by measures such as capping coaches' salaries, capping recruiting expenditures or prohibiting recruiting altogether, limiting the revenues colleges could earn from sports or the number of television appearances their teams could make, and requiring greater revenue sharing by college teams.[153] Each of these changes would require either direct government regulation of college sports or an antitrust exemption for the NCAA.[154]

Direct government regulation is unlikely, because it runs counter to the enduring American passion for limited government. Indirect regulation, by means of Congress conferring an antitrust exemption on the NCAA, is more consistent with the American ethos. A legislative proposal that would confer an antitrust exemption on the NCAA while requiring it to adopt the due process protections discussed in the previous section of this chapter is the subject of chapter 8.

Chapter 8

TRUST REPLACES ANTITRUST
A New Legal Structure for College Sports

The College Sports Legal Reform Act
Congress Must Act

Only the United States Congress can undo the adverse effects of *NCAA v. Board of Regents* and *NCAA v. Tarkanian*. The NCAA cannot declare itself exempt from the antitrust laws, and it has refused thus far to adopt the procedural protections for accused parties recommended in chapter 7. Therefore, Congress should confer on the NCAA a limited antitrust exemption in return for requiring it to adopt those protections. Specifically, Congress should give the NCAA an "educational exemption" from the antitrust laws. This exemption would enable the Association to promulgate rules designed to make college sports compatible with the academic institutions sponsoring them, without fear that a federal court would invalidate those rules on antitrust grounds. The College Sports Legal Reform Act, which this chapter will present, would exempt from antitrust scrutiny any NCAA rule reasonably related to the purposes of enhancing the academic lives of college athletes or making college sports and higher education compatible. If the Association could not show that a challenged rule was reasonably related to one of those purposes, a court would be free to evaluate the rule according to customary antitrust principles.

The proposed legislation would not necessarily entitle the NCAA to be the czar of televised college football again. To reclaim that lofty perch, the NCAA would have to show that its determination of how many times a particular school's team could appear on television during a season or how many games could be televised on a given Saturday served an educational end. Even if it could make that showing, it might be unwilling to impose such restrictions, for fear of invalidating numerous contracts and alienating its many members whose teams now appear on television, thanks to a proliferation of cable networks. But an educational purpose is evident in eliminating football games on weeknights and in shortening the length of the regular season; both changes would enable athletes to better attend to their studies. An educational purpose is also evident in a rule capping coaches' salaries, such as by prohibiting coaches from earning more in salary than the highest paid professor on campus or more than 90 percent of what the university president earns. The proposed law would facilitate the adoption of such rules by the NCAA, while also affording greater protection to accused parties during NCAA enforcement proceedings. Thus, the College Sports Legal Reform Act would effectively reverse *Board of Regents v. NCAA* and *NCAA v. Tarkanian,* thereby making college sports less commercial and fairer to the participants than they are today.

In other words, the proposed law derives from Justice White's dissents in those two cases. One commentary has observed, "Justice White seemed to know in 1984 [when *Board of Regents* was decided] that without broad NCAA oversight powers, college athletics was in danger of becoming over-commercialized."[1] And so it has become, triggering the need for the exercise of broad powers to tame the college sports monster, which feeds on commercial excess. One way to tame the monster would be to require that football games be played exclusively on Saturdays and that basketball games begin no later than 7:30 p.m. on a weeknight.[2] Former congressman Tom McMillen (D-MD), who played college and professional basketball, has called the Thursday night football telecasts "a giant step backward" and has criticized them for "breaking the tradition of Saturday games and ensuring that even more student-athletes will miss another day or two of classes."[3] Under present law, a rule prohibiting weeknight football games or restricting the starting times of basketball games would be subject to an antitrust challenge, and the NCAA would have to show that the rule's procompetitive virtues outweighed its anticompetitive aspect, namely, limiting the time when the market for college sports was accessible to consumers.[4]

Other ways to tame the monster—ways that the proposed exemption would permit—include prohibiting corporate-sponsored advertisement in college sports facilities and placing spending caps on college athletic departments, perhaps by sport.[5] Both rules would signal that college sports are a part of the academic community, not the world of corporate entertainment. The spending cap would tell the athletic department that it cannot spend lavishly when the rest of the institution is cutting budgets and programs, and the cap would reduce pressure on the academic side of the institution for annual contributions to the athletic department to erase budget deficits. Institutions could also tame the monster by limiting coaches' salaries in return for increasing their job security, perhaps by offering them five-year, renewable contracts. Professor Raymond Yasser has written, in this regard, "It must be made clear that coaches work for the university and they are not independent, roving entrepreneurs."[6] Toward this end, according to Yasser, "Coaches' contracts ought to contemplate that money paid for the P.R. aspects of coaching (e.g. camps, T.V., and radio shows, etc.) belongs to the university, not the coach."[7]

Admittedly, the proposed exemption is similar to the dual standard that federal courts already use when considering antitrust challenges to NCAA rules. Those courts have generally upheld NCAA rules that serve educational purposes or promote amateurism, while often invalidating, as anticompetitive, plainly commercial rules.[8] For example, *Board of Regents v. NCAA* appears to have endorsed what one commentator has termed "the two-pronged antitrust approach to NCAA regulation."[9] In *Board of Regents,* the Supreme Court suggested that coordinated economic activity by NCAA member institutions on matters unrelated to the eligibility of athletes (e.g., the NCAA Football Television Plan) should be subject to a rule-of-reason analysis under the Sherman Act when challenged on antitrust grounds.[10] But rules governing player eligibility and amateurism could be exempt from the antitrust laws or at least subject to less stringent antitrust scrutiny.[11]

Thus, in *Board of Regents,* the Supreme Court laid the foundation for the two-pronged antitrust approach to NCAA regulation noted previously.[12] Therefore, the results in antitrust cases concerning college sports tend to mirror those in antitrust cases concerning professional sports when the issues at hand are unrelated to the athletes who play the games. But when the athletes themselves are at the center of the dispute, the results of antitrust disputes in college sports vary considerably from those in professional sports cases.[13] Indeed, even before *Board of Regents,* in *Justice v. NCAA* in 1983, a federal district court distinguished between commercial and noncommercial rules of the NCAA, reasoning that the former warrant much stricter antitrust analysis, under the rule of reason, than the latter do.[14] After *Board of Regents,* in *United States v. Walters* in 1989, a federal district court held that, among other things, neither the NCAA's eligibility rules restricting compensation to college athletes nor the enforcement of those rules violated the antitrust laws.[15] According to scholar of sports law Walter Champion, the *Walters* court viewed the eligibility rules as substantially different from the NCAA's former television plan, which was purely commercial. Champion argued that the *Walters* court viewed the eligibility rules as "a justifiable means of encouraging competition among amateur teams and therefore procompetitive because they enhance public interest in intercollegiate sports."[16]

Similarly, in *Adidas America, Inc. v. NCAA,* a federal district court upheld, against an antitrust challenge, NCAA Bylaw 12.5.5, which limits the number and size of manufacturers' logos on college athletes' uniforms.[17] The court held that the rule did not violate the antitrust laws because it aimed to (1) protect athletes against commercial exploitation, (2) prevent colleges from turning their athletes into billboards in pursuit of advertising revenues, and (3) avoid excessive advertising that could interfere with the basic function of uniforms (i.e., to identify an athlete's number and team to teammates and referees). Thus, the court concluded that Bylaw 12.5.5 had no commercial purpose; hence the NCAA's enforcement of it was a noncommercial activity not subject to the antitrust laws. Finally, the court concluded that the NCAA did not realize any competitive or financial advantage from limiting manufacturers' logos on uniforms.

The judicially created dichotomy between commercial and noncommercial NCAA rules is not chiseled in stone, though; hence it may not survive in the future. Professor Daniel Lazaroff has observed in this regard,

> If courts continue to accept the idea that NCAA restrictions on athletes' compensation are somehow noncommercial, the *Board of Regents* dichotomy will apply. However, if courts begin to recognize that the academic ideal offered by the NCAA is more of a historical anachronism or a modern fiction, they will no longer be able to justify summary dismissal of student-athlete antitrust claims by simply relying on the dicta that athletes must not be paid. Rather, these courts will be required to assess the anticompetitive and procompetitive effects of challenged restraints within well-defined markets.[18]

Under the new circumstances, if the plaintiffs who challenged a particular NCAA rule could show that the rule had anticompetitive effects within one or more discernible "markets," the NCAA would have to "offer procompetitive justifications" for its rule.[19] The legality of the rule would ultimately depend on its "net competitive effects."[20]

The Consequences of Congressional Inaction

Professor Lazaroff argues that courts should abandon the *Board of Regents* dichotomy and should instead "apply the typical rule of reason analysis found in most Sherman Act litigation" to the NCAA's eligibility rules as well as to its more overtly commercial endeavors.[21] In Lazaroff's view, "Plaintiffs should be required to allege and prove NCAA market power and anticompetitive effects within well-defined product and geographic markets."[22] For example, he argues, college football players could allege that current rules for athletic scholarships "restrain and distort competition within the market for Division I-A collegiate football players in the United States."[23] The rule-of-reason approach would then "afford the NCAA an opportunity to offer proof to offset the plaintiffs' evidence of competitive harm," that is, "to demonstrate procompetitive justifications for its actions."[24]

Forcing the NCAA to defend its eligibility rules against antitrust challenges could end "college sports" as we know them, namely, games played by full-time university students whose only compensation is the opportunity to earn a college degree and who must make reasonable progress toward a degree in order to continue competing. If courts begin to view college athletes as employees and members of a particular labor market, the NCAA will be hard pressed to defend limiting the athletes' "wages" to tuition, fees, room, board, and necessary course books and materials, the benefits of an athletic scholarship.[25] To be sure, enough commercialism has injected itself into college sports that a judge, especially one devoted to free-market economics, could well conclude that NCAA rules limiting the compensation of athletes (i.e., the dollar amount of athletic scholarships) violate the antitrust laws. A 2003 commentary anticipated this possibility, observing, "As more money flows into the pockets of collegiate athletic departments and the NCAA as a whole, there will likely be more challenges to NCAA rules and policies as being violative of antitrust laws."[26]

Antitrust lawsuits could also challenge limits on (1) the number of athletic scholarships an institution can award (see *Agnew v. NCAA,* discussed in chapter 1), (2) wages per season for college athletes who have jobs during the school year, and (3) the size of coaching staffs.[27] The result would be a further blurring, if not an obliteration, of the line between college and professional sports. That unpleasant prospect is the reason why a limited antitrust exemption is necessary for NCAA rules designed to make college sports compatible with higher education. Absent this exemption, the colleges' penchant for excess in athletics, combined with free-market zealotry on the bench, could produce successful antitrust challenges to NCAA rules, challenges that would make college sports virtually indistinguishable from their professional counterparts.

The Major "Economic Reality" of College Sports

Overlooking the current commercial excesses threatening academic values and the integrity of college sports is no solution either. Critics of the *Board of Regents* dichotomy often charge that the courts put their heads in the sand when creating that dichotomy, because the NCAA's rules supposedly protecting "amateurism" actually protect a system whereby the NCAA and the colleges profit immensely while the athletes whose "labor" generates those profits are uncompensated beyond their athletic scholarships. A favorite target of the critics is the language of the United States Court of Appeals for the Seventh Circuit in *Banks v. NCAA,* in which that court upheld, against antitrust challenges, NCAA rules that strip athletes of their eligibility for college sports if they hire an agent or enter the professional draft in a particular sport.[28] In rejecting a college football player's challenge to both rules because they were noncommercial and had no anticompetitive effect, the Seventh Circuit stated that it considered "college football players as student-athletes simultaneously pursuing academic degrees that will prepare them to enter the employment market in non-athletic occupations."[29] The court added, "None of the NCAA rules affecting college football eligibility restrain trade in the market for college football players because the NCAA does not exist as a minor-league training ground for future NFL players but rather to provide an opportunity among amateur students pursuing a collegiate education."[30]

These statements fail to recognize that (1) all or almost all the players drafted each year by the National Football League have played college football; (2) many of those players attended college because they knew playing college football was necessary if they wished to play professional football someday; (3) they may have chosen a college primarily for athletic, not academic, reasons; and (4) once in college, football consumed so much of their time that many of them, especially the less academically prepared players, abandoned thoughts of earning a degree and concentrated on football instead. These conditions prompted one commentator to chastise federal judges for being "blind" to the current commercial realities of big-time college sports. He wrote, "Federal judges, whatever their own personal beliefs, should no longer uphold an aristocratic, Victorian notion of the 'proper' education of young men as a valid defense to Sherman Act violations, particularly when that notion is enforced by a cartel whose own leaders and supporters admit its rampant hypocrisy."[31] Rather, he emphasized that "[j]udges hearing future antitrust challenges to the NCAA's amateurism rules must require the NCAA to prove its various assertions about those rules with actual evidence."[32] Similarly, Professor Lazaroff has observed that some NCAA rules directed at athletes, "such as those addressing academic requirements or the use of performance-enhancing substances, would seem to generate no significant antitrust concerns."[33] But he adds, "The amateurism rules that restrict compensation and other economic benefits to NCAA athletes should not escape antitrust scrutiny by means of a dichotomy that does not comport with real world economic models."[34] Thus, critics of the *Board of Regents* dichotomy would, at a minimum, reduce the category of NCAA rules deemed to be "noncommercial" and, therefore, beyond the reach of the antitrust laws.

Unfortunately, neither the "nostalgic amateurism" model of college sports reflected in the *Banks* decision nor the "economic reality" model offered by critics of *Banks* fully captures the hybrid nature of big-time college sports. On the one hand, commercialism and professionalism are rampant in Division I football and men's basketball, as evidenced by the corporate names attached to college stadiums and football bowl games, the princely sums paid to top coaches in those sports, and the large amount of time players are expected to devote to their respective sports both in and out of season. On the other hand, players must still be full-time students in order to compete, must choose a major and make regular progress toward a degree to continue competing, and can be declared ineligible for competition if they fail to satisfy those requirements.[35] Beyond that, the NCAA operates an Academic Performance Program under which its Committee on Academic Performance calculates an Academic Progress Rate (APR) for each Division I institution, that is, a quantitative measure of the institution's "success in retaining and graduating" its athletes.[36] The committee reviews data supplied by member institutions and conducts analyses revealing (1) the academic progress rates among all Division I teams of both genders from every sport, (2) the academic progress rates among all Division I teams of the same gender in the same sport, and (3) the graduation rate of each of a particular institution's athletic teams compared to the minimum rate required by the NCAA.[37] Failure to meet the Association's minimum requirements on these measures results in a succession of penalties, beginning with a "public warning" for the first instance, increasing to lost scholarships and restrictions on recruiting for the second instance, and culminating in ineligibility for postseason competition after the third instance.[38]

Admittedly, "academic success" and graduation rates are imperfect measures, because academic requirements are subject to manipulation through nonrigorous curricula, grade inflation, and outright academic fraud. But whether or not an institution takes its athletes' academic lives seriously, all but a select few athletes will have to earn a living outside professional sports when their college playing days are over. According to the National Football League Players Association, of the 100,000 high school seniors who play football every year, only 215, or 0.002 percent, will earn a position on an NFL roster.[39] Looked at another way, of the 9,000 players who play college football each season, only 310, or 3 percent, will receive invitations to the NFL scouting combine, the pool of players from whom the NFL teams will select their picks in the annual draft.[40] The 215 who earn roster positions represent 2.4 percent of the total number of college players. The average length of an NFL career is about 3.5 seasons.[41]

No comparable data are available from the National Basketball Players Association, but an estimate of the chances of playing in the National Basketball Association is possible by comparing the number of NBA players to the number of players on college teams. The NBA consists of 30 teams, each with a 12-man roster, for a total of 360 players. That number compares to more than 300 college teams in Division I alone, or a total of more than 3,600 players. Thus, even if one excludes college players from Division II and III teams, the number of college players who earn a position on an NBA roster is approximately 360 of 3,600, or 10 percent.[42] When Divisions II and III are included, the number of college teams increases to 900, and the number of college players increases to more than 10,000. The 360 who play in the NBA represent less than 1 percent of the total number of college players. Additional professional opportunities are available overseas and in the NBA Development League, but they are not so numerous as to improve dramatically the odds of playing professional basketball.

The major "economic reality" of college sports, then, is that regardless of their chances of playing a sport professionally, college athletes need to prepare themselves for careers outside of professional sports. The legal structure underlying college sports and the rules governing college sports ought to help them do that. A legal structure that views college sports primarily as a commercial venture, as the Supreme Court did in *Board of Regents,* will not achieve this goal. Scholar of sports law Gary Roberts recognized this when he observed that "[p]reserving some modicum of educational integrity in the academy is simply not reconcilable with maximizing consumer welfare in the sports entertainment marketplace."[43]

Instead of focusing on "consumer welfare," the legal structure of college sports ought to emphasize the welfare of college athletes, as President Scott Cowan of Tulane University has recommended. According to President Cowan, institutions should "continue to enhance student-athlete welfare, not by paying them more money, but by reducing time requirements, pressures, and expectations."[44] An important means toward that end would be the limited antitrust exemption for college sports alluded to earlier in this chapter. Former congressman Tom McMillen has observed that "only the Congress, through an antitrust exemption, can restore the power of the purse string to the NCAA, since the Supreme Court stripped the NCAA of control over the football broadcasting contracts in 1984."[45] Similarly, only Congress has the constitutional authority to require the NCAA to honor due process in its enforcement system;[46] as noted in chapter 7, courts have consistently invalidated state legislative efforts to impose due process on the NCAA.[47] The College Sports Legal Reform Act, proposed in this chapter, would confer a limited antitrust exemption on the NCAA while also requiring the Association to provide persons accused of violating its rules with the procedural protections introduced in chapter 7.

The Proposed Legislation

The Act would read as follows:

A BILL

To exempt from the antitrust laws certain conduct engaged in by the National Collegiate Athletic Association (NCAA) jointly with member institutions for the purpose of enabling the NCAA to improve educational opportunities for college athletes and to provide due process for persons accused of violating NCAA rules.

Be it enacted by the Senate and House of Representatives of the United States of America in Congress assembled,

Sec.1 Short Title

This Act may be cited as the College Sports Legal Reform Act.

Sec. 2 Findings

Congress finds that

(1) the National Collegiate Athletic Association (NCAA) and college sports have a direct and substantial effect on interstate commerce;

(2) NCAA member institutions conduct amateur athletic events in the 50 states;

(3) the NCAA and its member institutions receive revenue from these amateur athletic events through a variety of means, including broadcasting rights, cable television rights, sponsorship of amateur athletic events, endorsement of products, licensing agreements, event ticket sales, and advertising;

(4) the numerous means of earning revenue through college sports and the vast sums that can potentially be earned have created powerful incentives to commercialize college sports, which commercialization threatens the institutions housing and sponsoring college teams by encouraging the construction of elaborate and costly athletic facilities, the compensation of football and men's basketball coaches at levels far exceeding the compensation of top institutional executives, and insufficient attention to the academic success and nonathletic career preparation of college athletes;

(5) despite the potential loss of a livelihood or a college scholarship faced by coaches and athletes accused of violating NCAA rules, the procedural protections they receive in such circumstances fail to meet constitutional standards of due process; and

(6) NCAA member institutions are limited in their authority to combat commercial excesses in college sports and have been reluctant to enact the reforms necessary to correct the deficiencies in the NCAA rule enforcement process.

Sec. 3 Definitions

For purposes of this Act,

(1) *amateur athletic events* means regular season and postseason athletic contests between teams sponsored by NCAA member institutions and played under rules promulgated by the NCAA;

(2) *antitrust laws* has the meaning given to it in subsection (a) of the first section of the Clayton Act (15 U.S.C. 12(a)), except that such term includes section 5 of the Federal Trade Commission Act (15 U.S.C. 45) to the extent section 5 applies to unfair methods of competition;

(3) *member institutions* means postsecondary educational institutions belonging to the NCAA;

(4) *coaches* means individuals who

(A) are employed, full-time or part-time, by NCAA member institutions to instruct, manage, and prepare for competition institutionally sponsored athletic teams or

(B) are graduate students who receive educational financial assistance from the institutions they attend in return for assisting in coaching athletic teams sponsored by those institutions or

(C) are volunteers who assist in coaching institutionally sponsored athletic teams for the purpose of acquiring experience in coaching;

(5) *discovery, depositions,* and *document production* have the meanings given to them by the Federal Rules of Civil Procedure; and

(6) *representative of an institution's athletic interests* has the meaning given to it by the *NCAA Division I Manual,* published annually by the NCAA.

TITLE I — ANTITRUST EXEMPTION

Sec. 101 Limited Exemption from Antitrust Laws
If the requirements of Section 201 are met within one year after the date of the enactment of this Act, then the antitrust laws shall not apply to any conduct engaged in by the NCAA, a principal purpose of which is to enhance educational opportunities for college athletes or to make intercollegiate athletic programs compatible with the educational missions of colleges and universities. This antitrust exemption shall extend to NCAA actions having commercial consequences, as long as at least one principal purpose of any such action is educational. But the exemption shall not extend to NCAA actions for which the NCAA cannot show an educational purpose. No antitrust exemption shall apply to any conduct engaged in by the NCAA if the NCAA fails to meet the requirements of Section 201 within one year of the date of the enactment of this Act.

TITLE II — DUE PROCESS

Sec. 201 Protections Afforded

(a) In General — The requirements of this section are met if the NCAA puts in place and enforces rules providing for due process before

(1) suspending or reprimanding a coach or an athlete from a team representing an NCAA member institution;

(2) suspending the telecommunications privileges of a member institution; or

(3) prohibiting a member institution from participating in an amateur athletic event.

(b) Required Procedures—Not later than one year after the date of the enactment of this Act, the NCAA shall

   (1) hire professional judges, from among candidates with experience as trial or appellate judges or administrative law judges, to preside at enforcement hearings and appeals, issue subpoenas when necessary, and issue final judgments in enforcement matters;

   (2) institute a prehearing discovery process, including depositions and document production, during which NCAA staff and counsel for accused parties may gather and exchange pertinent information;

   (3) permit accused parties, including coaches, athletes, institutional employees, and institutions themselves, to confront and cross-examine opposing witnesses at hearings;

   (4) at the discretion of the hearing judge, permit that a nonparty whom the NCAA or the accused institution has identified as having engaged in wrongdoing or having enabled wrongdoing to occur may present an oral or written statement at the hearing, subject to rebuttal by the institution; at any party's request, the judge shall require the statements to be given under oath or affirmation;

   (5) when the NCAA and the accused institution have identified an employee or representative of the institution's athletic interest as having engaged in or enabled wrongdoing, prohibit a member institution from firing or permanently reassigning the employee or disassociating itself from the representative until after the case has been resolved and the nonparty's role in it has been determined; and

   (6) open all hearings and appellate proceedings to the public, except when an accused party objects; this rule shall not apply to the posthearing deliberations of the appellate panels, which shall be closed to the public.

(c) Automatic Operation of Required Procedures—If the NCAA fails to put in place the procedures identified in part (b) of this section within one year of the date of the enactment of this Act, those procedures shall take effect automatically as of that date.

Beginning on the effective date, the NCAA must observe those procedures before a coach, athlete, or institution of higher learning can be suspended or reprimanded as a result of sanctions or the threat of sanctions imposed by the NCAA on the coach, athlete, or institution.

(d) Special Enforcement Fund—Not later than 90 days after the date of the enactment of this Act, the NCAA shall create a special fund to defray the expenses associated with the changes to the rule enforcement process described in this section.

(e) Report Relating to Progress in Instituting Due Process—Not later than 180 days after the date of the enactment of this Act, the president of the NCAA shall submit a report to Congress that

(1) identifies the actions the NCAA has taken to date to implement the procedures required by Section 201; and

(2) describes the remaining actions to be taken and the NCAA's plans for implementing them on or before the one-year deadline established by Section 201.

A Carrot and a Stick

Enactment of the College Sports Legal Reform Act would mitigate the adverse effects of *NCAA v. Board of Regents* and *NCAA v. Tarkanian* on the governance of college sports. On the one hand, the act would empower the NCAA to counter the commercial excesses plaguing college sports, thereby honoring its stated purpose, namely, "to maintain intercollegiate athletics as an integral part of the educational program and the athlete as an integral part of the student body and, by so doing, retain a clear line of demarcation between intercollegiate athletics and professional sports."[48] This authority, conferred by the limited antitrust exemption, would also enable the NCAA to avoid or at least to defend itself successfully in lawsuits challenging Association rules that pursue educational ends but have commercial consequences, such as capping coaches' salaries or requiring football games to be played on Saturdays. Therefore, the act offers an important "carrot" to the NCAA, namely, reduced exposure to antitrust challenges.[49]

On the other hand, the act requires the NCAA to be more athlete-friendly than it has historically been, by including in its enforcement proceedings due process protections akin to those applicable in federal and state administrative hearings. This requirement is a "stick" because (1) the NCAA cannot enjoy the antitrust exemption without implementing due process and (2) the due process protections will take effect automatically if the NCAA fails to implement them voluntarily within one year of the act's passage. Therefore, even if the NCAA fails to enhance due process voluntarily, the act would change the NCAA's behavior permanently by requiring it to make its enforcement proceedings fairer and more professional.

But the due process requirement is also a carrot, because increased due process is likely to improve the image of the NCAA in the eyes of the public generally and coaches and athletes in particular. Moreover, voluntary adoption of the act's due process protections would entitle the NCAA to an antitrust exemption, enabling it to implement educationally sound, athlete-friendly reforms while avoiding antitrust suits that might otherwise flow from those reforms. In this way, the act would shift the Association's focus away from antitrust and toward building trust with its member institutions, their coaches, and their athletes. It would also offer the NCAA's president, Mark Emmert, who took office in October 2010, a chance to make good on his claim that his job is "all about the student-athletes."[50]

Thus, the College Sports Legal Reform Act would increase the NCAA's authority to honor its own constitution by making college sports compatible with higher education. In return, the NCAA must provide coaches, athletes, and institutions accused of violating its rules with due process protections reflecting the high stakes involved in its enforcement proceedings. As a result, institutions would benefit from reduced commercialism, coaches and athletes would benefit from a fairer enforcement process, and the NCAA would enjoy an improved public image.

Why Reward the NCAA?

The reader might reasonably ask why the College Sports Legal Reform Act would reward the NCAA with an antitrust exemption despite the Association's reputation for being more interested in revenues than in the welfare of athletes.[51] After all, the Association created its Football Television Plan to maximize revenue by limiting televised games, thereby presumably keeping live attendance high. No educational purpose motivated the architects of the Football Television Plan. The Association also resisted adopting any due process protections until the early 1990s, and it continues to resist using professional judges in its enforcement proceedings and opening those proceedings to the public.

The answer to the question about rewarding the NCAA is twofold. First, the proposed statute is limited in its generosity to the NCAA, reflecting an awareness of the Association's history and skepticism about its commitment to the educational values it espouses. After all, the statute would confer only a limited antitrust exemption, which would serve educational ends, and the exemption is conditioned on the NCAA adopting the due process protections specified in the statute. Second, as the most powerful regulatory body governing college sports and the only one governing big-time college sports, the NCAA is the logical entity to implement any new legal arrangements Congress creates on this subject. In short, despite the NCAA's history of promoting commercialism and rejecting due process, Congress must work with it in order to make the governance of college sports less commercially driven and more respectful of individual rights.

The College Sports Legal Reform Act is skeptical about the NCAA but also hopeful that the NCAA can make college sports more compatible with higher education and fairer to individuals and institutions when given the right combination of inducements and directives to achieve those ends. The act sends an unmistakable message to the NCAA that it should focus less on revenues and more on educational integrity and procedural fairness. An equally unmistakable message of the act is that when Congress thinks that the NCAA has failed to govern college sports in a fair and educationally sound manner, it will intervene.

Waking the Sleeping Giant

Congress tends to be a sleeping giant regarding college sports; by and large, it prefers to remain on the sidelines and let the NCAA govern the games. Occasionally, it is spurred to hold hearings on a particular issue, but those hearings rarely result in legislation. Moreover, at this writing, in 2011, Congress is preoccupied with revitalizing an anemic economy; hence, reforming the legal structure of college sports is unlikely to be a high priority or the subject of early action.

But the giant is sleepy, not dead. During the 1990s Congress enacted two statutes directed specifically at college sports. The Student Athlete Right-to-Know Act, which was enacted in 1990 and took effect in 1992, requires every institution awarding athletic scholarships to disclose annually to the secretary of education graduation rates for recipients of athletic scholarships, according to race, gender, and sport, as compared to their nonathlete classmates, and to provide this information to every athlete whom it offers an athletic scholarship and to the athlete's parents, guidance counselor, and high school coach.[52]

The Equity in Athletics Disclosure Act, which Congress enacted in 1994, requires each coeducational college or university receiving federal funds and sponsoring intercollegiate athletic teams to annually report to the secretary of education data regarding participation and employment opportunities in sports for males and females at the responding institution, along with revenues and expenditures of the men's and women's teams at that institution.[53] The reporting institution must provide the data to students and potential students, upon request, and to the public, and it must notify students of their right to request such information. The secretary of education must make the annual reports submitted by institutions available to the public within a reasonable period of time after their submission. Thus, the enactment by Congress of a statute designed to make college sports fairer and more educationally sound would not be unprecedented.

Moreover, the College Sports Legal Reform Act is written in a manner designed to encourage its enactment. It is cautious and not overly ambitious. It does not designate the NCAA a "state actor" for purposes of the enforcement program, as did the Coach and Athlete's Bill of Rights (1991), which failed to become law.[54] A federal court would likely have found the latter unconstitutional had it been enacted, because Congress is not authorized to designate an institution a state actor under the Constitution. Only a court can make that determination. Instead, under the College Sports Legal Reform Act, if the NCAA failed to adopt the due process protections listed in the act by the stated deadline date, they would take effect automatically as of that date. But the NCAA's failure to adopt them voluntarily would cost it an antitrust exemption.

In conditioning an antitrust exemption on only one action—namely, the adoption of due process protections—the College Sports Legal Reform Act is sufficiently narrow that it would likely be referred only to the judiciary committee in each house of Congress, thereby enhancing the chances for passage. In this way, the proposed law is different from the ill-fated Collegiate Athletics Reform Act (1991), which was multifaceted, requiring referral to several committees in the House of Representatives.[55] The latter bill conditioned an antitrust exemption for the NCAA on its agreement to changes in its governance, a new plan of revenue distribution for member institutions, and the awarding of athletic scholarships for five years instead of one.[56] That bill would also have stripped the NCAA and its members of their respective exemptions from federal income taxation had the NCAA refused to adopt constitutional standards of due process.[57]

In its limited focus, the proposed law is also different from legislation advocated in a recent commentary, which would condition an antitrust exemption for the NCAA on its agreement to (1) make athletic scholarships at least four-year grants instead of the one-year grants they are now, (2) require member institutions to provide free medical care or health insurance for all sports-related injuries, (3) furnish remedial assistance and tutoring for athletes whose academic credentials are below a certain percentile for their institution's freshman class, and (4) establish a postgraduate scholarship program for former college athletes. This proposal, although laudable, could be difficult to enact because its financial, medical, and educational components would likely trigger consideration by more than one committee in each house of Congress.[58]

The narrow tailoring of the College Sports Legal Reform Act follows the advice of former congressman Lee Hamilton (D-IN), who has written that "[o]ne of the concerns in bill drafting is to decide how broadly or narrowly to draft a bill to avoid it being referred to too many committees."[59] Similarly, Congressional scholar Walter Oleszek has written that the more committees a bill is referred to, the more "opportunities arise for delay, negotiation, compromise, and bargaining."[60] Oleszek notes that in order to avoid this problem when introducing Internet legislation several years ago, two members of the House Judiciary Committee drafted their bill to amend the Sherman Antitrust Act, which is within that committee's exclusive jurisdiction. Had they drafted the bill more broadly, it might have also been referred to the House Commerce Committee, whose jurisdiction includes the Telecommunications Act of 1996.[61]

The proposed bill's narrowness also makes it relatively easy for the public to understand, especially the due process portion, and for journalists to explain. These features are important because, as Lee Hamilton explains, "[m]oving legislation today requires both an 'inside' and an 'outside' strategy—working to develop not only member interest but also public support."[62] In building public support for legislation, he notes, "the media can be a powerful friend or a powerful adversary."[63] The proposed law is designed to be media-friendly so as to encourage the media to be friendly to it.

Beyond that, the College Sports Legal Reform Act would not cost the American taxpayer any money. No appropriation of federal funds would be necessary, because the NCAA would incur the costs associated with implementing the due process protections the act requires. Furthermore, the specificity, simplicity, and frugality of the act would address the concerns of the Knight Commission on Intercollegiate Athletics, whose June 2010 report lamented excessive spending in college sports but decided against recommending an antitrust exemption for the NCAA. According to the commission, obtaining such an exemption is "a complicated, time-consuming, and expensive endeavor that is by no means assured of success."[64] The act's features would make its consideration less complicated, time-consuming, and expensive and its passage more likely than the commission suggests.

Still, Congress may refuse to do its part. If Congress fails to act, the prediction offered by Gary Roberts several years ago will come true. He wrote that unless Congress changes the legal foundation of college sports, "we are probably doomed to a future where random challenges to NCAA rules will succeed or fail based largely on the appeal of the plaintiffs and the personal predilections of the judge, and where the legal doctrine is so vague and malleable that any result is possible."[65] Roberts is correct, but vague, malleable legal doctrines ensure only more costly litigation, not wise public policy. The coaches and athletes who devote themselves to college sports deserve better. The ball is in Congress's court.

Parting Thoughts

Commercial excess and procedural unfairness plagued college sports long before the Supreme Court decided *NCAA v. Board of Regents* and *NCAA v. Tarkanian*. But those decisions exacerbated both problems. *Board of Regents* treated college sports as just another entertainment enterprise, using the antitrust laws to maximize consumer welfare. Among the results of this decision have been Thursday night college football telecasts, multimillion-dollar compensation packages for coaches, and an increasingly blurry distinction between college and professional sports. *Tarkanian* added insult to injury by not requiring the NCAA to provide due process to those accused of violating its rules while working in the entertainment enterprise that *Board of Regents* fostered. Because of the *Tarkanian* decision, no process is due even though accused individuals stand to lose an educational opportunity or a livelihood if found culpable.

The respective legacies of *Board of Regents* and *Tarkanian* live on, more than ten years into the new millennium. College sports are riddled with commercial excess, yet the NCAA faces antitrust challenges if it tries to rein in athletic commerce. It cannot give itself an antitrust exemption. Individuals and institutions accused of violating NCAA rules face an enforcement process that appears to be stacked against them. The NCAA could adopt fairer due process protections for accused individuals and institutions but thus far has declined to do so. Only Congress can provide both an antitrust exemption and due process simultaneously. The College Sports Legal Reform Act would do precisely that.

The act is necessary because amateurism is worth saving. Indeed, saving amateurism is crucial because the overwhelming majority of college athletes will not become professional athletes. Therefore, athletes must use their college years primarily to prepare for nonathletic careers, and institutions must enable athletes to prepare for careers beyond sports, just as they enable nonathletes to do. The first and most important step toward saving amateurism is for Congress to mitigate the adverse effects of *NCAA v. Board of Regents* and *NCAA v. Tarkanian* by enacting the College Sports Legal Reform Act. The sooner Congress does so, the sooner college sports will become educationally sound and fair to their participants.

NOTES

CHAPTER I

1. Jay Weiner, Chip Scoggins, and Rachel Blount, "College Football: TV Coverage Is Court's Gift to Sports Fans," *Minneapolis Star Tribune,* November 9, 2004.

2. Ibid.

3. Robert H. Frank, *Challenging the Myth: A Review of the Links among College Athletic Success, Student Quality, and Donations,* May 2004, http://www.knightcommission.org/images/pdfs/kcia_frank_report_2004.pdf.

4. Ibid., 6. See also Keith Dunnavant, *The Fifty-Year Seduction: How Television Manipulated College Football, from the Birth of the Modern NCAA to the Creation of the BCS* (New York: St. Martin's, 2004), 262.

5. Steve Wieberg, Jodi Upton, A. J. Perez, and Steve Burkowitz, "College Football Coaches' Salaries Rise in Down Economy," *USA Today,* November 9, 2009.

6. 468 U.S. 85 (1984).

7. 15 U.S.C. § 1.

8. See Weiner, Scoggins, and Blount, "College Football."

9. Ibid.

10. *NCAA v. Board of Regents of the University of Oklahoma,* 468 U.S. 85, 94 (1984).

11. Ibid., 91 n. 4.

12. Ibid., 107.

13. Ibid., 121.

14. Ibid., 124.

15. Ibid., 128.

16. Dennis J. Hutchinson, *The Man Who Once Was Whizzer White: A Portrait of Justice Byron R. White* (New York: Free Press 1998), 1.

17. Ibid., 53.

18. Ibid., 55–57.

19. Ibid., 4.

20. Ibid., 60–61.

21. Ibid., 64.

22. Ibid., 86–87.

23. Ibid., 93.

24. Ibid., 142.

25. Ibid., 160.

26. Ibid., 170.

27. Ibid.

28. Ibid.

29. Ibid., 178.

30. Ibid., 227. White's desire to keep his name out of the newspapers reflected his fatigue and irritation with the relentless press coverage that had attended his athletic celebrity. But it also reflected his innate modesty, to which one of his former law clerks attested in a tribute published in the *Stanford Law Review* after Justice White's death. See David C. Frederick, *Justice White and the Virtues of Modesty*, 55 Stanford Law Review 21, 23 (2002).

31. Ibid., 450.

32. Alfred Wright, "A Modest All-American Who Sits on the Highest Bench," *Sports Illustrated*, December 10, 1962, 85–98.

33. Welch Suggs, "Football, Television, and the Supreme Court," *Chronicle of Higher Education*, July 9, 2004, A32–A33.

34. Dunnavant, *Fifty-Year Seduction*, 226.

35. Ibid., 264.

36. Brad Wolverton, "5 Questions for the Fall," *Chronicle of Higher Education*, September 2, 2005, A63–A65.

37. Ibid.

38. Ibid.

39. See Associated Press, "Boise State to Join Mountain West Conference," June 11, 2010.

40. Ibid., 267.

41. Brian L. Porto, *A New Season: Using Title IX to Reform College Sports* (Westport, CT: Praeger, 2003), 65.

42. Ibid., 66.

43. Erik Brady and Jodi Upton, "NCAA Recognizes Growing Problem with Costs," *USA Today*, November 17, 2005, C10.

44. Ibid.

45. Ibid.

46. Ibid.

47. Ibid.

48. Jack Gillum, Jodi Upton, and Steve Berkowitz, "Amid Funding Crisis College Athletics Soak Up Subsidies, Fees," *USA Today*, January 15, 2010.

49. Ibid.

50. Art and Science Group, LLC, *Knight Commission on Intercollegiate Athletics: Quantitative and Qualitative Research with Football Bowl Subdivision University Presidents on the Costs and Financing of Intercollegiate Athletics: Report of Findings and Implications*, October 2009, 8, http://www.knightcommissionmedia.org/images/President_Survey_FINAL.pdf.

51. Knight Commission on Intercollegiate Athletics, *Restoring the Balance: Dollars, Values, and the Future of College Sports,* June 2010, 4, http://www.knightcommission .org.

52. Only 1.3 percent of seniors playing college basketball and 2 percent of seniors playing college football become professionals in their respective sports. *Supporting Our Intercollegiate Student-Athletes: Proposed NCAA Reforms; Hearings before the Subcommittee on Commerce, Trade, and Consumer Protection of the House Committee on Energy and Commerce,* 108th Cong., 2d sess., May 18, 2004, 4 (comments of Representative Cliff Stearns [R-FL]).

53. Brad Wolverton, "23 of 56 Bowl Teams Fail to Meet New NCAA Academic Standards, Report Says," *Chronicle of Higher Education,* December 16, 2005, A36.

54. Welch Suggs, "Low Graduation Rates for Top Basketball Teams Spur Criticism of Colleges and Education Department," *Chronicle of Higher Education,* March 24, 2004.

55. Ibid.

56. Ibid.

57. Brad Wolverton, "NCAA Rescinds Scholarships at 65 Colleges," *Chronicle of Higher Education,* March 10, 2006, A35.

58. Brad Wolverton, "Graduation Rates Remain at Record High," *Chronicle of Higher Education,* January 27, 2006.

59. Brad Wolverton, "23 of 56 Bowl Teams Fail to Meet New NCAA Academic Standards, Report Says," *Chronicle of Higher Education,* December 16, 2005, A36.

60. Ibid.

61. Ibid.

62. Press release, Institute for Diversity and Ethics in Sport, "Academic Progress/Graduation Rate Study of Division I NCAA Men's Basketball Tournament Teams Reveals Marked Improvement in Overall Graduation Rates But Large Continuing Disparities of the Success of White and African-American Student-Athletes," March 12, 2006, 1.

63. Ibid., 2.

64. Ibid.

65. Ibid.

66. Ibid., 3.

67. Institute for Diversity and Ethics in Sport, *Academic Progress/Graduation Success Rate Study of Division I NCAA Women's and Men's Basketball Tournament Teams,* March 16, 2010, http://www.tidesport.org.

68. Institute for Diversity and Ethics in Sport, *Keeping Score When It Counts: Assessing the 2009–10 Bowl-Bound College Football Teams—Academic Performance Improves, but Race Still Matters,* December 7, 2009, http://www.tidesport.org.

69. Brad Wolverton, "The Clicker Crowd," *Chronicle of Higher Education,* March 3, 2006, 38.

70. Jeff Rabjohns, "College Football's Exposure Explodes," *Indianapolis Star,* November 15, 2004.

71. Sara Lipka, "Intense Pressure of College Sports Begins with Recruiting Process, College Athletes Tell Knight Commission," *Chronicle of Higher Education,* January 31, 2006.

72. Libby Sander, "Athletes' Graduation Rates Hit Another High, NCAA Says," *Chronicle of Higher Education,* November 27, 2009, A20.

73. Brad Wolverton, "Athletes' Hours Renew Debate over College Sports," *Chronicle of Higher Education,* January 25, 2008, A1.

74. Kendra Nichols, "Men's Basketball Program at U. of Georgia Faces Probation and Loss of Scholarships," *Chronicle of Higher Education,* August 6, 2004.

75. David Shieh, "NCAA Orders Florida State U. to Forfeit Wins over Cheating Scandal," *Chronicle of Higher Education,* March 6, 2009.

76. Regarding the history and the consequences of the contract between Notre Dame and NBC, see generally Mark Yost, *Varsity Green: A Behind the Scenes Look at the Culture and Corruption in College Sports* (Stanford, CA: Stanford University Press, 2010).

77. 488 U.S. 179 (1988).

78. Ibid., 193.

79. Ibid., 197 n. 18.

80. Ibid., 199.

81. Ibid.

82. Ibid.

83. Ibid., 202.

84. Kevin E. Broyles, *NCAA Regulation of Intercollegiate Athletics: Time for a New Game Plan,"* 46 Alabama Law Review 487–568 (1995).

85. *Due Process and the NCAA: Hearing before the Subcommittee on the Constitution of the House Committee on the Judiciary,* 108th Cong., 2d sess., September 14, 2004, 20 (statement of Professor Gary Roberts), http://www.house.gov/judiciary.

86. Gary R. Roberts, *Resolution of Disputes in Intercollegiate Athletics,* 35 Valparaiso Law Review 431, 447 (2001).

87. Broyles, *NCAA Regulation of Intercollegiate Athletics,* 513.

88. Welch Suggs, "The NCAA's Scapegoat Question," *Chronicle of Higher Education,* May 6, 2005, A39–A41.

89. Ibid.

90. Ibid.

91. *Due Process and the NCAA* (statement of Dr. B. David Ridpath).

92. Ibid.

93. *Ridpath v. Board of Governors of Marshall University, et al.,* United States District Court for the Southern District of West Virginia, Docket Number 3:03-2037, Plaintiff's Complaint, 4. On February 1, 2009, Dr. Ridpath and Marshall reached a settlement whereby Marshall agreed to write a letter to the NCAA's Committee on Infractions stating that Ridpath's removal from his athletic post was not connected to the major rules violations that occurred at Marshall and to pay Ridpath a mone-

tary settlement in return for his decision not to proceed to trial (e-mail message to the author from B. David Ridpath, February 2, 2009).

94. *Due Process and the NCAA* (statement of Dr. Ridpath).

95. Ibid.

96. *Ridpath v. Board of Governors of Marshall University, et al.,* Complaint, 5.

97. Ibid., 6.

98. Ibid.

99. Ibid., 7.

100. Ibid.

101. *Due Process and the NCAA* (statement of Dr. Ridpath).

102. Ibid., 67–68.

103. National Symposium on Athletics Reform, New Orleans, LA, November 11, 2003, 6, http://symposium.tulane.edu/.

104. Ibid.

105. Tom McMillen and Paul Coggins, *Out of Bounds: How the American Sports Establishment Is Being Driven by Greed and Hypocrisy—and What Needs to Be Done about It* (New York: Simon and Schuster 1992), 226.

106. Ibid., 222–23.

107. Ibid., 224.

108. Ibid.

109. Ibid.

110. James L. Musselman, *Recent Federal Income Tax Issues regarding Professional and Amateur Sports,* 13 Marquette Sports Law Review 195–209 (2003).

111. McMillen and Coggins, *Out of Bounds,* 225.

112. Arthur A. Fleischer, III, Brian L. Goff, and Robert D. Tollison, *The National Collegiate Athletic Association: A Study in Cartel Behavior* (Chicago: University of Chicago Press 1992).

113. 388 F.3d 955 (6th Cir. 2004).

114. Ibid., 957.

115. Ibid.

116. Ibid.

117. Ibid.

118. The NFL's antitrust exemption appears in the Sports Broadcasting Act, 15 U.S.C. § 1291.

119. Suggs, "Football, Television, and the Supreme Court." This article is correct that the NCAA passed up the chance for an antitrust exemption, but incorrect in stating that the NFL obtained its exemption in 1951 rather than 1961.

120. Ibid.

121. Gary R. Roberts, *The NCAA, Antitrust, and Consumer Welfare,* 70 Tulane Law Review 2631 (1996).

122. Ibid.

123. Ibid., 2673.

124. Ibid., 2673–74.

125. Tom Price, "Reforming Big-Time College Sports," *CQ Researcher,* undated.

126. National Symposium on Athletics Reform, 28.

127. Ibid., 29.

128. Fleischer, Goff, and Tollison, *National Collegiate Athletic Association: A Study in Cartel Behavior,* 15.

129. 134 F.3d 1010 (10th Cir. 1998).

130. Porto, *New Season,* 210.

131. Ibid.

132. Ibid.

133. Ibid.

134. 977 F.2d 1081 (7th Cir. 1992).

135. Ibid., 1090.

136. Richard J. Hunter and Ann M. Mayo, *Issues in Antitrust, the NCAA, and Sports Management,* 10 Marquette Sports Law Journal 69, 74–75 (1999).

137. Brad Wolverton, "Former College Athletes Accuse NCAA of Antitrust Violations in Vast Lawsuit over Scholarship Cap," *Chronicle of Higher Education,* March 10, 2006.

138. Ibid.

139. Ibid.

140. Ibid.

141. Ibid. See also *White et al. v. NCAA,* United States District Court for the Central District of California, Case No. CV06-0999 RGK, February 17, 2006, Complaint, 2.

142. *White et al. v. NCAA,* Complaint, 16, quoting NCAA Operating Bylaw 15.02.5.

143. Porto, *New Season,* 208.

144. Ibid.

145. Ibid., 209.

146. Ibid.

147. Ibid.

148. Brad Wolverton, "NCAA Will Pay Big to Settle Antitrust Lawsuit," *Chronicle of Higher Education,* February 8, 2008, A15. See also "*White v. NCAA*" at http://www.ncaa.org/wps/portal/ncaahome?WCM_GLOBAL_CONTEXT=/ncaa/ncaa/academics+and+athletes/education+and+research/white+v+ncaa.

149. "Suit Against NCAA Now In Court In Indy," http://indianalawblog.com/archives/2011/03/ind_courts_suit_8.html (accessed May 26, 2011).

150. "Frequently Asked Questions," http://www.ncaa.org/wps/wcm/connect/public/NCAA/Enforcement/resources/FAQ.

CHAPTER 2

1. Benjamin G. Rader, *American Sports: From the Age of Folk Games to the Age of Televised Sports,* Fourth Edition (Upper Saddle River, NJ: Prentice Hall, 1999), 181.

2. John Sayle Watterson, *College Football: History, Spectacle, Controversy* (Baltimore: Johns Hopkins University Press 2000), 72.

3. Rader, *American Sports,* 181.

4. Ronald A. Smith, *Sports and Freedom: The Rise of Big-Time College Athletics* (New York: Oxford University Press, 1988), 202; Watterson, *College Football,* 78.

5. Allen L. Sack and Ellen J. Staurowsky, *College Athletes for Hire: The Evolution and Legacy of the NCAA's Amateur Myth* (Westport, CT: Praeger, 1998), 34.

6. Brian L. Porto, *A New Season: Using Title IX to Reform College Sports* (Westport, CT: Praeger, 2003), 31.

7. Andrew Zimbalist, *Unpaid Professionals: Commercialism and Conflict in Big-Time College Sports* (Princeton, NJ: Princeton University Press, 1999), 91–92.

8. Porto, *New Season,* 33.

9. Ibid.

10. Paul R. Lawrence, *Unsportsmanlike Conduct: The National Collegiate Athletic Association and the Business of College Football* (Westport, CT: Praeger, 1987), 29.

11. John R. Thelin, *Games Colleges Play: Scandal and Reform in Intercollegiate Athletics* (Baltimore: Johns Hopkins University Press, 1996), 60.

12. Zimbalist, *Unpaid Professionals,* 93.

13. Rader, *American Sports,* 263.

14. Thelin, *Games Colleges Play,* 125.

15. Ira Horowitz, "The Reasonableness of Horizontal Restraints: NCAA," in John E. Kwoka, Jr., and Lawrence J. White, eds., *The Antitrust Revolution: The Role of Economics,* Second Edition (New York: HarperCollins, 1994), 214–37.

16. Ibid.

17. Porto, *New Season,* 34.

18. Zimbalist, *Unpaid Professionals,* 94.

19. Ibid.

20. Keith Dunnavant, *The Fifty-Year Seduction: How Television Manipulated College Football, from the Birth of the Modern NCAA to the Creation of the BCS* (New York: St. Martin's, 2004), 9.

21. Ibid., 14.

22. Porto, *New Season,* 35.

23. Dunnavant, *Fifty-Year Seduction,* 14.

24. Point-shaving is winning by fewer points than the quoted point spread. The point spread is a guess as to the number of points by which a particular team is likely to win a game. Gamblers pay players to "fix" games by shaving points because point-shaving enables the gamblers to profit by "beating the point spread." See Porto, *New Season,* 37.

25. Dunnavant, *Fifty-Year Seduction,* 28.

26. Zimbalist, *Unpaid Professionals,* 94.

27. Ibid., 96; see also Walter Byers and Charles Hammer, *Unsportsmanlike Conduct: Exploiting College Athletes* (Ann Arbor: University of Michigan Press, 1995), 90.

28. Zimbalist, *Unpaid Professionals,* 96.

29. Lawrence, *Unsportsmanlike Conduct,* 78.

30. Porto, *New Season*, 35.

31. Lawrence, *Unsportsmanlike Conduct*, 78.

32. Dunnavant, *Fifty-Year Seduction*, 32.

33. Ibid., 124.

34. Horowitz, "Reasonableness of Horizontal Restraints," 217.

35. Ibid., 134.

36. Dunnavant, *Fifty-Year Seduction*, 123.

37. Ibid., 123–24.

38. John J. Siegfried and Molly Gardner Burba, *The College Football Association Television Broadcast Cartel*, 49 Antitrust Bulletin 799, 801 (Fall 2004).

39. Dunnavant, *Fifty-Year Seduction*, 64.

40. Watterson, *College Football*, 342.

41. Ibid., 343.

42. Ibid.

43. Ibid.

44. Ibid., 344.

45. Ibid.

46. Ibid.

47. Ibid.

48. Ibid.

49. Ibid.

50. Siegfried and Burba, *College Football Association Television Broadcast Cartel*, 801.

51. Ibid., 345.

52. Ibid., 345–46. See also Dunnavant, *Fifty-Year Seduction*, 152.

53. Siegfried and Burba, *College Football Association Television Broadcast Cartel*, 801.

54. Dunnavant, *Fifty-Year Seduction*, 154.

55. Ibid.

56. Ibid.

57. 392 F. Supp. 295 (D. Mass. 1975).

58. Ibid., 296.

59. The Sherman Antitrust Act appears in Title 15 of the United States Code, beginning at Section 1.

60. 392 F. Supp. at 303.

61. Ibid.

62. Ibid., quoting *Eastern R.R. Presidents Conference v. Noerr Motor Freight, Inc.*, 365 U.S. 127, 81 S.Ct. 523, 5 L.Ed.2d 464 (1961).

63. 392 F. Supp. at 304.

64. Ibid.

65. Ibid.

66. 564 F.2d 1136 (5th Cir. 1977).

67. Ibid., 1149.

68. Ibid.

69. Ibid., 1151.

70. Ibid., 1152.

71. Ibid., 1153.

72. Ibid., 1154.

73. 577 F. Supp. 356 (D. Ariz. 1983). *Justice* was decided after both the trial and appellate courts had ruled in *Regents v. NCAA* but before the Supreme Court heard *Regents*. This chapter discusses *Justice* before discussing *Regents* partly because the final decision in *Justice* preceded the final decision in *Regents* but also, more important, because *Justice* illustrates the reasoning that enabled the NCAA to win antitrust cases prior to *Regents*.

74. Ibid., 362.

75. Ibid., 378.

76. Ibid., 379.

77. Ibid.

78. Ibid., 382.

79. Ibid.

80. Ibid., 383.

81. Ibid.

82. Ibid. Recall that by the time *Justice* was decided, both a federal trial court and a federal appellate court had already ruled in *Regents,* so the court in *Justice* was able to consult and cite both *Regents* opinions in drawing its distinction between NCAA rules designed primarily to preserve amateurism and NCAA rules with a more pronounced economic purpose and more direct anticompetitive consequences.

83. 499 F. Supp. 537 (S.D. Ohio 1980).

84. Ibid., 545.

85. Ibid.

86. Ibid., 546.

87. 546 F. Supp. 1276, 1292 (W.D. Okla. 1982).

88. Ibid.

89. Ibid.

90. This purpose is reflected in the language of the *Ground Rules for Two-Network Scheduling,* which accompanied the 1982–85 television contracts the NCAA signed with ABC and CBS, respectively. Paragraph 6 of Article 10 states that the purpose of the equity games "shall be to establish an equitable foundation of games chosen by each network for its schedule." This information is available in *NCAA v. Regents,* Joint Appendix, 50.

91. 546 F. Supp. at 1292.

92. Ibid., 1293.

93. Ibid.

94. Ibid.

95. Ibid., 1294.

96. Ibid.

97. Ibid.

98. Ibid.

99. Ibid., 1295.

100. Ibid., 1296.

101. Ibid., 1313.

102. Ibid.

103. Ibid., 1315.

104. Ibid., 1316.

105. Ibid.

106. Ibid., 1317.

107. Ibid., 1319.

108. *Board of Regents v. NCAA,* 707 F.2d 1147, 1153 (10th Cir. 1983).

109. Ibid.

110. Ibid., 1154.

111. Ibid., citing *National Society of Professional Engineers v. United States,* 435 U.S. 679, 98 S.Ct. 1355, 55 L.Ed.2d 637 (1978), in which the Supreme Court, based on a rule-of-reason analysis, held that the society's ethical rule prohibiting competitive bidding by its members violated the Sherman Act.

112. Ibid., 1160.

113. Ibid.

114. Ibid., 1161.

115. Ibid., 1163.

116. Ibid., 1165.

117. Ibid., 1167.

118. Ibid.

119. Ibid.

120. Ibid.

121. Ibid., 1168.

122. Ibid.

CHAPTER 3

1. 468 U.S. at 94.

2. Ibid., 93.

3. *NCAA v. Board of Regents of the University of Oklahoma,* Transcript of Oral Argument, March 20, 1984, 3.

4. Ibid.

5. 468 U.S. at 94.

6. Ibid.

7. Ibid., 99.

8. Ibid.

9. Ibid.

10. Ibid.

11. Ibid.

12. Ibid., 99–100.

13. Ibid., 100.

14. Ibid., quoting *Broadcast Music, Inc. v. Columbia Broadcasting System, Inc.,* 444 U.S. 1, 19–20 (1979).

15. Ibid.

16. Ibid., 101.

17. Ibid.

18. Ibid.

19. Ibid., 102.

20. Ibid.

21. Ibid.

22. Ibid.

23. Ibid., 103.

24. Ibid.

25. Ibid., 104.

26. Ibid.

27. Ibid., 106–7.

28. Ibid., 107, quoting *Reiter v. Sonotone Corp.,* 442 U.S. 330, 343 (1970).

29. Ibid., 107.

30. Ibid., 108.

31. Ibid.

32. Ibid., 109.

33. *NCAA v. Regents,* Petitioner's Brief, 41.

34. Ibid.

35. 468 U.S. at 109.

36. Ibid., 110.

37. Ibid., 111.

38. Ibid.

39. *Board of Regents v. NCAA,* 546 F. Supp. 1276, 1297 (1982).

40. Ibid.

41. *NCAA v. Regents,* 468 U.S. at 113.

42. Ibid., 114.

43. Ibid., 91 n. 4.

44. *NCAA v. Regents,* Petitioner's Brief, 20.

45. Ibid.

46. Ibid.

47. Ibid., 48.

48. Ibid., 17.

49. Ibid., 21.

50. Ibid., 20.

51. *NCAA v. Regents,* 468 U.S. at 114.

52. Ibid.

53. Alvin K. Klevorick, *The Fractured Unity of Antitrust Law and the Antitrust Jurisprudence of Justice Stevens,* 27 Rutgers Law Journal 637 (Spring 1996).

54. Robert H. Lande, *Consumer Choice as the Ultimate Goal of Antitrust,* 62 University of Pittsburgh Law Review 503, 503 (2001).

55. Ibid., 504.

56. Ibid., 525.

57. Ibid., 648.

58. Ibid.

59. Ibid.

60. Ibid., 655.

61. *NCAA v. Regents,* 468 U.S. at 116.

62. Ibid.

63. Ibid.

64. Ibid.

65. Ibid., 117.

66. Ibid.

67. Ibid.

68. Ibid., 119, citing *Board of Regents v. NCAA,* 546 F. Supp. 1276, 1296, 1309–10.

69. *Regents v. NCAA,* 546 F. Supp. at 1310.

70. *NCAA v. Regents,* 468 U.S. at 119.

71. Ibid., 120.

72. In 1986 Chief Justice Warren Burger, who had held that post since 1969, retired, and President Ronald Reagan appointed Rehnquist chief justice. Rehnquist had served on the Court since 1971.

73. *NCAA v. Regents,* 468 U.S. at 121.

74. Ibid., 122, quoting *Association for Intercollegiate Athletics for Women v. NCAA,* 558 F. Supp. 487, 494 (D.C. 1983), *affirmed,* 735 F.2d 577 (1984).

75. 468 U.S. at 122.

76. Ibid., 123.

77. Ibid.

78. Ibid.

79. Ibid.

80. Ibid., quoting *Kupec v. Atlantic Coast Conference,* 399 F. Supp. 1377, 1380 (M.D.N.C. 1975).

81. Ibid., 123–24.

82. Ibid., 124.

83. Ibid.

84. Ibid., 126.

85. Ibid., 128.

86. Ibid., 129.

87. Ibid.

88. Ibid.

89. Ibid., 130.

90. Ibid.

91. Ibid., 131.

92. Ibid., 128.

93. Ibid.

94. Ibid.

95. Ibid., 131.

96. Ibid., 133, quoting *NCAA v. Regents,* 707 F.2d at 1168.

97. Ibid.

98. Ibid., 134, quoting *Goldfarb v. Virginia State Bar,* 421 U.S. 773, 788 n. 17, 95 S.Ct. 2004 (1975).

99. 421 U.S. 773, 95 S.Ct. 2004 (1975).

100. Ibid., 775–76.

101. Ibid., 776–77.

102. Ibid., 779.

103. Ibid., 786.

104. Ibid., 788.

105. Ibid.

106. Ibid., 788 n. 17.

107. 468 U.S. at 134.

108. 435 U.S. 679 (1978).

109. 468 U.S. at 134.

110. *NCAA v. Regents,* Transcript of Oral Argument, March 20, 1984, 24.

111. Ibid.

112. Ibid.

113. Ibid.

114. 435 U.S. at 683.

115. Ibid., 684.

116. Ibid., 685.

117. Ibid.

118. Ibid., 686.

119. Ibid., 687.

120. Ibid., 688.

121. Ibid., 689.

122. Ibid., 689–90.

123. Alan J. Meese, *Competition and Market Failure in the Jurisprudence of Justice Stevens,* 74 Fordham Law Review 1775, 1778 (2006).

124. *National Society of Professional Engineers,* 435 U.S. at 691.

125. Meese, *Competition and Market Failure,* 1789.

126. Ibid.

127. Ibid., 694.

128. Ibid., 696.

129. Ibid.

130. Ibid., 697.

131. *NCAA v. Regents,* 468 U.S. at 135, quoting Eugene D. Gulland, J. Peter Byrne, and Sheldon Elliot Steinbach, *Intercollegiate Athletics and Television Contracts: Beyond Economic Justifications in Antitrust Analysis of Agreements Among Colleges,* 52 Fordham Law Review 717, 728 (1984).

132. Ibid.

133. Ibid.

134. Ibid., quoting *NCAA v. Regents*, 707 F.2d at 1167.

135. Ibid., 136, citing *Tackling Intercollegiate Athletics: An Antitrust Analysis*, 87 Yale Law Journal 655, 676 n. 106 (1978).

136. Ibid., quoting Gulland, Byrne, and Steinbach, *Intercollegiate Athletics and Television Contracts*, 722.

137. Ibid.

138. James T. Malysiak, *Justice White on Antitrust: Protecting Freedom to Compete*, 58 no. 3 University of Colorado Law Review 497, 514 (Summer 1987).

139. Ibid., 512.

140. Ibid.

141. Ibid., 497.

142. Ibid., 512.

143. Dennis J. Hutchinson, *The Man Who Once Was Whizzer White: A Portrait of Justice Byron R. White* (New York: Free Press, 1998), 60.

144. Keith Dunnavant, *The Fifty-Year Seduction: How Television Manipulated College Football, from the Birth of the Modern NCAA to the Creation of the BCS* (New York: St. Martin's, 2004), 166.

145. Richard A. Posner, *Antitrust Law*, Second Edition (Chicago: University of Chicago Press, 2001), 32 (emphasis in original).

146. Ibid., 2.

147. Robert H. Bork, *The Antitrust Paradox: A Policy at War with Itself* (New York: Free Press, 1978, 1993), 435.

148. Ibid.

149. Ibid.

150. Ibid.

151. *NCAA v. Regents*, Transcript of Oral Argument, March 20, 1984, 32.

152. Ibid.

153. Ibid., 41.

154. Ibid.

155. Ibid., 50.

156. Ibid.

157. Ibid., 51.

158. *NCAA v. Regents*, Respondents' Brief, 27.

159. Ibid., 28.

160. Peter C. Corstensen and Paul Olszowka, *Antitrust, Student-Athletes, and the NCAA: Limiting the Scope and Conduct of Private Economic Regulation*, 1995 Wisconsin Law Review 545, 589 (1995).

161. Ibid., 590.

162. *NCAA v. Regents*, Respondents' Brief, 12 (emphasis in original).

163. *NCAA v. Regents*, Petitioner's Reply Brief, 3–14.

164. Ibid., 18–19.

165. See Supreme Court Rule 37, http://www.supreme court.gov.

166. *NCAA v. Regents,* Amicus Curiae Brief of the National Federation of State High School Associations, at 1.

167. Ibid., 2. Unlike the NCAA, though, the National Federation has jurisdiction over academic competitions, such as speech and music, in addition to sports. The NCAA's jurisdiction pertains exclusively to sports.

168. Ibid., 14.

169. Ibid.

170. Ibid.

171. Ibid., 3.

172. Ibid., 4.

173. Ibid.

174. Ibid., 17.

175. The National Federation's fear that invalidation of the Football Television Plan would result in collegiate encroachment on Friday night high school football appears to have been unfounded. Encroachment has not occurred, perhaps because of the Professional Sports Telecasting Act (15 U.S.C. §§ 1291 et seq.), enacted by Congress in 1966, which provides that the National Football League's antitrust exemption for sales of the television rights to its members' games would not apply if the NFL sought to televise its games on Friday nights or Saturday afternoons during the regular high school and college football seasons. Technically, this law only protects high schools from encroachment by professional football telecasts, but its spirit reflects an apparent congressional intent to protect both Friday night high school football and Saturday afternoon college football. Therefore, if television networks and the NCAA had tried to schedule college games on Friday nights after *NCAA v. Regents,* either Congress, the federal courts, or both would likely have thwarted the attempt by means of legislation or the finding of an antitrust violation.

176. *NCAA v. Regents,* 468 U.S. at 136.

177. *NCAA v. Regents,* NCAA's Brief, 20.

CHAPTER 4

1. Michael S. Serrill, "Taking Away the NCAA's Ball," *Time,* July 9, 1984, 77–78.

2. Ibid.

3. Ibid.

4. Keith Dunnavant, *The Fifty-Year Seduction: How Television Manipulated College Football, From the Birth of the Modern NCAA to the Creation of the BCS* (New York: St. Martin's, 2004), 170.

5. *The Supreme Court Decision in NCAA v. University of Oklahoma: Hearing before the U.S. Senate Committee on the Judiciary,* 98th Cong., 2d sess., November 19, 1984, 27 (statement of Neal H. Pilson, executive vice president, CBS Broadcast Group).

6. Ibid.

7. Ibid.

8. Dunnavant, *Fifty-Year Seduction,* 170.

9. Ibid.

10. David Greenspan, *College Football's Biggest Fumble: The Economic Impact of the Supreme Court's Decision in National Collegiate Athletic Association v. Board of Regents of the University of Oklahoma*, 33 Antitrust Bulletin 1, 26 (Spring 1988).

11. John J. Siegfried and Molly Gardner Burba, *The College Football Association Television Broadcast Cartel*, 49 no. 3 Antitrust Bulletin 799, 802 (Fall 2004).

12. Serrill, "Taking Away the NCAA's Ball," 77-78.

13. Dunnavant, *Fifty-Year Seduction*, 173.

14. Ibid.

15. Ibid.

16. Ibid., 174.

17. Ibid.

18. William Taafe, "A Supremely Unsettling Smorgasbord," *Sports Illustrated*, September 5, 1984, 150-51.

19. Ibid.

20. Ibid.

21. Greenspan, *College Football's Biggest Fumble*, 49.

22. Ibid. Syndicators act as brokers, buying the secondary rights to a team's or a conference's games (i.e., rights to games the major networks do not intend to telecast) and then reselling those rights to individual stations or networks. See D. Kent Meyers and Ira Horowitz, *Private Enforcement of the Antitrust Laws Works Occasionally: Board of Regents of the University of Oklahoma v. NCAA, A Case in Point*, 48 Oklahoma Law Review 669, 693 (Winter 1995).

23. Dunnavant, *Fifty-Year Seduction*, 185.

24. Ibid., 177.

25. Ibid., 233.

26. Title IX can be found in Title 20 of the United States Code, beginning at Section 1681 and ending at Section 1688.

27. Dunnavant, *Fifty-Year Seduction*, 185.

28. Ibid., 189.

29. Ibid., 195.

30. Ibid., 196.

31. Ibid.

32. Ibid., 198.

33. Ibid., 214.

34. Ibid., 224.

35. Ibid., 226.

36. Ibid.

37. Ibid., 227.

38. Ibid., 241.

39. Brian L. Porto, *A New Season: Using Title IX to Reform College Sports* (Westport, CT: Praeger, 2003), 39. Miami, along with Boston College and Virginia Tech, has since left the Big East in favor of the Atlantic Coast Conference.

40. Dunnavant, *Fifty-Year Seduction*, 233-34.

41. Ibid., 236.

42. Ibid., 237.

43. Porto, *New Season,* 39.

44. Ibid.

45. Ibid., 39–40.

46. Jasen R. Corns, *Pigskin Paydirt: The Thriving of College Football's Bowl Championship Series in the Face of Antitrust Law,* 39 Tulsa Law Review 167, 172 (2003).

47. Brad Wolverton, "5 Questions for the Fall," *Chronicle of Higher Education,* September 2, 2005, A63.

48. Ibid.

49. Ibid.

50. Ibid.

51. Ibid.

52. Siegfried and Burba, *College Football Association Television Broadcast Cartel,* 804.

53. Ibid.

54. Ibid.

55. Ibid.

56. Ibid., 804–5.

57. Ibid., 809.

58. Ibid., 805.

59. Ibid., 810.

60. Dunnavant, *Fifty-Year Seduction,* 262.

61. Brad Wolverton and Sara Lipka, "Experts Urge Knight Commission to Try to Cap Coaches' Salaries and Curtail Recruiting," *Chronicle of Higher Education,* January 23, 2007.

62. Adam R. Schaefer, *Slam Dunk: The Case for an NCAA Antitrust Exemption,* 83 North Carolina Law Review 555, 560 (2005).

63. Robert H. Frank, *Challenging the Myth: A Review of the Links among College Athletic Success, Student Quality, and Donations,* May 2004, 6, http://www.knightcommission.org/images/pdfs/kcia_frank_report_2004.pdf.

64. Jay Weiner, Chip Skoggins, and Rachel Blount, "College Football: TV Coverage Is Court's Gift to Sports Fans," *Minneapolis Star Tribune,* November 9, 2004.

65. Ibid.

66. Chad Pekron, *The Professional Student-Athlete: Undermining Amateurism as an Antitrust Defense in NCAA Compensation Challenges,* 24 Hamline Law Review 24, 64 (2000).

67. Meyers and Horowitz, *Private Enforcement of the Antitrust Laws,* 689.

68. Ibid.

69. Ibid.

70. *NCAA v. Board of Regents of the University of Oklahoma,* 468 U.S. 85, 128 (1984).

71. Welch Suggs, "Jock Majors," *Chronicle of Higher Education,* January 17, 2003.

72. Welch Suggs, "New Grades on Academic Progress Show Widespread Failings among Teams," *Chronicle of Higher Education,* March 11, 2005.

73. Ibid.

74. Ibid.

75. Brad Wolverton, "NCAA Penalizes 112 Teams for Failing to Meet Its Academic-Progress Requirements," *Chronicle of Higher Education,* May 3, 2007.

76. Ibid.

77. Ibid.

78. Murray Sperber, "When Academic Progress Isn't," *Chronicle of Higher Education,* April 15, 2005.

79. Suggs, "Jock Majors."

80. Ibid.

81. Ibid.

82. Brad Wolverton, "Athletics Participation Prevents Many Players from Choosing Majors They Want," *Chronicle of Higher Education,* January 8, 2007.

83. Dunnavant, *Fifty-Year Seduction,* 239.

84. Ibid., 239.

85. Brad Wolverton and Sara Lipka, "Experts Urge Knight to Fight High Salaries and Recruiting Pressures," *Chronicle of Higher Education,* February 2, 2007, A28–A30.

86. Brad Wolverton, "NCAA Ruling on Preparatory Schools Could Send More Athletes to Junior Colleges," *Chronicle of Higher Education,* May 11, 2007.

87. Ibid.

88. Robin Wilson, "Where Have All the Women Gone?" *Chronicle of Higher Education,* May 4, 2007, A40–A44.

89. Porto, *New Season,* 65.

90. Ibid., 65–66.

91. David Scott Moreland, *The Antitrust Implications of the Bowl Championship Series: Analysis through Analogous Reasoning,* 21 Georgia State University Law Review 721, 724 (Spring 2005).

92. Ibid.

93. Ibid., 724–25.

94. Jodi M. Warmbrod, *Antitrust in Amateur Athletics: Fourth and Long; Why Non-BCS Universities Should Punt Rather Than Go For an Antitrust Challenge to the Bowl Championship Series,* 57 Oklahoma Law Review 333, 341 (2004).

95. Corns, *Pigskin Paydirt,* 177.

96. Moreland, *Antitrust Implications,* 738.

97. Ibid., 725.

98. Ibid., 736–37.

99. Ibid., 741–42.

100. Ibid., 745.

101. Ibid.

102. Corns, *Pigskin Paydirt,* 193.

103. Ibid., 188.

104. Ibid.

105. Ibid., 189.

106. Ibid.

107. Ibid., 187.

108. Ibid.

109. Ibid., 195.

110. Warmbrod, *Antitrust in Amateur Athletics,* 372.

111. Corns, *Pigskin Paydirt,* 195.

112. Ibid.

113. Ibid., 200.

114. Ibid.

115. Ibid., 201.

116. Moreland, *Antitrust Implications,* 748.

117. Gary R. Roberts, *The NCAA, Antitrust, and Consumer Welfare,* 70 Tulane Law Review 2631, 2673 (1996).

118. Ibid.

119. Howard J. Savage, Harold W. Bentley, John T. McGovern, and Dean F. Smiley, *American College Athletics,* Bulletin No. 23 (New York: Carnegie Foundation for the Advancement of Teaching, 1929), 240. See also Porto, *New Season,* 32.

120. Lindsay J. Rosenthal, *From Regulating Organization to Multi-Billion Dollar Business: The NCAA Is Commercializing the Amateur Competition It Has Taken Almost a Century to Create,* 13 Seton Hall Journal of Sport Law 321, 328 (2003).

121. Ibid., 329.

122. Stanton Wheeler, *Rethinking Amateurism and the NCAA,* 15 Stanford Law and Policy Review 213, 217 (2004).

123. Ibid.

124. Ibid., 227.

125. Richard J. Hunter and Ann H. Mayo, *Issues in Antitrust, the NCAA, and Sports Management,* 10 Marquette Sports Law Journal 69, 82 (1999).

126. *Gaines v. NCAA,* 746 F. Supp. 738 (M.D. Tenn. 1990); *Banks v. NCAA,* 977 F.2d 1081 (7th Cir. 1992); *Law v. NCAA,* 134 F.3d 1010 (10th Cir. 1998); *Worldwide Basketball and Sport Tours, Inc. et al. v. NCAA,* 388 F.3d 955 (6th Cir. 2004).

127. 746 F. Supp. at 740.

128. Ibid.

129. Ibid., 740–41.

130. Ibid., 741.

131. Ibid., 742.

132. Ibid., 744.

133. Ibid.

134. Ibid.

135. Ibid., 744–45.

136. Ibid., 746.

137. Ibid.

138. Ibid.

139. Ibid., 747.

140. Ibid.

141. Ibid.

142. 977 F.2d 1081 (7th Cir. 1992).

143. Ibid., 1083.

144. Ibid.

145. Ibid., 1087.

146. Ibid., 1089–90.

147. Ibid., 1090.

148. Ibid., 1094.

149. Ibid.

150. Ibid., 1095.

151. Ibid., 1097.

152. Ibid., 1098.

153. Ibid., quoting *NCAA v. Regents,* 468 U.S. at 117, 104 S.Ct. at 2969.

154. Ibid.

155. Ibid., 1099.

156. Ibid., 1099–1100.

157. In 1999 the NCAA signed a contract for $6 billion giving CBS the rights to televise the men's basketball tournament for 11 years. See Schaefer, *Slam Dunk,* 560.

158. *Gaines v. NCAA,* 746 F. Supp. 738, 744 (M.D. Tenn. 1990).

159. Ibid.

160. 134 F.3d 1010 (10th Cir. 1998).

161. Ibid., 1013.

162. Ibid., 1014–15.

163. Ibid., 1015.

164. The district court's decision is located at 902 F. Supp. 1394 (D. Kan. 1995).

165. 134 F.3d 1010, 1019 (10th Cir. 1998).

166. Ibid.

167. Ibid.

168. Ibid., 1020.

169. Ibid., 1021.

170. Ibid.

171. Ibid., 1022.

172. Ibid.

173. Ibid., 1023.

174. Ibid.

175. Ibid., 1024.

176. Ibid.

177. Ibid.

178. Ibid. Affirming the district court's injunction did not resolve the damages portion of the lawsuit, though. In April 1999, the NCAA paid the plaintiffs $54.5 million to settle the lawsuit. The NCAA member institutions contributed $18.125

million to this amount, and the rest came directly from the Association's funds. Even institutions belonging to Divisions II and III, which did not employ RECs, were required to contribute to the settlement fund. See Porto, *New Season,* 210.

179. 388 F.3d 955 (6th Cir. 2004).

180. This rule appeared in Article 17.5.5.4 of the NCAA's operating bylaws. See Michael B. Licalsi, *The Whole Situation Is a Shame, Baby! NCAA Self-Regulations Categorized as Horizontal Combinations under the Sherman Act's Rule of Reason Standard: Unreasonable Restraints of Trade or an Unfair Judicial Test?* 12 George Mason Law Review 831, 851 (Spring 2004).

181. Ibid., 851–52.

182. Ibid., 852.

183. *Worldwide Basketball and Sport Tours, Inc. et al v. NCAA,* 273 F. Supp.2d 933, 935 (S.D. Ohio 2003). Under the previous rule, a Division I team could play in an exempt tournament every year, as long as it did not play in the same tournament twice within four years. See Schaefer, *Slam Dunk,* 559.

184. *Worldwide Basketball,* 273 F. Supp.2d at 935.

185. Ibid., 936.

186. Schaefer, *Slam Dunk,* 559.

187. *Worldwide Basketball,* 273 F. Supp.2d at 936.

188. Ibid., 953–54.

189. Ibid., 954.

190. Ibid.

191. Ibid., 953.

192. Ibid.

193. *Worldwide Basketball and Sport Tours, Inc. et al. v. NCAA,* 388 F.3d 955, 959 (6th Cir. 2004).

194. Ibid., 961.

195. Ibid., 962.

196. Ibid., 963–64.

197. Schaefer, *Slam Dunk,* 566.

198. 488 U.S. 179 (1988).

CHAPTER 5

1. Robert C. Berry and Glen M. Wong, *Law and Business of the Sports Industries: Common Issues in Amateur and Professional Sports,* Volume 2, Second Edition (Westport, CT: Praeger, 1993), 102.

2. Don Yeager, *Undue Process: The NCAA's Injustice For All* (Champaign, IL: Sagamore, 1991), 13.

3. Ibid.

4. Ibid.

5. Ibid., 131.

6. Ronald J. Thompson, *Due Process and the National Collegiate Athletic Association: Are There Any Constitutional Standards?* 41 UCLA Law Review 1651, 1663 (1994).

7. Berry and Wong, *Law and Business of the Sports Industries,* 104.

8. Ibid.

9. Ibid.

10. Ibid.

11. Ibid.

12. Ibid.

13. Ibid.

14. Ibid., 106.

15. Ibid.

16. Charles Alan Wright, *Responding to an NCAA Investigation, or, What to Do When an Official Inquiry Comes,* 1 Entertainment and Sports Law Journal 19, 31 (1984).

17. Ibid.

18. Berry and Wong, *Law and Business of the Sports Industries,* 104.

19. Ibid.

20. Ibid.

21. C. A. Wright, *Responding to an NCAA Investigation,* 33.

22. Berry and Wong, *Law and Business of the Sports Industries,* 104.

23. Ibid.

24. Ibid.

25. Ibid.

26. Ibid.

27. Ibid., 107.

28. Arthur A. Fleischer, III, Brian L. Goff, and Robert D. Tollison, *The National Collegiate Athletic Association: A Study in Cartel Behavior* (Chicago: University of Chicago Press, 1992), 71, 134.

29. Ibid.

30. Ibid.

31. Ibid., 106.

32. C. A. Wright, *Responding to an NCAA Investigation,* 24.

33. Quoted in Richard Harp and Joseph McCullough, *Tarkanian: Countdown of a Rebel* (New York: Leisure Press, 1984), 171.

34. Ibid., 154.

35. *Enforcement Program of the National Collegiate Athletic Association: Report together with Minority Views by the Subcommittee on Oversight and Investigations of the Committee on Interstate and Foreign Commerce,* House of Representatives, 95th Cong., 2d sess., 1978, 4 (statement of Norman Sloan).

36. Ibid.

37. Ibid., 1.

38. Ibid. See also Tom McMillen and Paul Coggins, *Out of Bounds: How the American Sports Establishment Is Being Driven by Greed and Hypocrisy—and What Needs to be Done about It* (New York: Simon and Schuster, 1992), 211.

39. Ibid. See also Pete Thamel, "With Eye on Football, Big East Adds T.C.U.," *New York Times,* November 29, 2010.

40. Ibid., 6.

41. Ibid., 32. See also Ronald J. Thompson, *Due Process and the National Collegiate Athletic Association: Are There Any Constitutional Standards?* 41 UCLA Law Review 1651, 1666 (1994).

42. *Enforcement Program of the National Collegiate Athletic Association,* 18.

43. Ibid., 26.

44. Ibid., 33.

45. Ibid., 34.

46. Ibid., 38.

47. Ibid., 40.

48. Ibid.

49. Ibid., 34.

50. Ibid.

51. Ibid., 22.

52. Ibid.

53. Ibid., 24–26.

54. Ibid., 27.

55. Ibid.

56. Ibid.

57. Yeager, *Undue Process,* 244.

58. *Enforcement Program of the National Collegiate Athletic Association,* 40.

59. Ibid.

60. Ibid., 42.

61. Ibid., 51.

62. Ibid.

63. Ibid.

64. Ibid., 55.

65. McMillen and Coggins, *Out of Bounds,* 212.

66. Harp and McCullough, *Tarkanian,* 171.

67. Ibid.

68. C. Peter Goplerud, III, *NCAA Enforcement Process: A Call for Procedural Fairness,* 20 Capital University Law Review 543, 548 (1991).

69. Yeager, *Undue Process,* 254.

70. Ibid., 255.

71. Ibid., 259.

72. Ibid., 259–60.

73. Ibid., 261–62.

74. Jerry Tarkanian and Dan Wetzel, *Runnin' Rebel: Shark Tales of "Extra Benefits," Frank Sinatra, and Winning It All* (Champaign, IL: Sports Publishing, 2005), 229. Tarkanian was nearly as successful in 19 years of coaching at UNLV as he had been during 5 years at Long Beach State. His UNLV teams won 509 games, while losing only 105, for a remarkable .829 winning percentage. His 1990 UNLV team won the NCAA Men's Basketball Championship. Tarkanian ranks among the top five Division I coaches of all time in winning percentage (ibid., xv).

75. Thompson, *Due Process and the National Collegiate Athletic Association,* 1661.

76. Ibid.

77. Stephen R. Van Camp, *National Collegiate Athletic Association v. Tarkanian: Viewing State Action Through the Analytical Looking Glass,* 92 West Virginia Law Review 761, 761 (1990).

78. Don Yeager, *Shark Attack: Jerry Tarkanian and his Battle with the NCAA and UNLV* (New York: HarperCollins, 1992), 80–81.

79. Christopher V. Carlyle, *NCAA Due Process: Its Past and Its Future,* 12 SPG Entertainment and Sports Lawyer 10, 10 (Spring 1994).

80. *NCAA v. Tarkanian,* No. 87-1061, United States Supreme Court, October Term, 1987, Joint Appendix, 122–40.

81. Ibid., 140–41.

82. Ibid., 141–42.

83. Ibid., 156.

84. Ibid., 158–59.

85. Ibid., 161.

86. Ibid., 163.

87. Ibid., 166–67.

88. Ibid., 171.

89. Ibid., 174–75.

90. Ibid., 176.

91. Ibid., 177.

92. Tarkanian and Wetzel, *Runnin' Rebel,* 59.

93. Ibid., 64.

94. Ibid.

95. Matthew M. Keegan, *Due Process and the NCAA: Are Innocent Student-Athletes Afforded Adequate Protection from Improper Sanctions? A Call for Change in the NCAA Enforcement Procedures,* 25 Northern Illinois University Law Review 297, 311–12 (Spring 2005).

96. Ibid.

97. Ibid.

98. Ibid.

99. Yeager, *Undue Process,* 203.

100. Ibid.

101. Keegan, *Due Process and the NCAA,* 312.

102. Ibid.

103. Ibid.

104. Keegan, *Due Process and the NCAA,* 312.

105. Yeager, *Undue Process,* 202.

106. Ibid.

107. Ibid.

108. Harp and McCullough, *Tarkanian,* 153.

109. Ibid.

110. Ibid., 153–54.

111. Yaeger, *Undue Process*, 202–3.

112. *NCAA v. Tarkanian*, Joint Appendix, 76.

113. Ibid., 203.

114. Keegan, 312.

115. Ibid.

116. *NCAA v. Tarkanian*, Joint Appendix, 37–38.

117. Ibid.

118. Ibid.

119. *University of Nevada v. Tarkanian*, 95 Nev. 389, 397, 594 P.2d 1159, 1164 (1979).

120. Ibid.

121. Ibid.

122. See, e.g., *Buckton v. NCAA*, 366 F. Supp. 1152 (D. Mass. 1973); *Associated Students, Inc. v. NCAA*, 493 F.2d 1251 (9th Cir. 1974); *Parish v. NCAA*, 506 F.2d 1028 (5th Cir. 1975); *Howard University v. NCAA*, 510 F.2d 213 (D.C. Cir. 1975); *Regents of the University of Minnesota v. NCAA*, 560 F.2d 352 (8th Cir. 1977).

123. Thompson, *Due Process and the National Collegiate Athletic Association*, 1657–58.

124. Carlyle, *NCAA Due Process*, 10.

125. Thompson, *Due Process and the National Collegiate Athletic Association*, 1658.

126. Ibid., 1659.

127. 366 F. Supp. 1152 (D. Mass. 1973).

128. Ibid.

129. Thompson, *Due Process and the National Collegiate Athletic Association*, 1659–60. See also note 122 to the present chapter for the names of cases decided after *Buckton* that followed the *Buckton* court's reasoning.

130. The citations for these cases are, respectively, 457 U.S. 830, 457 U.S. 991, and 457 U.S. 922.

131. James Potter, *The NCAA as State Actor: Tarkanian, Brentwood, and Due Process*, 155 University of Pennsylvania Law Review 1269, 1275 (May 2007).

132. Ibid., 1280.

133. Ibid., 1279.

134. *Rendell-Baker v. Kohn*, 457 U.S. 830, 837, 102 S.Ct. 2764, 2769 (1982).

135. Potter, *NCAA as State Actor*, 1279–80.

136. *Blum v. Yaretsky*, 457 U.S. 991, 1005, 102 S.Ct. 2777, 2786 (1982).

137. *Arlosoroff v. NCAA*, 746 F.2d 1019 (4th Cir. 1984).

138. Ibid., 1020.

139. Ibid.

140. Ibid.

141. Ibid.

142. Ibid.

143. Ibid., 1021, citing *Regents of the University of Minnesota v. NCAA*, 560 F.2d 352 (8th Cir. 1977); *Howard University v. NCAA*, 510 F.2d 213 (D.C. Cir. 1975); *Parish v. NCAA*, 506 F.2d 1028 (5th Cir. 1975); and *Associated Students, Inc. v. NCAA*, 493 F.2d 1251 (9th Cir. 1974).

144. Ibid.

145. Ibid.

146. Ibid., citing *Rendell-Baker v. Kohn,* 457 U.S. 830, 102 S.Ct. 2764, 73 L.Ed.2d 418 (1982), and *Blum v. Yaretsky,* 457 U.S. 991, 102 S.Ct. 2777, 73 L.Ed.2d 534 (1982).

147. *Arlosoroff v. NCAA,* 746 F.2d 1019, 1021 (4th Cir. 1984).

148. Ibid.

149. Ibid.

150. Ibid., 1022.

151. Ibid.

152. Ibid.

153. Thompson, *Due Process and the National Collegiate Athletic Association,* 1661.

154. Ibid.

155. Potter, *NCAA as State Actor,* 1284.

156. Ibid.

157. *NCAA v. Tarkanian,* Joint Appendix, 26.

158. Ibid.

159. *Tarkanian v. NCAA,* 103 Nev. 331, 333, 741 P.2d 1345 (1987).

160. Ibid. Ordinarily, both plaintiffs and defendants in civil cases decided by American courts pay their own attorney's fees, regardless of which party wins. This is known as the "American Rule." But in the *Tarkanian* case, the coach was able to recover his attorney's fees under 42 U.S.C. § 1988, a federal statute that authorizes the recovery of attorney's fees by plaintiffs who suffered civil rights violations perpetrated by government officials.

161. Ibid. On July 17, 1984, after the second trial, the NCAA tried to remove the *Tarkanian* case to federal court, but the federal court rejected that attempt and returned the case to state court on November 15, 1984.

162. Ibid.

163. Ibid., 335.

164. Ibid., 336.

165. Ibid.

166. Ibid., 337.

167. Ibid.

168. Ibid.

169. *Lugar v. Edmonson Oil Company,* 457 U.S. 922, 937, 102 S.Ct. 2744, 2753 (1982).

170. *Tarkanian v. NCAA,* 103 Nev. 331, 337, 741 P.2d 1345 (1987).

171. Ibid.

172. Ibid.

173. Ibid.

174. Ibid., 338.

175. Ibid.

176. Ibid.

177. Ibid.

178. Ibid., citing *Paul v. Davis,* 424 U.S. 693, 711, 965 S.Ct. 1155, 1165, 47 L.Ed.2d 405, *rehearing denied,* 425 U.S. 985, 96 S.Ct. 2194, 48 L.Ed.2d 811 (1976).

179. Ibid.

180. Ibid., 338–39.

181. Ibid., 339.

182. Ibid.

183. Ibid., 340.

184. Ibid., 340–41.

185. Ibid.

186. Ibid.

187. Ibid.

188. Ibid.

189. Ibid.

190. Ibid.

191. Ibid., 342.

192. Ibid.

193. Ibid.

194. Ibid.

195. Potter, *NCAA as State Actor,* 1284.

CHAPTER 6

1. *NCAA v. Tarkanian,* No. 87-1061, April 29, 1988, Petitioner's Brief, i.

2. 457 U.S. 922, 102 S.Ct. 2744 (1982).

3. *NCAA v. Tarkanian,* No. 187-1061, April 29, 1988, Petitioner's Brief, 24–25.

4. Ibid., 25.

5. Ibid.

6. Ibid.

7. Ibid.

8. Ibid.

9. 746 F.2d 1019 (4th Cir. 1984).

10. See, e.g., *McHale v. Cornell University,* 620 F. Supp. 67 (N.D.N.Y. 1985); *Kneeland v. NCAA,* 650 F. Supp. 1047 (W.D. Tex. 1986); *Graham v. NCAA,* 804 F.2d 953 (6th Cir. 1986); *Hawkins v. NCAA,* 652 F. Supp. 602 (C.D. Ill. 1987).

11. *NCAA v. Tarkanian,* No. 87-1061, April 29, 1988, Petitioner's Brief, 18.

12. Ibid.

13. Ibid.

14. Ibid., 22.

15. Ibid., 25.

16. Ibid., 22.

17. Ibid.

18. Ibid., 25.

19. Ibid.

20. Ibid.

21. Ibid., 26.

22. Ibid.

23. Ibid., 27.

24. Ibid., 28.

25. Ibid.

26. Ibid., 29.

27. Ibid.

28. Ibid.

29. Ibid.

30. Ibid., 31.

31. Ibid.

32. *NCAA v. Tarkanian,* No. 87-1061, April 29, 1988, Respondent's Brief, 22.

33. Ibid.

34. Ibid.

35. Ibid., 23.

36. Ibid., 24.

37. Ibid.

38. Ibid., 26, citing Nev. Rev. Stat. §§ 281.370(1), 396.320(1).

39. Ibid.

40. Ibid.

41. Ibid.

42. Ibid., 27.

43. Ibid., 32.

44. Ibid.

45. Ibid.

46. Ibid., 33.

47. Ibid.

48. Ibid., 29–30 n. 33.

49. Ibid., 34.

50. *NCAA v. Tarkanian,* No. 87-1061, April 29, 1988, Petitioner's Reply Brief, 4.

51. Ibid., 5.

52. Ibid., 7.

53. Ibid.

54. Ibid.

55. Ibid., 8.

56. Ibid., 10.

57. Available at http://www.oyez.org/cases/1980-1989/1988/1988_87_1061/argument.

58. *NCAA v. Tarkanian,* No. 87-1061, Transcript of Oral Argument, October 5, 1988, 3.

59. Ibid.

60. Ibid.

61. Ibid., 5.
62. Ibid., 8.
63. Ibid., 9.
64. Ibid.
65. Ibid., 12.
66. Ibid.
67. Ibid.
68. Ibid., 16.
69. Ibid.
70. Ibid., 17.
71. 488 U.S. 179 (1988).
72. Ibid., 191.
73. Ibid., quoting *Burton v. Wilmington Parking Authority,* 365 U.S. 715, 722 (1961).
74. Ibid.
75. Ibid.
76. Ibid.
77. Ibid.
78. Ibid.
79. Ibid.
80. Ibid.
81. Ibid., 193.
82. Ibid., 194.
83. Ibid.
84. Ibid., 195.
85. Ibid., 196–97.
86. Ibid., 197.
87. Ibid.
88. Ibid., 198.
89. Ibid.
90. Ibid., 199.
91. Ibid.
92. Ibid.
93. Ibid., 200.
94. Ibid., 199.
95. 398 U.S. 144 (1970).
96. 449 U.S. 24 (1980).
97. *NCAA v. Tarkanian,* 488 U.S. 179, 200 (1988).
98. Ibid.
99. Ibid., citing *Dennis,* 449 U.S. at 27.
100. Ibid., quoting *Dennis,* 449 U.S. at 27.
101. Ibid., citing *Adickes,* 398 U.S. at 152.
102. Ibid.
103. Ibid., 201.

104. Ibid.

105. Ibid.

106. Ibid.

107. Ibid., 202.

108. Ibid.

109. Ibid.

110. Ibid.

111. Ibid., 202–3.

112. Ibid., 203.

113. Ibid.

114. Ibid.

115. Ibid.

116. Stephen R. Van Camp, *National Collegiate Athletic Association v. Tarkanian: Viewing State Action through the Analytical Looking Glass,* 92 West Virginia Law Review 761, 772 (1990).

117. Ibid., 770.

118. Ibid., 771.

119. Ibid., 772.

120. *Jackson v. Metropolitan Edison Co.,* 419 U.S. 345, 352–53 (1974).

121. *Flagg Brothers, Inc. v. Brooks,* 436 U.S. 149 (1978).

122. *Rendell-Baker v. Kohn,* 457 U.S. 830, 102 S.Ct. 2764 (1982); *Blum v. Yaretsky,* 457 U.S. 991 (1982).

123. Van Camp, *National Collegiate Athletic Association v. Tarkanian,* 775.

124. Ibid., 782.

125. Ibid., 782–83.

126. Ibid., 783.

127. Ibid., 772.

128. Kevin M. McKenna, *The Tarkanian Decision: The State of College Athletics Is Everything but State Action,* 40 DePaul Law Review 459, 461 (1991).

129. James L. Arslanian, *The NCAA and State Action: Does the Creature Control Its Master?* 16 Journal of Contemporary Law 333, 355 (1990).

130. Robin J. Green, *Does the NCAA Play Fair? A Due Process Analysis of NCAA Enforcement Regulations,* 42 Duke Law Journal 99, 109 (1992).

131. Ibid.

132. Ibid.

133. Ibid., 110.

134. Branden Tedesco, *National Collegiate Athletic Association v. Tarkanian: A Death Knell for the Symbiotic Relationship Test?* 18 Hastings Constitutional Law Quarterly 237, 244 (Fall 1990).

135. Ibid., 252.

136. Ibid.

137. Ibid., 253.

138. Ibid., 253–54.

139. Arslanian, *NCAA and State Action,* 351.

140. Ibid., 350.

141. Ibid., 351.

142. Ibid.

143. Ibid., 355.

144. See, e.g., Tedesco, *National Collegiate Athletic Association v. Tarkanian,* 253.

145. Ibid.

146. McKenna, *Tarkanian Decision,* 495.

147. Green, *Does the NCAA Play Fair?* 109–10.

148. Ibid., 111, citing 123 University of Pennsylvania Law Review 1267 (1975).

149. Ibid., 111–12.

150. Ibid., 123.

151. Ibid., 125.

152. Ibid., 127.

153. Ibid.

154. Ibid.

155. Ibid.

156. Ibid., 129.

157. Ibid., 132.

158. *Due Process and the NCAA: Hearing before the Subcommittee on the Constitution of the House Committee on the Judiciary,* 108th Cong., 2d sess., September 14, 2004, 75, http://www.house.gov/judiciary.

159. Ibid.

160. Ibid.

161. Ibid., 5.

162. Ibid.

163. Ibid., 7.

164. *Ridpath v. Board of Governors of Marshall University, et al.,* United States District Court for the Southern District of West Virginia, Docket Number 3:03-2037, Plaintiff's Complaint, 7.

165. *Due Process and the NCAA* (testimony of B. David Ridpath).

166. Ibid.

167. Ibid., 19.

168. Ibid. (testimony of Professor Gary Roberts).

169. Ibid.

170. Ibid., 17.

171. Ibid., 20.

172. Ibid.

CHAPTER 7

1. See *UNLV v. Tarkanian,* 110 Nev. 581, 586, 879 P.2d 1180 (1994).

2. Don Yeager, *Shark Attack: Jerry Tarkanian and His Battle with the NCAA and UNLV* (New York: HarperCollins, 1992), 183.

3. Ibid., 183.

4. Ibid., 229.

5. Ibid., 253.

6. Ibid., 233. Point-shaving is a scheme whereby basketball players, cooperating with gamblers, try to win a game by fewer points than the quoted "point spread." That is what Richard Perry did in 1978–79. See chapter 2, note 24 for an explanation of point-shaving.

7. Ibid., 1.

8. Jerry Tarkanian and Dan Wetzel, *Runnin' Rebel: Shark Tales of "Extra Benefits," Frank Sinatra, and Winning It All* (Champaign, IL: Sports Publishing, 2006), xv.

9. Christopher V. Carlyle, *NCAA Due Process: Its Past and Its Future,* 12 Entertainment and Sports Lawyer 10, 10 (Spring 1994).

10. Ibid.

11. Sherry Young, *The NCAA Enforcement Program and Due Process: The Case for Internal Reform,* 43 Syracuse Law Review 747, 803 (1992).

12. Ibid., 805.

13. 10 F.3d 633 (9th Cir. 1993), *cert. denied,* 511 U.S. 1033, 114 S.Ct. 1543, 128 L. Ed. 2d 195 (1994).

14. Ibid., 635.

15. Ibid., 638.

16. Ibid.

17. Ibid.

18. Ibid., 639.

19. Ibid.

20. Ibid., 640, citing *Southern Pacific Co. v. Arizona,* 325 U.S. 761, 65 S.Ct. 1515, 89 L. Ed. 1915 (1945).

21. 1994 WL 750585 (N.D. Fla).

22. John Kitchin, *The NCAA and Due Process,* 5 Kansas Journal of Law and Public Policy 71, 79–80 (Spring 1996). The Illinois statute can be found at 110 Ill. Comp. Stat. §§ 25/1-13, and the Nebraska statute can be found at Neb. Rev. Stat. §§ 85-1201–10.

23. NCAA news release, "NCAA and Jerry Tarkanian Agree to Settlement," April 2, 1998 (on file with the author).

24. Young, *The NCAA Enforcement Program and Due Process: The Case for Internal Reform,* 43 Syracuse Law Review 747, 814 (1992).

25. Ibid., 817–18.

26. Ibid., 818.

27. Ibid., 817–18.

28. Ibid., 818.

29. "Enforcement Panel Issues Report," *NCAA News,* November 4, 1991, 13.

30. Ibid.

31. Ray L. Yasser, James R. McCurdy, C. Peter Goplerud, and Maureen A. Wes-

ton, *Sports Law: Cases and Materials,* Sixth Edition (Newark, NJ: Matthew Bender, 2006), 98–99.

32. David Williams, II, *Is the Federal Government Suiting Up to Play in the Reform Game?* 20 Capital University Law Review 621, 627 (1991).

33. Robin J. Green, *Does the NCAA Play Fair? A Due Process Analysis of NCAA Enforcement Regulations,* 42 Duke Law Journal 99, 140 (October 1992).

34. LeRoy Pernell, *A Commentary on Professor Goplerud's Article, "NCAA Enforcement Process: A Call for Procedural Fairness,"* 20 Capital University Law Review 561, 566 (1991).

35. Williams, *Is the Federal Government Suiting Up to Play in the Reform Game?* 631. Mr. McMillen was well placed to be a leader in Congress on issues concerning college and professional sports. Before being elected to the House, he had been an All-American basketball player at the University of Maryland and had spent more than a decade playing professionally in the National Basketball Association. In college, he was as good a student as he was a basketball player, and his success in both settings earned him a Rhodes Scholarship to Oxford University after college.

36. Ibid., 632.

37. Ibid., 635.

38. Ibid.

39. *See* NCAA news release, "NCAA and Jerry Tarkanian Agree to Settlement," April 2, 1998 (on file with the author).

40. Ibid., 6.

41. Ibid.

42. Ibid., 7.

43. Ibid., 1.

44. Ibid.

45. 531 U.S. 288.

46. Ibid., 293.

47. Ibid.

48. Ibid.

49. Ibid.

50. Ibid., 294. The district court's decision can be found at 13 F. Supp.2d 670 (M.D. Tenn. 1998).

51. Ibid. The Sixth Circuit's decision can be found at 180 F.3d 758 (1999).

52. Ibid., 297.

53. Ibid.

54. Ibid., 299.

55. Ibid., 300.

56. 382 U.S. 296, 86 S.Ct. 486 (1966).

57. 382 U.S. at 299.

58. *Brentwood Academy v. Tennessee Secondary School Athletic Association,* 531 U.S. 288, 302 (2001).

59. Ibid., 305.

60. Ibid., 312.

61. Kadence Otto and Kristal Stippich, *Revisiting Tarkanian: The Entwinement and Interdependence of the NCAA and State Universities and Colleges 20 Years Later,* 18 Journal of Legal Aspects of Sport 243, 245–246 (Summer 2008).

62. The commentary previously cited points to *Cohane v. NCAA,* 215 Fed. Appx. 13, 2007 WL 247710 (C.A.2 (N.Y.)), as evidence to the contrary. In *Cohane,* the appellate court reversed part of a trial court's order holding that a basketball coach whom the State University of New York at Buffalo had fired could prove no set of facts showing that the NCAA was a willful participant in joint activity with the state university in firing him. The appellate court reasoned that the coach's allegations, if proven, could show that the university and the NCAA had acted jointly to deprive the coach of his livelihood, a liberty interest. Therefore, the trial court had erred in interpreting *Tarkanian* to mean that the NCAA can never be a state actor when it investigates one of its members. Still, *Cohane* is less important than the commentary suggests, and not just because it is an unpublished opinion, hence lacking in precedential value. Besides that, it merely holds that a fired coach ought to have the chance to prove that the NCAA and a public university acted jointly in terminating his or her employment. That holding is consistent with *Tarkanian* and is a far cry from a ruling that the NCAA is always (or even presumably) a state actor when investigating one of its members.

63. *Due Process and the NCAA: Hearing before the Subcommittee on the Constitution of the House Committee on the Judiciary,* 108th Cong., 2d sess., September 14, 2004, 15 (testimony of Professor Gary Roberts), http://www.house.gov/judiciary.

64. Yasser et al., *Sports Law,* 100.

65. *Due Process and the NCAA,* 15 (testimony of Professor Roberts).

66. "Frequently Asked Questions about NCAA Enforcement," available at http://news.minnesota.publicradio.org/features/199903/11_newsroom_cheating/enforce.shtml. For a more current but less detailed version of this document, see http://ncaa.org/wps/wcm/connect/public/NCAA/Enforcement/Resources/.

67. Ibid., 13.

68. Ibid.

69. See *2008–2009 NCAA Division I Manual,* 296, Bylaw 19.02.2.2 (Indianapolis: NCAA, 2008).

70. Ibid.

71. Mike Rogers and Rory Ryan, *Navigating the Bylaw Maze in NCAA Infractions Cases,* 37 Seton Hall Law Review 749, 768 (2007).

72. Ibid.

73. Ibid.

74. Ibid., 769.

75. See "Frequently Asked Questions about the NCAA Enforcement Process," 1, http://news.minnesota.publicradio.org/features/199903/11_newsroom_cheating/enforce.shtml.

76. Rogers and Ryan, *Navigating the Bylaw Maze,* 770.

77. Ibid., 755–56.

78. Ibid., 770–71. See also *2008–2009 NCAA Division I Manual,* 300.

79. Rogers and Ryan, *Navigating the Bylaw Maze,* 770–71.

80. Ibid.

81. Ibid., 771.

82. Ibid.

83. Ibid.

84. Ibid.

85. Ibid.

86. Ibid.

87. Ibid.

88. Ibid., 790.

89. Ibid.

90. See National Collegiate Athletic Association, *Procedures Followed during Hearings before the NCAA Committee on Infractions,* July 28, 2007, 5, http://www.ncaa.org.

91. Rogers and Ryan, *Navigating the Bylaw Maze,* 791.

92. *Due Process and the NCAA,* 13 (testimony of Professor Roberts).

93. Rogers and Ryan, *Navigating the Bylaw Maze,* 792.

94. Ibid.

95. National Collegiate Athletic Association, *Procedures Followed before the NCAA Committee on Infractions,* 4.

96. Rogers and Ryan, *Navigating the Bylaw Maze,* 792.

97. National Collegiate Athletic Association, *Procedures Followed before the NCAA Committee on Infractions,* 3.

98. Ibid.

99. Ibid.

100. Ibid.

101. Ibid.

102. Ibid., 4.

103. Rogers and Ryan, *Navigating the Bylaw Maze,* 793.

104. Ibid., 794.

105. National Collegiate Athletic Association, *Procedures Followed before the NCAA Committee on Infractions,* 4.

106. Ibid.

107. Rogers and Ryan, *Navigating the Bylaw Maze,* 795.

108. Ibid., 795–96.

109. "Frequently Asked Questions about the NCAA Enforcement Process," 4–5.

110. Ibid., 22.

111. Ibid.

112. NCAA Division I Infractions Appeals Committee, *Policies and Procedures Guide,* January 26, 2009, 2, http://www.ncaa.org.

113. Ibid., 3.

114. Ibid.

115. Ibid.

116. Ibid., 4.

117. Ibid.

118. Ibid., 5.

119. Ibid., 6. See also NCAA Operating Bylaw 32.10.5.

120. Ibid.

121. Ibid., 9.

122. Ibid., 10.

123. *Due Process and the NCAA,* 12 (testimony of Professor Gary Roberts).

124. Richard R. Hilliard, Angel F. Shelton, and Kevin E. Pearson, *An Update on Recent Decisions Rendered by the NCAA Infractions Appeals Committee: Further Guidance for NCAA Member Institutions,* 28 Journal of College and University Law 605, 630 (2002).

125. Ibid., 631–32.

126. NCAA Division I Infractions Appeals Committee, *Policies and Procedures Guide,* 11.

127. *NCAA: Who's in Control of Intercollegiate Athletics? Hearings before the Subcommittee on Energy, Consumer Protection, and Competitiveness of the Committee on Energy and Commerce,* House of Representatives, 102nd Cong., 1st sess., 1991, 67 (testimony of Professor Burton Brody).

128. Alfred C. Aman, Jr., and William T. Mayton, *Administrative Law* (St. Paul, MN: West, 1993), 148, quoting *Bi-Metallic Investment Co. v. State Board of Equalization,* 239 U.S. 441, 446, 36 S.Ct. 141, 142, 60 L.Ed. 372 (1996).

129. Aman and Mayton, *Administrative Law,* 163–64.

130. Ibid., 176.

131. Ibid., 173, 177.

132. Daniel Hall, *Administrative Law: Bureaucracy in a Democracy,* Second Edition (Upper Saddle River, NJ: Prentice Hall, 2002), 57–58.

133. See 5 U.S.C. § 554(d)(2).

134. 5 U.S.C. § 556(a)(3).

135. See Indiana Code 4-21.5-3-22(a)(1).

136. 5 U.S.C. § 556(d).

137. Ibid.

138. Indiana Code 4-21.5-3-25(c).

139. Ibid., 4-21.5-3-25(d).

140. Ibid., 4-21.5-3-25(f).

141. Ronald J. Thompson, *Due Process and the National Collegiate Athletic Association: Are There Any Constitutional Standards?* 41 UCLA Law Review 1651, 1663 (1994).

142. These recommendations are adapted from recommendations offered in C. Peter Goplerud, III, *NCAA Enforcement Process: A Call for Procedural Fairness,* 20 Capital University Law Review 543, 559–60 (1991).

143. Rogers and Ryan, *Navigating the Bylaw Maze,* 766.

144. Ibid., 766–67.

145. Ibid., 767.

146. See *2008–2009 NCAA Division I Manual,* 483, Bylaw 32.8.8.2.

147. Rogers and Ryan, *Navigating the Bylaw Maze,* 795.

148. Ibid.

149. William J. Fox, *Understanding Administrative Law,* Fifth Edition (Newark, NJ: LexisNexis, 2008), 218–19, citing 5 U.S.C. § 556(d).

150. See Indiana Code 4-21.5-3-25(f).

151. *Due Process and the NCAA,* 18 (testimony of Professor Roberts).

152. Ibid., 15.

153. Ibid., 19.

154. Ibid.

CHAPTER 8

1. Adam R. Schaefer, *Slam Dunk: The Case for an NCAA Antitrust Exemption,* 83 North Carolina Law Review 555, 560 (January 2005).

2. Ibid., 566.

3. Tom McMillen and Paul Coggins, *Out of Bounds: How the American Sports Establishment Is Being Driven by Greed and Hypocrisy—and What Needs to Be Done About It* (New York: Simon and Schuster, 1992), 132.

4. Schaefer, *Slam Dunk,* 566–67.

5. Ibid., 567.

6. Raymond L. Yasser, "A Comprehensive Blueprint for the Reform of Intercollegiate Athletics," in Joseph Gordon Hylton and Paul M. Anderson, eds., *Sports Law and Regulation* (Milwaukee, WI: Marquette University Press / National Sports Law Institute, 1999), 391.

7. Ibid. For a more recent discussion of this topic, see Michael Oriard, *Bowled Over: Big-Time College Football from the Sixties to the BCS Era* (Chapel Hill: University of North Carolina Press, 2009), 197.

8. See Gary R. Roberts, *Resolution of Disputes in Intercollegiate Athletics,* 35 Valparaiso Law Review 431, 433 (2001), citing *Board of Regents v. NCAA,* 468 U.S. 85 (1984), *Smith v. NCAA,* 139 F.3d 180 (3d Cir. 1998), and *Banks v. NCAA,* 977 F.2d 1081 (7th Cir. 1992).

9. Daniel E. Lazaroff, *The NCAA in Its Second Century: Defender of Amateurism or Antitrust Recidivist?* 86 Oregon Law Review 329, 340 (2007).

10. Ibid.

11. Ibid.

12. Ibid.

13. Ibid.

14. 577 F. Supp. 356 (D. Ariz. 1983).

15. See 711 F. Supp. 1435 (N.D. Ill. 1989), cited in Walter T. Champion, Jr., *Fundamentals of Sports Law,* Second Edition (St. Paul, MN: Thomson/West, 2004), 557, § 19:5.

16. Ibid., 557–58, § 19:5.

17. 40 F. Supp. 2d 1275 (D. Kan. 1999).

18. Lazaroff, *NCAA in Its Second Century,* 336.

19. Ibid., 357.

20. Ibid.

21. Ibid., 363.

22. Ibid.

23. Ibid.

24. Ibid., 363–64.

25. *2008–9 NCAA Division I Manual,* 172–74, Bylaw, Articles 15.2.1–15.2.3 (Indianapolis: NCAA, 2008).

26. Adam Epstein, *Sports Law* (Clifton Park, NY: Thomson Delmar Learning, 2003), 233.

27. Richard J. Hunter and Ann M. Mayo, *Issues in Antitrust, the NCAA, and Sports Management,* 10 Marquette Sports Law Journal 69, 74–75 (1999).

28. 977 F.2d 1081 (7th Cir. 1992).

29. See ibid., 1090, cited in Lazaroff, *NCAA in Its Second Century,* 349.

30. 977 F. 2d. at 1089–90.

31. Tibor Nagy, *The "Blind Look" Rule of Reason: Federal Courts' Peculiar Treatment of NCAA Amateurism Rules,* 15 Marquette Sports Law Review 331, 335 (Spring 2005).

32. Ibid., 368.

33. Lazaroff, *NCAA in Its Second Century,* 355.

34. Ibid.

35. See, e.g., *2008–2009 NCAA Division I Manual,* 127, Bylaw, Articles 14.01.2 and 14.01.2.1; 148, Bylaw, Article 14.4.

36. Ibid., 351, Bylaw, Article 23.02.1.

37. Ibid., 352, Bylaw, Articles 23.2.1.1.1–23.2.1.1.3.

38. Ibid., 353, Bylaw, Articles 23.2.1.2, 23.2.1.2.2, and 23.2.1.2.3.

39. See http://www.nflplayers.com/user/template.aspx?fmid=181&lmid=349&pid=0&type=t&we (last visited December 16, 2009).

40. Ibid.

41. Ibid.

42. See http://wiki.answers.com/Q/What_percentage_of_NCAA_basketball_players_make_NBA (last visited December 15, 2009).

43. Gary R. Roberts, *The NCAA, Antitrust, and Consumer Welfare,* 70 Tulane Law Review 2631, 2673 (1996).

44. See National Symposium on Athletics Reform, New Orleans, LA, November 11, 2003, 28, http://symposium.tulane.edu.

45. McMillen and Coggins, *Out of Bounds,* 207.

46. Ronald J. Thompson, *Due Process and the National Collegiate Athletic Association: Are There Any Constitutional Standards?* 41 UCLA Law Review 1651, 1683 (1994).

47. See *NCAA v. Miller,* 10 F.3d 633 (9th Cir. 1993), *cert. denied,* 511 U.S. 1033, 114 S.Ct. 1543, 128 L.Ed.2d 195 (1994); *NCAA v. Roberts,* 1994 WL 75085 (N.D. Fla).

48. *2008–9 NCAA Division I Manual*, 1, NCAA Constitution, Article 1.3.1.

49. The exemption would not protect the NCAA from antitrust challenges to its purely commercial activities, though. For example, the exemption would not protect the NCAA from lawsuits such as the one filed by former UCLA basketball star Ed O'Bannon, who alleges that "the NCAA has illegally deprived former student-athletes from receiving any compensation for the use of their images and likenesses in numerous revenue-generating formats, including DVD sales and rentals, photograph sales, video games, 'stock footage' clips sold to corporate advertisers, jersey and other apparel sales, and rebroadcasts of 'classic' games" (David Moltz, "The Right Profile," *Inside Higher Ed,* July 23, 2009, http://www.insidehighered.com/layout/set/print/news/2009/07/23/ caa).

50. "A Greeting from NCAA President Mark Emmert," *NCAA News,* October 5, 2010, http://www.ncaa.org/wps/wcm/connect/public/ncaa/resources/latest+news/2010+news+stories/october/a+greeting+from+mark+emmert.

51. See, e.g., John R. Thelin, *Games Colleges Play: Scandal and Reform in Intercollegiate Athletics* (Baltimore: Johns Hopkins University Press, 1996); Arthur A. Fleischer, III, Brian L. Goff, and Robert D. Tollison, *The National Collegiate Athletic Association: A Study in Cartel Behavior* (Chicago: University of Chicago Press, 1992).

52. See 20 U.S.C. § 1092(e).

53. See 20 U.S.C. § 1092(g).

54. H.R. 2157 (May 1, 1991), available at http://thomas.loc.gov.

55. H.R. 3046 (July 25, 1991), available at http://thomas.loc.gov.

56. See summary of H.R. 3046 at http://thomas.loc.gov/cgi-bin/query/C?r102:./temp/-102IXXb4d. See also David Williams, II, *Is The Federal Government Suiting Up to Play in the Reform Game?* 20 Capital University Law Review 621, 640 (1991).

57. Williams, *Is The Federal Government Suiting Up?* 636.

58. Matthew J. Mitten, James J. Musselman, and Bruce W. Burton, *Targeted Reform of Commercialized Intercollegiate Athletics,* 47 San Diego Law Review 779 (2010). A condensed version of this article appears in the Fall 2010 issue of *Marquette Lawyer,* beginning at page 23.

59. Lee H. Hamilton, *How Congress Works (and Why You Should Care)* (Bloomington: Indiana University Press, 2004), 56.

60. Walter J. Oleszek, *Congressional Procedures and the Policy Process,* Seventh Edition (Washington, DC: CQ Press, 2007), 89.

61. Ibid., 84.

62. Hamilton, *How Congress Works,* 57.

63. Ibid.

64. Knight Commission on Intercollegiate Athletics, *Restoring the Balance: Dollars, Values, and the Future of College Sports,* June 2010, 18, http://www.knightcommis sion.org.

65. Roberts, *NCAA, Antitrust, and Consumer Welfare,* 2674.

BIBLIOGRAPHY

ARTICLES AND BOOKS

Aman, Alfred C., Jr., and Mayton, William T., *Administrative Law* (St. Paul, MN: West, 1993).

Arslanian, James L., *The NCAA and State Action: Does the Creature Control Its Master?* 16 Journal of Contemporary Law 333 (1990).

Art and Science Group, LLC, *Knight Commission on Intercollegiate Athletics: Quantitative and Qualitative Research with Football Bowl Subdivision University Presidents on the Costs and Financing of Intercollegiate Athletics; Report of Findings and Implications,* October 2009, http://www.knightcommission.media.org/images/President_Survey_FINAL.pdf..

Berry, Robert C., and Wong, Glen M., *Law and Business of the Sports Industries: Common Issues in Amateur and Professional Sports,* Volume 2, Second Edition (Westport, CT: Praeger, 1993).

Bork, Robert H., *The Antitrust Paradox: A Policy at War with Itself* (New York: Free Press, 1978, 1993).

Brady, Erik, and Upton, Jody, "NCAA Recognizes Growing Problem with Costs," *USA Today,* November 17, 2005, C10.

Broyles, Kevin E., *NCAA Regulation of Intercollegiate Athletics: Time for a New Game Plan,* 46 Alabama Law Review 487 (1995).

Byers, Walter, and Hammer, Charles, *Unsportsmanlike Conduct: Exploiting College Athletes* (Ann Arbor: University of Michigan Press, 1995).

Carlyle, Christopher V., *NCAA Due Process: Its Past and Its Future,* 12 SPG Entertainment and Sports Lawyer 10 (Spring 1994).

Champion, Walter T., Jr., *Fundamentals of Sports Law,* Second Edition (St. Paul, MN: Thomson/West, 2004).

Corns, Jasen R., *Pigskin Paydirt: The Thriving of College Football's Bowl Championship Series in the Face of Antitrust Law,* 39 Tulsa Law Review 167 (2003).

Corstensen, Peter C., and Olszowka, Paul, *Antitrust, Student-Athletes, and the NCAA: Limiting the Scope and Conduct of Private Economic Regulation,* 1995 Wisconsin Law Review 545 (1995).

Dunnavant, Keith, *The Fifty-Year Seduction: How Television Manipulated College Football, from the Birth of the Modern NCAA to the Creation of the BCS* (New York: St. Martin's, 2004).

Epstein, Adam, *Sports Law* (Clifton Park, NY: Thomson Delmar Learning, 2003).

Fleischer, Arthur A., III, Goff, Brian L., and Tollison, Robert D., *The National Collegiate Athletic Association: A Study in Cartel Behavior* (Chicago: University of Chicago Press, 1992).

Fox, William J., *Understanding Administrative Law,* Fifth Edition (Newark, NJ: Lexis-Nexis, 2008).

Frank, Robert H., *Challenging the Myth: A Review of the Links among College Athletic Success, Student Quality, and Donations,* May 2004, http://www.knightfoundation.org/dotAsset/131763.pdf.

Frederick, David C., *Justice White and the Virtues of Modesty,* 55 Stanford Law Review 21 (2002).

Gillum, Jack, Upton, Jodi, and Berkowitz, Steve, "Amid Funding Crisis College Athletics Soak Up Subsidies, Fees," *USA Today,* January 15, 2010, http://www.usatoday.com/sports/college/2010-01-13-ncaa-athletics-funding-analysis-N.htm.

Goplerud, C. Peter, III, *NCAA Enforcement Process: A Call for Procedural Fairness,* 20 Capital University Law Review 543 (1991).

Green, Robin J., *Does the NCAA Play Fair? A Due Process Analysis of NCAA Enforcement Regulations,* 42 Duke Law Journal 99 (1992).

Greenspan, David, *College Football's Biggest Fumble: The Economic Impact of the Supreme Court's Decision in National Collegiate Athletic Association v. Board of Regents of the University of Oklahoma,* 33 Antitrust Bulletin 1 (Spring 1988).

Gulland, Eugene D., Byrne, J. Peter, and Steinbach, Sheldon Elliot, *Intercollegiate Athletics and Television Contracts: Beyond Economic Justifications in Antitrust Analysis of Agreements among Colleges,* 52 Fordham Law Review 717 (1984).

Hall, Daniel, *Administrative Law: Bureaucracy in a Democracy,* Second Edition (Upper Saddle River, NJ: Prentice Hall, 2002).

Hamilton, Lee H., *How Congress Works (and Why You Should Care)* (Bloomington: Indiana University Press, 2004).

Harp, Richard, and McCullough, Joseph, *Tarkanian: Countdown of a Rebel* (New York: Leisure Press, 1984).

Hilliard, Richard R., Shelton, Angel F., and Pearson, Kevin E., *An Update on Recent Decisions Rendered by the NCAA Infractions Appeals Committee: Further Guidance for NCAA Member Institutions,* 28 Journal of College and University Law 605 (2002).

Horowitz, Ira, "The Reasonableness of Horizontal Restraints: NCAA," in John E. Kwoka, Jr., and Lawrence J. White, eds., *The Antitrust Revolution: The Role of Economics,* Second Edition (New York: HarperCollins, 1994), 214–37.

Hunter, Richard J., and Mayo, Ann M., *Issues in Antitrust, the NCAA, and Sports Management,* 10 Marquette Sports Law Journal 69 (1999).

Hutchinson, Dennis, *The Man Who Once Was Whizzer White: A Portrait of Justice Byron R. White* (New York: Free Press, 1998).

Institute for Diversity and Ethics in Sport, *Academic Progress/Graduation Success Rate Study of Division I NCAA Women's and Men's Basketball Tournament Teams,* March 16, 2010, http://www.tidesport.org.

Institute for Diversity and Ethics in Sport, *Keeping Score When It Counts: Assessing the 2009–10 Bowl-Bound College Football Teams—Academic Performance Improves, but Race Still Matters,* December 7, 2009, http://www.tidesport.org.

Keegan, Matthew M., *Due Process and the NCAA: Are Innocent Student-Athletes Afforded Adequate Protection from Improper Sanctions? A Call for Changes in the NCAA Enforcement Procedures,* 25 Northern Illinois University Law Review 297 (Spring 2005).

Kitchin, John, *The NCAA and Due Process,* 5 Kansas Journal of Law and Public Policy 71 (Spring 1996).

Klevorick, Alvin K., *The Fractured Unity of Antitrust Law and the Antitrust Jurisprudence of Justice Stevens,* 27 Rutgers Law Journal 637 (Spring 1996).

Knight Commission on Intercollegiate Athletics, *Restoring the Balance: Dollars, Values, and the Future of College Sports,* June 2010, http://www.knightcommission.org.

Lande, Robert H., *Consumer Choice as the Ultimate Goal of Antitrust,* 62 University of Pittsburgh Law Review 503 (2001).

Lawrence, Paul R., *Unsportsmanlike Conduct: The National Collegiate Athletic Association and the Business of College Football* (Westport, CT: Praeger, 1987).

Lazaroff, Daniel E., *The NCAA in Its Second Century: Defender of Amateurism or Antitrust Recidivist?* 86 Oregon Law Review 329 (2007).

Licalsi, Michael B., *The Whole Situation Is a Shame, Baby! NCAA Self-Regulations Categorized as Horizontal Combinations under the Sherman Act's Rule of Reason Standard: Unreasonable Restraints of Trade or an Unfair Judicial Test?* 12 George Mason Law Review 831 (Spring 2004).

Malysiak, James T., *Justice White on Antitrust: Protecting Freedom to Compete,* 58 no. 3 University of Colorado Law Review 497 (Summer 1987).

McKenna, Kevin M., *The Tarkanian Decision: The State of College Athletics Is Everything but State Action,* 40 DePaul Law Review 459 (1991).

McMillen, Tom, and Coggins, Paul, *Out of Bounds: How the American Sports Establishment Is Being Driven by Greed and Hypocrisy—and What Needs to Be Done about It* (New York: Simon and Schuster, 1992).

Meese, Alan J., *Competition and Market Failure in the Jurisprudence of Justice Stevens,* 74 Fordham Law Review 1775 (2006).

Meyers, D. Kent, and Horowitz, Ira, *Private Enforcement of the Antitrust Laws Works Occasionally: Board of Regents of the University of Oklahoma v. NCAA, a Case in Point,* 48 Oklahoma Law Review 669 (Winter 1995).

Mitten, Matthew J., Musselman, James J., and Burton, Bruce W., *Targeted Reform of Commercialized Intercollegiate Athletics,* 47 San Diego Law Review 779 (2010).

Moltz, David, "The Right Profile," *Inside Higher Ed,* July 23, 2009, http://www.inside highered.com/layout/set/print/news/2009/07/23/ncaa.

Moreland, David Scott, *The Antitrust Implications of the Bowl Championship Series: Analysis through Analogous Reasoning,* 21 Georgia State University Law Review 721 (Spring 2005).

Musselman, James L., *Recent Federal Income Tax Issues regarding Professional and Amateur Sports,* 13 Marquette Sports Law Review 195 (Spring 2003).

Nagy, Tibor, *The "Blind Look" Rule of Reason: Federal Courts' Peculiar Treatment of NCAA Amateurism Rules,* 15 Marquette Sports Law Review 331 (Spring 2005).

National Symposium on Athletics Reform, New Orleans, LA, November 11, 2003, http://symposium.tulane.edu.

NCAA, *2008–09 NCAA Division I Manual* (Indianapolis: NCAA, 2008).

Oleszek, Walter J., *Congressional Procedures and the Policy Process,* Seventh Edition (Washington, DC: CQ Press, 2007).

Oriard, Michael, *Bowled Over: Big-Time College Football from the Sixties to the BCS Era* (Chapel Hill: University of North Carolina Press, 2009).

Otto, Kadence, and Stippich, Kristal, *Revisiting Tarkanian: The Entwinement and Interdependence of the NCAA and State Universities and Colleges 20 Years Later,* 18 Journal of Legal Aspects of Sport 243 (Summer 2008).

Pekron, Chad, *The Professional Student-Athlete: Undermining Amateurism as an Antitrust Defense in NCAA Compensation Challenges,* 24 Hamline Law Review 24 (2000).

Pernell, Leroy, *A Commentary on Professor Goplerud's Article, "NCAA Enforcement Process: A Call for Procedural Fairness,"* 20 Capital University Law Review 561 (1991).

Porto, Brian L., *A New Season: Using Title IX to Reform College Sports* (Westport, CT: Praeger, 2003).

Posner, Richard A., *Antitrust Law,* Second Edition (Chicago: University of Chicago Press, 2001).

Potter, James, *The NCAA as State Actor: Tarkanian, Brentwood, and Due Process,* 155 University of Pennsylvania Law Review 1269 (May 2007).

Rader, Benjamin G., *American Sports: From the Age of Folk Games to the Age of Televised Sports,* Fourth Edition (Upper Saddle River, NJ: Prentice Hall, 1999).

Roberts, Gary R., *The NCAA, Antitrust, and Consumer Welfare,* 70 Tulane Law Review 2631 (1996).

Roberts, Gary R., *Resolution of Disputes in Intercollegiate Athletics,* 35 Valparaiso Law Review 431 (2001).

Rogers, Mike, and Ryan, Rory, *Navigating the Bylaw Maze in NCAA Infractions Cases,* 37 Seton Hall Law Review 749 (2007).

Rosenthal, Lindsay J., *From Regulating Organization to Multi-Billion Dollar Business: The NCAA Is Commercializing the Amateur Competition It Has Taken Almost a Century to Create,* 13 Seton Hall Journal of Sport Law 321 (2003).

Sack, Allen L., and Staurowsky, Ellen J., *College Athletes for Hire: The Evolution and Legacy of the NCAA's Amateur Myth* (Westport, CT: Praeger, 1998).

Sander, Libby, "Athletes' Graduation Rates Hit Another High, NCAA Says," *Chronicle of Higher Education,* November 27, 2009, A20.

Savage, Howard J., Bentley, Harold W., McGovern, John T., and Smiley, Dean F., *American College Athletics,* Bulletin No. 23 (New York: Carnegie Foundation for the Advancement of Teaching, 1929).

Schaefer, Adam R., *Slam Dunk: The Case for an NCAA Antitrust Exemption,* 83 North Carolina Law Review 555 (2005).

Serrill, Michael S., "Taking Away the NCAA's Ball," *Time,* July 9, 1984, 77–78.

Siegfried, John J., and Burba, Molly Gardner, *The College Football Association Television Broadcast Cartel,* 49 Antitrust Bulletin 799 (Fall 2004).

Smith, Ronald A., *Sports and Freedom: The Rise of Big-Time College Athletics* (New York: Oxford University Press, 1988).

Sperber, Murray, "When Academic Progress Isn't," *Chronicle of Higher Education,* April 15, 2005, http://chronicle.com/article/When_Academic_Progress_Isnt/ 2131/.

Suggs, Welch, "Football, Television, and the Supreme Court," *Chronicle of Higher Education,* July 9, 2004, A32–A33.

Suggs, Welch, "Jock Majors," *Chronicle of Higher Education,* January 17, 2003, http://chronicle.com/article/Jock_Majors/32843.

Suggs, Welch, "The NCAA's Scapegoat Question," *Chronicle of Higher Education,* May 6, 2005, A39–A41.

Suggs, Welch, "New Grades on Academic Progress Show Widespread Failings among Teams," *Chronicle of Higher Education,* March 11, 2005, http://chronicle .com/article/New_Grades_on_Academic/28317/.

Taafe, William, "A Supremely Unsettling Smorgasbord," *Sports Illustrated,* September 5, 1984, 150–51.

Tarkanian, Jerry, and Wetzel, Dan, *Runnin' Rebel: Shark Tales of "Extra Benefits," Frank Sinatra, and Winning It All* (Champaign, IL: Sports Publishing, 2006).

Tedesco, Brandon, *National Collegiate Athletic Association v. Tarkanian: A Death Knell for the Symbiotic Relationship Test?* 18 Hastings Constitutional Law Quarterly 237 (Fall 1990).

Thamel, Pete, "With Eyes on Football, Big East Adds T.C.U.," *New York Times,* November 29, 2010.

Thelin, John R., *Games Colleges Play: Scandal and Reform in Intercollegiate Athletics* (Baltimore: Johns Hopkins University Press, 1996).

Thompson, Ronald J., *Due Process and the National Collegiate Athletic Association: Are There Any Constitutional Standards?* 41 UCLA Law Review 1651 (1994).

Van Camp, Stephen R., *National Collegiate Athletic Association v. Tarkanian: Viewing State Action through the Analytical Looking Glass,* 92 West Virginia Law Review 761 (1990).

Warmbrod, Jodi M., *Antitrust in Amateur Athletics: Fourth and Long; Why Non-BCS Universities Should Punt Rather Than Go For an Antitrust Challenge to the Bowl Championship Series,* 57 Oklahoma Law Review 333 (2004).

Wheeler, Stanton, *Rethinking Amateurism and the NCAA,* 15 Stanford Law and Policy Review 213 (2004).

Williams, David, II, *Is the Federal Government Suiting Up to Play in the Reform Game?* 20 Capital University Law Review 621 (1991).

Wilson, Robin, "Where Have All the Women Gone?" *Chronicle of Higher Education,* May 4, 2007, A40–A44.

Wolverton, Brad, "Athletes' Hours Renew Debate over College Sports," *Chronicle of Higher Education,* January 25, 2008, A1.

Wolverton, Brad, "Athletics Participation Prevents Many Players from Choosing Majors They Want," *Chronicle of Higher Education,* January 8, 2007, http://chronicle.com/article/Athletics-Participation/122712/.

Wolverton, Brad, "The Clicker Crowd," *Chronicle of Higher Education,* March 3, 2006, 38.

Wolverton, Brad, "5 Questions for the Fall," *Chronicle of Higher Education,* September 2, 2005, A63–A65.

Wolverton, Brad, "Former College Athletes Accuse NCAA of Antitrust Violations in Vast Lawsuit over Scholarship Cap," *Chronicle of Higher Education,* March 10, 2006, http://chronicle.com/article/Former_College_Athletes_Acc/29199/.

Wolverton, Brad, "NCAA Penalizes 112 Teams for Failing to Meet Its Academic-Progress Requirements," *Chronicle of Higher Education,* May 3, 2007, http://chronicle.com/article/NCAA_Penalizes_112_Teams_for/122159/.

Wolverton, Brad, "NCAA Rescinds Scholarships at 65 Colleges," *Chronicle of Higher Education,* March 10, 2006, A35.

Wolverton, Brad, "NCAA Ruling on Preparatory Schools Could Send More Athletes to Junior Colleges," *Chronicle of Higher Education,* May 11, 2007, http://chronicle.com/article/NCAA_Ruling_on_Preparatory_/25735/.

Wolverton, Brad, "NCAA Will Pay Big to Settle Antitrust Lawsuit," *Chronicle of Higher Education,* February 8, 2008, A15.

Wolverton, Brad, "23 of 56 Bowl Teams Fail to Meet New NCAA Academic Standards, Report Says," *Chronicle of Higher Education,* December 16, 2005, A36.

Wolverton, Brad, and Lipka, Sara, "Experts Urge Knight Commission to Try to Cap Coaches' Salaries and Curtail Recruiting," *Chronicle of Higher Education,* January 23, 2007, http://chronicle.com/article/Experts_Urge_Knight_Commiss/122794/.

Wright, Alfred, "A Modest All-American Who Sits on the Highest Bench," *Sports Illustrated,* December 10, 1962, 85–98.

Wright, Charles Alan, *Responding to an NCAA Investigation, or, What to Do When an Official Inquiry Comes,* 1 Entertainment and Sports Law Journal 19 (1984).

Yasser, Raymond L., "A Comprehensive Blueprint for the Reform of Intercollegiate Athletics," in Joseph Gordon Hylton and Paul M. Anderson, eds., *Sports Law and Regulation* (Milwaukee, WI: Marquette University Press / National Sports Law Institute, 1999), 363–402.

Yasser, Ray, McCurdy, James R., Goplerud, C. Peter, and Weston, Maureen A., *Sports Law: Cases and Materials,* Sixth Edition (Newark, NJ: Matthew Bender, 2006).

Yeager, Don, *Shark Attack: Jerry Tarkanian and His Battle with the NCAA and UNLV* (New York: HarperCollins, 1992).

Yeager, Don, *Undue Process: The NCAA's Injustice for All* (Champaign, IL: Sagamore, 1991).

Yost, Mark, *Varsity Green: A Behind the Scenes Look at the Culture and Corruption in College Sports* (Stanford, CA: Stanford University Press, 2010).

Young, Sherry, *The NCAA Enforcement Program and Due Process: The Case for Internal Reform*, 43 Syracuse Law Review 747 (1992).

Zimbalist, Andrew, *Unpaid Professionals: Commercialism and Conflict in Big-Time College Sports* (Princeton, NJ: Princeton University Press, 1999).

CONGRESSIONAL HEARINGS AND REPORTS

Due Process and the NCAA: Hearing before the Subcommittee on the Constitution of the House Committee on the Judiciary, 108th Cong., 2d sess., September 14, 2004.

Enforcement Program of the National Collegiate Athletic Association: Report together with Minority Views by the Subcommittee on Oversight and Investigations of the Committee on Interstate and Foreign Commerce, House of Representatives, 95th Cong., 2d sess., 1978.

NCAA: Who's in Control of Intercollegiate Athletics? Hearings before the Subcommittee on Energy, Consumer Protection, and Competitiveness of the Committee on Energy and Commerce, House of Representatives, 102nd Cong., 1st sess., 1991.

COURT DECISIONS

Adickes v. S. H. Kress & Co., 398 U.S. 144 (1970).

Arlosoroff v. NCAA, 746 F.2d 1019 (4th Cir. 1984).

Associated Students, Inc. v. NCAA, 493 F.2d 1251 (9th Cir. 1974).

Association for Intercollegiate Athletics for Women v. NCAA, 558 F. Supp. 487 (D.D.C. 1983), *affirmed,* 735 F.2d 577 (D.C. Cir. 1984).

Banks v. NCAA, 977 F.2d 1081 (7th Cir. 1992).

Blum v. Yaretsky, 457 U.S. 991 (1982).

Board of Regents v. NCAA, 546 F. Supp. 1276 (W.D. Okla. 1982).

Board of Regents v. NCAA, 707 F.2d 1147 (10th Cir. 1983).

Brentwood Academy v. Tennessee Secondary School Athletic Association, 531 U.S. 288 (2001).

Buckton v. NCAA, 366 F. Supp. 1152 (D. Mass. 1973).

Dennis v. Sparks, 449 U.S. 24 (1980).

Eastern R.R. Presidents Conference v. Noerr Motor Freight, Inc., 365 U.S. 127 (1961).

Flagg Brothers, Inc. v. Brooks, 436 U.S. 149 (1978).

Gaines v. NCAA, 746 F. Supp. 738 (M.D. Tenn. 1990).

Goldfarb v. Virginia State Bar, 421 U.S. 773 (1975).

Graham v. NCAA, 804 F.2d 953 (6th Cir. 1986).

Hawkins v. NCAA, 652 F. Supp. 602 (C.D. Ill. 1987).

Hennessey v. NCAA, 564 F.2d 1136 (5th Cir. 1977).

Howard University v. NCAA, 510 F.2d 213 (D.C. Cir. 1975).

Jackson v. Metropolitan Edison Co., 419 U.S. 345 (1974).

Jones v. NCAA, 392 F. Supp. 295 (D. Mass. 1975).

Justice v. NCAA, 577 F. Supp. 356 (D. Ariz. 1983).

Kneeland v. NCAA, 650 F. Supp. 1047 (W.D. Tex. 1986).

Kupec v. Atlantic Coast Conference, 399 F. Supp. 1377 (M.D.N.C. 1975).

Law v. NCAA, 134 F.3d 1010 (10th Cir. 1998).

Lugar v. Edmonson Oil Company, 457 U.S. 922 (1982).

McHale v. Cornell University, 620 F. Supp. 67 (N.D.N.Y. 1985).

National Society of Professional Engineers v. United States, 435 U.S. 679 (1978).

NCAA v. Board of Regents of the University of Oklahoma, 468 U.S. 85 (1984).

NCAA v. Miller, 10 F.3d 633 (9th Cir. 1993), *cert. denied*, 511 U.S. 1033 (1994).

NCAA v. Roberts, 1994 WL 75085 (N.D. Fla.).

NCAA v. Tarkanian, 488 U.S. 179 (1988).

Parish v. NCAA, 506 F.2d 1028 (5th Cir. 1975).

Regents of the University of Minnesota v. NCAA, 560 F.2d 352 (8th Cir. 1977).

Rendell-Baker v. Kohn, 457 U.S. 830 (1982).

Smith v. NCAA, 139 F.3d 180 (3d Cir. 1998).

United States v. Walters, 711 F. Supp. 1435 (N.D. Ill. 1989).

Warner Amex Cable Communications, Inc. v. American Broadcasting Companies, Inc. et al., 499 F. Supp. 537 (S.D. Ohio 1980).

Worldwide Basketball and Sport Tours, Inc. et al. v. NCAA, 388 F.3d 955 (6th Cir. 2004).

INDEX

Academic Progress Rate (APR), 8, 81, 184
Adickes v. S. H. Kress & Co., 138–39
Adidas America, Inc. v. NCAA, 181
Administrative Procedure Act (federal), 110, 171
Administrative Procedure Act (Indiana), 171, 172
Agnew v. NCAA, 24, 182
Air Force Academy, 9
Alltel, 89
Amateurism, 25, 196. *See also* National Collegiate Athletic Association: philosophy at founding
American Broadcasting Company (ABC), 1, 39, 78
Angel, Dan, 15
Antitrust exemption for NCAA, 20, 21–22, 178–79, 180–81. *See also* College Sports Legal Reform Act
Appalachian State University, 29, 42
Arizona State University, 84
Arlosoroff v. NCAA, 120–22, 123, 128, 141
"arms race" (among colleges in recruiting, facility construction, etc.), 80
Atlantic Coast Conference (ACC), 6, 75–76, 85

Bachus, Spencer, 148
Baepler, Donald, 115, 130, 134, 139
Banks v. NCAA, 21, 90, 92, 93, 94, 96, 183–84
Barrett, James, 47–48, 64
Baylor University, 77
Big East Conference, 6, 77
Big 10 Conference, 1, 77, 85
Big 12 Conference, 1, 74, 77, 85
Black Entertainment Television (BET), 1
Blum v. Yaretsky, 119, 120, 121, 123, 129, 130, 133, 141
Boise State University, 6

Bork, Robert, 66
Boston College, 6, 75, 78
Bowl Championship Series (BCS), 84–88
Brand, Myles, 7
Brentwood Academy v. Tennessee Secondary School Athletic Association, 158–60
Brigham Young University, 86
Brody, Burton, 104–5, 109, 169
Brown, Dave, 83
Buckton v. NCAA, 119
Burciaga, Juan, 32, 37, 39–46
Burger, Warren, 60, 141
Byers, Walter, 31, 100

Cable television, 80–81
California State University, Fresno. *See* Tarkanian, Jerry
California State University, Long Beach, 111
Carnegie Report, 88
Chabot, Steve, 148
Champion, Walter, 180
Christianson, Erik, 18
Chronicle of Higher Education, 82, 84
Citadel, the, 29
Clemson University, 86
Coach and Athlete's Bill of Rights, 156, 193
Coats, Andy, 67
College football
  increased salaries for coaches of, 1–2
  increased television coverage of, 1
College Football Association (CFA), 30–31, 48, 78–79
College Sports Legal Reform Act
  difference from existing law, 180
  due process protections included, 189
  educational purpose of, 179, 188
  features enhancing likelihood of enactment, 193–95
  likely consequences of, 179–80, 190–91

245